FACING
THE TRUTH
of Your Life

Marilyn,

thank you for your
kindness, support e
generousity.
　　　All the Best
　　　Gabe York
　　　3·24·18

FACING THE TRUTH
of Your Life

Merle James Yost, MA, LMFT

Merle Yost
Making sense of people

Cover Design by eBook DesignWorks
Book Design and Typesetting by eBook DesignWorks
Graphics by Made U Look Graphic Design
Author Photo by Ginger Hill, Marketing & Design Co.

Library of Congress Cataloging-In-Publication Data

Yost, Merle James
      Facing the Truth of Your Life / Merle Yost. — First Edition Merle James Yost
          Pages   cm
      Includes End Notes
          978-0-9991547-0-0
1. Psychology. 2. Self-Help. 3. Spirituality. 4. Gestalt Therapy. 5. Transpersonal
Psychology

Library of Congress Control Number: 2017915915

Printed in the United States of America

Also By Merle James Yost

Reflections for Managers

More Reflections for Managers

Reflections for the Workplace

When Love Lasts Forever

Demystifying Gynecomastia

For Alex

Everything can be taken from a man, but one thing: the last of the human freedoms — to choose one's attitude in any given set of circumstances, to choose one's own way.

— Viktor Frankl (b. 1905) *Man's Search for Meaning*

Table of Contents

Acknowledgments

Many people have helped me and graciously held my hand throughout this process. First and foremost I have to acknowledge Tim who was there at the beginning of my last book and has guided me throughout this one. Without him, it would not have come to fruition.

Each person listed has contributed a little to a lot. Hearing other voices and perspectives has only made this book stronger, for which I am immensely grateful.

Editors

Timothy Cassidy – *Primary*

Alan Cooney

Marcia Hootman

Dan Encarnacion

Zander Keig

Feedback Contributors

Alex Synan

David Valdez

Jeff Hall

Abby Volk Neuberg

Alex Synan

Chaqa Hill

Paul Inman

Rami Kouhana

Diana Barbieri

My Support Team

Joan Wager

Luis Alvarado

Jeff Hall

Mark Marion

Thomas Faupl

Cai Bristol

Introduction

Birth then, in the conventional meaning of the word, is only the beginning of birth in the broader sense. The whole life of the individual is nothing but the process of giving birth to himself; indeed, we should be fully born, when we die — although it is the tragic fate of most individuals to die before they are born.

—Erich Fromm (b. 1900)
Psychologist from *The Sane Society* 1956

Why would I be drawn to this book?

There are thousands of self-help books, past and present. Each book in its own way promises to change your life. None of them can. Only you can do that. However, there are some that can change the way you see the world. These few books will challenge you to see yourself, explain how you got where you are, and show you who contributed to your journey.

Facing the Truth of Your Life is a different kind of self-help book, covering a broad range of topics. Each theme is designed to explain how you became you and to make you aware of what you can do to heal yourself. Fritz Perls, the co-founder of Gestalt Therapy said, "Awareness in and of itself can be curative." Just the simple reframe of how you think you got where you are can change everything or nothing. It is always up to you to decide.

What is the source of pain in my life?

Most people are in pain of some kind, be it physical, emotional, somatic, intellectual, or psychic; what is yours? Few people are taught as children how to discriminate between or deal with the various types of pain. Most of the time, when we are in some kind of emotional pain, we either think it is something outside of us: our spouse, mother, neighbor, boss, or someone else who is the cause of our suffering. While these people unquestionably are players in our discomfort, the path to ending the suffering lies inside of us. Childhood is painful. We are trying to make sense of the world, and especially the bad things that happen to us, which we do not have the training or skills to process and resolve.

Searching for a solution is a great thing, and you should congratulate yourself on your willingness to look for a way out of your current situation and ameliorate your pain.

How many brides or grooms have told people later that as they walked down the aisle they knew that the marriage was a mistake? How many people went to school and studied something they had no interest in because it is what their parents wanted them to do? Or because it was what was expected of them? How many people do you know stay in a job or a relationship well after its expiration date? How many people give up and just numb out, waiting to die? The answer to all of these questions is "many of them," and most people are guilty of placing themselves in one or more of these categories. If you answered "yes" to any of these questions about yourself, then you are in pain, whether you choose to admit it or not. Avoidance equals pain. Holding on to well-intentioned, misguided beliefs or ideas trap us in the past and prevents us from living life now. If you want more out of life, you need to let go of the pain.

Many years ago, there was a useful question asked as part of EST (Erhard Seminars Training was a high profile San Francisco based self-help seminar during the 70s.) that I paraphrase: "What is it that you have been unwilling to give up, that if you gave it up, would let your life work?"

Why would I want to face the pain?

Many people live by the creed "better the devil you know than the devil you do not know." To risk facing the devil you do not know, who has probably haunted you your entire life, means risking pain, discomfort, and change. There are fundamental misunderstandings about life and yourself that, once placed into a new perspective, can change everything. Facing the pain increases the possibility of ending much suffering.

People considering Alcoholics Anonymous are often reluctant to stop drinking because all their friends drink, and if they stopped, they would need to find new friends. Change can be hard and lonely. If you change your perspective on life, it is possible that your current friends will not share your new perspective. We want to be around people who have similar views. We cluster as humans and migrate from one cluster to another along our life long journey. From singlehood to relationship, from childlessness to becoming a parent, each of these milestones will change the cluster of people that will be our friends and community.

Change makes most people uncomfortable. Coming to the conclusion that others may not understand our problem or perspective usually makes us uncomfortable. The question is: Are you ready to face your pain and end needless suffering?

What will I get out of reading this book?

Readers of early drafts have told me that these chapters reveal more and more upon being read multiple times. You may get the most out of the book by reading a chapter or two, stopping to contemplate what you've read, and consider how it might apply to your own life.

Some chapters will be more emotionally challenging than others. Where one person will find something difficult to consider, another person will simply think it confirms something they already know, or describes something outside their own experience. Because we are each uniquely different, each response will be unique as well.

Parts Two and Three generally bring up the most recollections and pain for the reader. **Take your time, particularly in these parts.** Please understand that the intent *is* to stir up questions as they may apply to you. If you are having a strong reaction to a particular chapter, slow down, pay attention and ask yourself where those feelings are coming from. The point is not to overwhelm you. The point is to assist you to see your life through a different lens.

Many of the chapters have one or more personal exercises that are designed to help you gain a deeper understanding of the material and how it applies to your own life.

Please take the time to do the exercises. Keeping a notebook of your responses will help keep track of what you've been working on, give you a record of your responses and demonstrate how you have changed as you work through the book.

Almost every chapter also has short stories designed to illustrate a point in the chapter. If they are depicted in a therapeutic setting, or any other setting, the situations and persons described are purely fictional and any resemblance to any person is purely coincidental.

I look forward to hearing how the book impacts you and your life. Feel free to write me at FTT@merleyost.com or join the discussion group at Facebook Group: FTT Community.

What should I expect other than just another self-help book?

What makes *Facing the Truth of Your Life* different is that it is designed to bring the pain to the surface. This is not a fast read for most people. It may bring up too much pain from your past and present. That is the point. If you cannot heal the pain, it will continue to haunt you. The path to freedom is to uncover the real you rather than to be stuck in the beliefs and pain of your past.

There is no guarantee this book will change your life, but reading it will challenge you on many levels. It is both compassionate and provocative. It is intended to be a new frame for you to look at your life. This frame can give you a starting point to make sense of your life, the purpose of life and how the world works.

Why did I write this book?

I am a veteran of 17 years of personal psychotherapy and two years of group therapy inside a professional training program, with over 25 years of working with individuals, couples, and groups to help them heal and to reclaim their lives. This book encapsulates much of what I have learned over the last 35 years about healing myself and healing others.

By working on healing my traumatic childhood and helping others, I understand and know how much can change through healing the past. This book grows out of my desire to teach people who have given up hope that tomorrow can be better and happier.

PART ONE

REFRAMING YOUR LIFE

— 1 —

Giving Meaning To Life

We only become what we are by the radical and deep-seated refusal of that which others have made of us.

—Jean-Paul Sartre (b. 1905)
from Preface to Frantz Fanon's *Wretched of the Earth*

SOME PEOPLE SEEM TO come out of the womb knowing what they want to do or what impact they want to have in the world. *I'm going to be a doctor and heal people. I'm going to solve the homeless problem. I'm going to find a way to end hunger. I'm going to be a parent and have amazing children.* These are worthy and laudable goals. But it is possible to get lost in goals and miss out on who you are. "Saving the world" is exhausting and can completely consume a person. If you cannot save the world or even attempt to, who are you otherwise? Do you have any value? Do you have any purpose? Can you justify being alive?

Why are we alive? What is the purpose of life? Most people ignore the question, over-intellectualize it or surrender their perspective to religious belief. There are plenty of Jim Joneses[1] offering answers so that individuals do not have to think for themselves.

Because of religion, for many, the point of this life is to avoid having a bad eternal afterlife. Again, that seems too limited. It is also a distraction from just being alive and enjoying your body and this moment in time.

Too many people have a shocking lack of curiosity. They might be curious about what they will have for dinner, but seemingly have little interest in asking:

Why are we alive?

What happens after we die?

Who am I?

What is going on inside of me?

Should I change?

Can I change?

How do I change?

What does it mean to be a better person?

Do I fit in the world?

Where should I fit and why should I fit?

How did I become me?

It is as if pondering these questions creates too much work. A typical person already has a lot of work being an employee, a parent, a lover or a friend. Why ponder theories that do not provide immediate material gain, when we live in a society that is about doing things fast, getting an immediate answer and moving on to the next thing?

Asking Questions

How willing are you to ask "why, when, and how?" How much time and interest do you have in exploring the great existential questions?

People have used science, religion and, most recently, psychology to try and make sense of the world. But for most, it is an outer exploration. We discount the vast unexplored world inside most of us. We cannot just question our external experience; we must question everything.

Much has been written about the meaning of life. Some claim there is no meaning. Perhaps they are right, but the exploration of that question is still of value. A simple answer, however, ends a conversation, rather than encouraging exploration. If you do get to an answer, it should open up more possibilities and excitement for potentialities.

Different people in different times have come to different conclusions. Freud[2] said, "The purpose of life is to pursue pleasure." Victor Frankl[3] said, "The purpose is to pursue meaning." Whatever your belief, and however you ponder the question of life's purpose, it has much to do with how introspective you are, how you are wired genetically and how your family has programmed you. Your belief in the purpose of life has much to do with how willing you are to go beneath the surface of yourself and, consequently, of life itself. How you answer these questions has much to do with how you feel you fit into the world.

Exploring questions about our purpose is the work of a lifetime, and from a Buddhist perspective, it takes many lifetimes. New discoveries will continually change and shift our perception and understanding of what is 'real' and what is 'important.' Exploration of these questions strengthens knowledge, and will consequently re-shape our worldviews. You will likely discover that the answers are constantly changing and evolving. That is great news. When you think you know it all, then it is time to reconsider what you think you know. It is impossible to know everything, the total sum of life and death and what, if anything comes next, in one lifetime, because our perspective is too small.

Asking questions can be revolutionary. Asking questions can and will create change. Werner Heisenberg said, *"The very act of observing disturbs the system."* That is true for both what goes on outside of us as well as on the inside. That is how the world changes, and that is how we change. We observe, we hypothesize, and we test to see if something is true. If the hypothesis confirms a new reality, we reach a new level of understanding and then move on to the next observation with more information.

In most ways, the answers are much less important than the questions. The purpose is not just exploring these questions from a thought-based perspective. We need to dig into ourselves fearlessly and honestly, burning away the programmed beliefs that do not fit, the ones that block us from a relationship with our 'self.' An integral part of 'self-discovery' is looking at our relationships with others and figuring out who they are and who you are.

I have no special talent. I am only passionately curious.

—Albert Einstein (b. 1921) Physicist, Philosopher

Going Inside

Exploration and questioning are not just about the external world. If anything, the most important investigation is inside. We need to dig deeper into who we think we are and to gain insight into how we came to believe this is "who we are." Once we take that belief system apart, dissecting it until it reveals the deepest understanding of what we are not, we can come to an awareness of who we are. That is the journey.

There is so much more to us than our thoughts and even our feelings. There is a multifaceted world inside that is waiting to be discovered and explored.

This is the world of the mind-body connection: our skin, muscles and organs, our intuition, emotion, and memory make us who we are. Much of modern life involves an endless flood of stimulus and information to deal with, creating multiple reactions that demand we stay focused on the external. All of that external distraction consumes us and keeps us from really knowing who we are on the inside.

It is a life long journey. Each awakening and emerging awareness, while perhaps painful at the moment, can lead to healing. By allowing more of who you are to emerge and become visible, you are creating space for the unique 'you' to be in the world.

Family

For the majority of the world's people and cultures, two concepts are the primary focus of life. First is family — maintaining the bloodline, creating progeny and repaying the debt of having been given life. God is the other focus. Most people are born into a religion, never questioning the religion's validity or if it serves them. They exist with a blind belief in the answers given through the Bible, the Koran and other sacred texts so that little else in life has to be questioned.

Family can be defined as a small, biological unit or as large as a race or nationality. We live in a world where the predominant paradigm is the family. Whether it is the Western nuclear family or the extended family of non-Western cultures, the family is the center of our universe. No matter how old we grow, it always seems to come back to the family. While the family is essential to children for survival, development, and instruction, focusing on the blood or cultural family is too restrictive a paradigm for humanity. We must redefine it. The family paradigm as we know it is the cause of most conflict and strife in the world. Wars are fought over "you hurt my family, I will hurt yours." We must move to a more inclusive paradigm that means all the people on our planet are as important as our biological family, our race, and our country. We are all the same. Only then will we be able to make choices that will be in all of our interests.

Conclusion

Most people are unhappy — maybe a little, maybe a lot — but unhappy to some degree. Now and then they stick their head out of their tortoise shells and wonder: is this all there is?

When you are stuck in that protective shell, it is important to stick your head out often enough to get a glimpse of what is happening in the world. Understanding your role and your impact on others is required to get a better sense of who you are and what possibilities the world holds for you.

At your core is someone who deserves to be loved. We are born with no shell and no protection. We start out dependent on others to care for us and to teach us to survive in the world. As we grow up, we lose touch with our *core being* that came into the world. Those outside forces then shape and form a protective covering. Underneath all of that sculpting, hurt and covering is someone worthy of love for just 'being.' The journey is important, starting with the defenseless being, and hopefully, in time, progresses to a solid sense of self. The journey of reconnecting to the core you were born with and finding your direct connection to the world is an essential part of what life is all about.

Psychologist Abraham Maslow's[4] hierarchy of needs theorized that the higher you ascend on the scale of having basic survival needs met, the more time, energy and luxury you have to explore other questions. If your biggest concern of the day is securing food or shelter, there is much less time and energy to focus on the meaning of being. If we are to evolve as a civilization, we need to meet the basic, needs (food, shelter, etc.) of people so that they can pursue the larger question of why they are alive. That will allow for people's vision and compassion to include others.

People have to find their own truth. Finding that truth is about the journey toward the inner self. Most people avoid, or get sidetracked from, the journey. Many on the path do not realize they have been sidetracked. Realization of this can mean the difference between a happy life with a good death and a long, miserable life with a fearful, terrifying death, or something in-between. Most people put off this process until the end of their lives and, unsurprisingly, never get there at all. The earlier you start searching and clearing your pain, the easier the exploration. There is much to do and many levels of understanding that have to be attained to achieve a more authentic way of being.

2

Defining Self

... the self is never to be found, but must be created, not the happy accident of passivity, but the product of a thousand actions, large and small, conscious or unconscious, performed not "away from it all," but in the face of "it all," for better or for worse, in work and leisure rather than in free time.

—Robert Penn Warren, (b. 1905) Poet

THIS ENTIRE BOOK IS ultimately a discussion about "the self" — what the self is, how it is formed, how it changes. Because there are so many words regarding development that are used somewhat interchangeably, such as, *self, ego, awareness, consciousness, truth, belief,* etc., this chapter focuses on the definition of *self* for the purpose of making sense of the discussion in the book.

Each of us, based on our own education and experience, has our own definition of these words. The meanings can vary: even in psychology, the meaning of *the self* depends entirely on context. In *Facing the Truth of Your Life,* when we refer to "self," it is defined in two specific ways, the **Public Self** and the **Root Self**. There are many stages of development a person goes through from birth through death. The public self and the root self in this book are condensations of those various stages of development to two basic stages of development.

The Public Self

The *Public Self* is initiated when we are born and start to conceptualize the world. We reach conclusions about who we are and how we fit into the world. We take in information and assemble it into the emotional structure of a personality. Generally, when people talk about 'self,' they are referring to their self-image, their self-perception and their separateness from others. This organization is the public self, and is often called the *ego*. I use 'self' rather than 'ego' because ego has too many different interpretations, many of them negative. The healthiness of a person's public self depends on the ability to deal with change and uncertainty. A lack of flexibility and resiliency suggests unresolved trauma that needs to be addressed, so that healthy growth can continue.

There are many stages and processes in a person's development. These graphics represent the development of the "self" as a compact overview of the developmental process through the life cycle. The first three combine the various stages of the public self. The fourth graphic depicts the root self.

At Birth

A newborn baby does not know it is separate from its mother. At birth, the child is unformed and unable to differentiate itself from others. As far as it is concerned, it is one with the mother.

At birth, we have no understanding of the world and no formed personality. (The lines in the figure represent genetic influences.) Genes play a role in personality development, yet nurture definitely impacts how nature's gifts will show up in the world. Through nurturing, we begin to construct a *pub-*

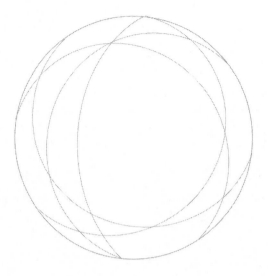

lic self in childhood that determines how separate we feel from others and how functional we are in the world. Love or lack of love, losses, trauma, and downloaded beliefs all play a role in our development. Each experience changes our public self in big and small ways as we continue to develop and change throughout our lives.

The formation of the public self allows you to separate from others, so you really know you are different from them. But it is just the beginning of your journey.

It is very possible to be 50 years old and still not progressed beyond this early stage of development, even though we're talking about the development of a 0-2 year old at the core level. A person's biological age does not guarantee emotional development.

Forming

As children mature, they download experiences and information, particularly as their external experience is reflected back to them. They then start

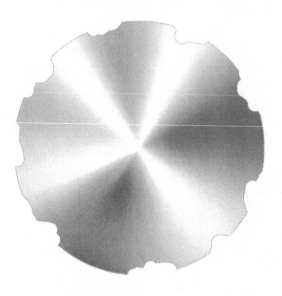

to come to conclusions about how the world works. They start to internally organize, and begin to form a sense of self. Over time, ideally through experience, trial and error, they will begin to coalesce into the person they will become. This is the beginning of forming a solid public self.

The craters in the graphic represent the unprocessed and unresolved pain and trauma that a person experiences throughout life. The "crater" means that the child or person is unable to be fully present in the moment with another when attempting to make emotional contact. If the 'wound (crater) is touched,' the individual will emotionally regress to the earlier experience. If you were six years old when your father died and that is an unresolved wound, anytime that memory is triggered, you will regress to that age and re-experience the unresolved feelings of that event. Everyone has unresolved experiences from the past, some more than others. The more unresolved wounds you have, the harder it is to function as an adult in the world.

If two people make contact where there are no craters, they can make full emotional contact. Each person is able to hear and see the other clearly.

Formed Adult

This graphic represents the adult who has a solid sense of public self — one who has formed into a person who is self-aware. There may still be craters from long past or current wounds, but hopefully, there has been progress in healing the wounds — the craters have "smoothed out" somewhat or are completely gone, and now the person is able to stay present and aware most of the time when coming in contact with others.

The craters, or unresolved events, can keep a person in a constant state of emotional turmoil. A person may react over and over to multiple things, rather than staying present in the moment, responding from an adult perspective. To be overly reactive is crazymaking for all involved. The person who unknowingly triggered their wounds may have no idea what is going on, or why the other person reacted strangely. The reactive person is in a regressed place, lost in the pain of the past and does not know how to find a way back to the present.

A more solidly formed adult will have enough self-awareness to know when they have been triggered, so they have some ability to handle the situation. To be able to respond to external stimuli, to do what is really in your own and others' best interests, it is crucial that you have a relationship with your inner self. That means observing your thoughts and feelings, having awareness and recognition of where they come from and to recognize their meanings.

If two people meet and they have compatible unresolved issues, that is to say "their craters match up," it may have the dynamic of a connection, but also a deeply pathological relationship can result. If two people from abusive

homes are programmed to see a relationship through the same lens, they may feel they have found their soul mate, because the other behaves the way they expect.

The interlocking of craters can be benign as well. This matching of perspectives happens in relationships of all kinds, not just romantic or sexual ones.

As a person works through trauma and begins to heal wounds, the craters get smaller and may even disappear. The benefit of making the effort to face and heal the pain in your life is that fuller emotional contact with others is easier, more satisfying and most of all, enjoyable. You could actually be aware of what is happening in the moment, and respond accordingly, instead of getting lost in each other's drama.

Where some people have a self, most people have a void, because they are too busy in wasting their vital creative energy to project themselves as this or that, dedicating their lives to actualizing a concept of what they should be like rather than actualizing their potentiality as a human being, a sort of "being" vs. having — that is, we do not "have" mind, we are simply mind. We are what we are.

— Bruce Lee (b. 1940) In My Own Process, Draft 9

The Root Self

The second 'self' referred to in this book is the *root self*: the self that transcends space and time. It is the self as defined in transpersonal psychology[5] that is beyond the personality and is core to the energy that we brought into the world. Some describe it as the soul, or Gaia consciousness, the part of us that existed before we were born and continues on after our body dies. This energy is connected to everything in the universe, with no boundaries of time. The root self is beyond the restraints of our personality, however it means to an individual to have a universal consciousness.

Before we can progress from the public self to the root self, it is necessary to solidify a public self by working though as many life traumas as possible. In this way, when confronted with abuse or drama, the adult does not regress to the wounded child's state of mind.

Only when the public self is solid can the process of deconstructing the core of the public self begin. This allows the emergence of the root self. While leaving the superstructure of the public self in place, the root self can be accessed for being in contact with both the divine and the world around you.

Deconstruction

If a person continues to work on themself to get to a deeper understanding of self and their connection to the universe, it is necessary to clear out more of the downloads preventing an awakening to the deepest self, the *root self.*

The graphic above shows the hollowed out center, but unlike the unformed At Birth graphic, the superstructure of the public self is intact. As a person continues to work through and clear downloads about how the world works, a deeper connection to the universe will be gained. The line between the public self and the root self will continue to grow thinner, but will not disappear. As illusions that prevent us from reaching deeper states of consciousness dissipate, there is the possibility of greater awareness of the totality of the world. The predominance of the root self represents awakening or enlightenment, a duality of consciousness that allows us to be present in the now, yet connected to everything in the world at the same time. Few are consciously interested in this journey, but for those who choose this path, the rewards can be enormous.

We tap into the root self by digging down to the essential elements of who we are. From the root self, we source deep intuition, knowledge of our place in the universe and consequently, our connectedness to everything and everyone. There may well be elements of the root self already present in everyone's public self, but most people will have to peel away the incongruent layers of beliefs and survival strategies to remember who they are and let their original energy reemerge.

Conclusion

Personal growth is not easy and often not fun. Each stage requires introspection and reflection from others to assist you in more clearly seeing yourself. The process of organizing and forming the self can be exhausting, as is the process of dismantling downloads, myths and delusions about who you thought you were. You do not exist in isolation. Children are dependent, and adults are supposed to be interdependent. Being alive is relational. We need feedback — good and bad, painful and nonsensical — to understand ourselves. At the same time, we need to discover who others are as well. To move through all the stages of development requires curiosity about our existence and purpose.

Few people will reach a full awareness of the root self. Since we do not know what the end point of enlightenment will look like, it is important to keep in mind that the journey is what is important. Understand that discovery is about striving to be the best you can be. Giving up because it is too hard, or seemingly unreachable misses so many possibilities of what life has to offer. The journey should take you to a place of deeper compassion, love, empathy, caring and a peace inside that, in the end, will allow for connection to the deepest you.

— 3 —

Moving Beyond
The Surface

Reality is what we take to be true.

What we take to be true is what we believe.

What we believe is based our perceptions.

What we perceive depends on what we look for.

What we look for depends on what we think.

What we think depends on what we perceive.

What we perceive determines what we believe.

What we believe determines what we take to be true.

What we take to be true is our reality.

— David Bohm, (b. 1917) Physicist

WHEN BABIES AND KIDS ride in a car with their parents, they do not have the education to understand all of the different parts that make up that experience, like having a job to buy the car, insurance and gas, or taking a test to be allowed to drive on the road. As children, we are unconscious. We have not expanded our awareness to include all of these things that make other things possible. As we grow up, hopefully, what our parents tell us about these various things teaches us so that we can have awareness, as well as learn skills to handle each of the tasks involved in driving a car.

This is a metaphor for our early life. When born, we simply go for the ride not knowing that there are others who are separate from us. As we grow, we start to differentiate people and experiences. Because of early programming, most people operate on autopilot, not understanding that they are simply acting out the script their parents taught them and not knowing that this is not the only way to see the world. It is only with effort that we bring the programming to the surface and can begin to make our own choices.

There is more than one way to drive a car. Perhaps when Mom felt wronged by another driver, she felt the need to show them how angry she felt. She would tailgate, flip them off, roll down her window and yell. Maybe she would even follow them for miles, stalking them, in hopes of making them as unhappy as she was.

If you grow up with this behavior as the norm, why would you question whether it would be the correct way for you to drive?

As you increase your awareness of the world around you, you will eventually have the opportunity to be authentic and more fully in control of the route you take and how you choose to drive through life.

One of the things that is striking is that most people have no idea who they truly are, and, subsequently, have no inner relationship with themselves. They are not conscious of what they feel and almost no idea of how they are seen by others. They usually have little idea of what they want — other than lots of sex (pleasure in whatever form) and/or to be rich and famous. Their awareness is almost all based on superficial external feedback. If you smile at them, they feel good. If you express anger toward them, they feel bad.

But sometimes, when you reach beneath a man's self-portrait
and reach deep down inside, what you find is nothing at all.

—Evolution, *Star Trek Next Generation*, S3 Ep1 (45-46)

The less sense of self inside a person, the greater the amount of narcissism that makes up that person's personality. Everyone possesses some degree of narcissism.

Narcissus, a beautiful young man whose story comes to us from the ancient Greeks, fell in love with the reflection of his face in the smooth surface of a pond. In the myth, he dies because he cannot stop looking at himself. The perception is that he was so in love with himself that he could not leave. The explanation that makes more sense is that only when he saw his reflection in the water did he exist to himself. If he stopped looking at his reflection, he would no longer exist and could not bear the pain. Narcissism is a psychological disorder in which a person has no internal sense of self. When a person is narcissistic, and dares to explore inside themself, they will find nothing but turmoil and pain agitated by a desire for love. A narcissist needs constant stimulation from the outside to submerge and attempt to suffocate the pangs of hunger for existence resonating below their skin. The only way a narcissist sees their own self is via the reflections of themself that are constructed from the reactions of another responding to the narcissist's actions. The narcissist can shape their own reflection by manipulating others' behavior to suit their own delusional, self-validating needs. What is described here is a narcissistic personality disorder (NPD).

Here is an example of a person needing constant external stimulation to avoid the emptiness and chaos inside:

Sheila was a pretty girl. She got lots of attention and was constantly the center of attention. She was a member of several social organizations and popular at work. Sheila almost never had a quiet moment. When she was alone, she would watch TV, listen to music, talk to someone on the phone or have endless text chats. She did not feel comfortable being alone. Being alone made her feel too much, it made her feel like she was not being loved. She had a long succession of boyfriends and an endless list of people to be entertained by. As she grew older she went to more and more extremes to make people like her and still smile when they saw her. Plastic surgery and doing volunteer work were two common examples. Her being okay required others to admire her, say nice things to her and most of all to reflect to her what a wonderful person she was. Sheila had built a life around not being alone with herself and especially alone with her feelings about herself.

It seems like a great deal of modern life is about skimming along the surface and not digging in, questioning or coming to your own individual conclusions. Most religions do not want you questioning their set beliefs too much or too deeply. A couple of notable exceptions are Judaism and Buddhism. Most religions expect you to take their beliefs 'on faith' — do not dig too deep, or it might bring down the house of cards your belief system is built on.

But it is not just religion that comes up short. The same failing is apparent in politics, education, family and so many institutions that we are supposed to accept "on faith."

More and more of modern life is about the avoidance of pain. Yet pain is one of the primary life experiences that shape us. Pain is not all that forms us,

They fuck you up, your mum and dad.

They may not mean to, but they do.

They fill you with the faults they had

And add some extra, just for you.

— Philip Larkin (b. 1922) British Poet, *This Be The Verse*

but we do learn from painful experiences. Most people respond to pain by figuring out how to avoid it.

People often think they are nothing but their thoughts, as in, "I think, therefore I am." The brain, however, is an input/output device that works like a computer. When the brain is stimulated through touch, sight, hearing or taste, its processes find the appropriate reaction, completing that reaction as a physical action. Who we are is something much deeper than a string of stimulated neurons. As long as people are lost inside their computer-like thoughts and think that is all there is, there will be little chance to learn, grow or heal. Thoughts are devices we use, but they are not 'us.' Thoughts come from various places inside of us.

Intuition may be heard in the brain, but it does not come from there. For most, intuition is a sense of knowing. Learning to identify intuition versus wishful thinking is one of the more profound tasks of knowing yourself. Separating thoughts from intuition is part of the process of learning how to tap into something deeper inside ourselves than our thoughts.

Being Programmed

It is essential to go inside ourselves and sort through the beliefs, values and morals that we downloaded (socialization) from our parents, family and society. These non-tangible, intellectual, emotional downloads can be as damaging as a physical trauma and for most, are harder to quantify or touch. But they can be nonetheless disrupting when we try to make contact with others and be fully present.

In Gestalt therapy, these downloaded beliefs are called Introjects.[6] From the moment of birth, we swallowed whatever food was put into our mouths because we did not yet have the skills to determine what was nourishment or not. We did not know what we liked or disliked. We do the same with feelings, values and beliefs, and things we hear people say — particularly our family members. Part of growing up and becoming your own person is to go inside and to look at the beliefs you swallowed. The task is to bring them up (some people literally throw up in the process), tear them apart, keep what works for you and then discard that which doesn't. This is a key part of the separation from your family, defining yourself and having your own experience in the world.

Kian went to college, where first he majored in music. His mother wanted him to be a professional singer. About two years into the process, Kian figured out that was his mother's dream, not his. Kian had a good voice and was an okay musician. But he neither had the passion, the drive, nor the desire to sing in front of crowds of people. It was the beginning of Kian really questioning and wondering what he wanted to be when he grew up and how he wanted his life to unfold. Kian largely dropped out of school. He began working in retail and found as he was promoted that he was good at running businesses. He liked being in charge, but it became clear to him that this wasn't satisfying either. Just because he could do it, did not mean he should do it or needed to do it. He quit his job and took some time for self-reflection and exploration. If Kian had been married with kids, it is very likely he would not have had the option of quitting, taking a year off and figuring out what he wanted for his own sense of fulfillment. To stay in that first job, or even that line of work, would have killed his soul. Kian was unwilling to be physically alive and yet be the walking dead, like so many people around him. His exploration led him to return to graduate school and become a social worker. He found his passion and was very happy.

To know what you want, you have to know who you are. Otherwise, it is all about living out the things you think you are supposed to want. And for most, when you actually get the physical things and "stuff" you think you are supposed to want, you feel disappointed and lost. Your inner landscape is easy to ignore and avoid — at least initially. Yet, this is the most important target as the first step in creating a relationship with yourself.

Once you have that awareness, it is important to maintain it. Self-awareness requires effort and continuity just like any other relationship. It requires downtime. It is about developing a deeper understanding of what is happening inside by building an *observing ego,*[7] so you have a much better understanding of why you are the way you are in the world. An observing ego is the ability or to step back and recognize your thoughts and feelings as just thoughts and feelings rather than who you are. It is the awareness that you are neither your feelings nor thoughts. They are just information that your body and brain are relaying to you. Once you have the distance to simply observe, you then have the ability to consciously respond instead of unconsciously react. Through the development and use of an observing ego, you can begin to be clear about the sources of your thoughts and feelings, which will allow to choose what you do with the information.

With that awareness, you then have choice about how you are going to be. Most of us get told that pain is bad, that it is to be avoided at all costs and if that is not possible, we should minimize it as much as possible. While not advocating an endless search for pain — that would be masochistic — we absolutely need to face our pain when it shows up. Pain tells us something is wrong. When your stomach feels upset, it is giving you a sign that something is not right. If you feel depressed, something is not right emotionally. Society tells us increasingly to deal with the symptom, rather than explore and figure out the cause. This leads to more suffering and a delay in dealing with the underlying pain causing the discomfort.

How we learn to deal with pain, disappointment and other unpleasant things shapes our view of the world and our role in it. Someone with the tools to face conflict and disappointment is going to be much more resilient than someone without them. A resilient person will process the experience, learn from it, and move on. Without a process of consideration, contemplation, acceptance and continuation, most people will live the life of a victim, with no way out of a life of seemingly endless pain.

Amy and John were in similar motorcycle accidents. Each lost a leg as a result of their accidents.

Amy had a healthy childhood. She learned that life is constant change and that you make adjustments to that change. She grieved her lost leg and, the same time, started to sort through how this was going to change her life. She considered the adjustments she would have to make and the challenges and opportunities her loss would bring. Amy acknowledged her lost leg and owned her responsibility in the accident. She began reconfiguring her world to deal with her new circumstance.

John took a different path. He awoke in the hospital to discover his leg was gone and he collapsed emotionally. He could not stop reliving the accident, always feeling angry. John could only see himself as a victim, so grieving was not possible. Nor was he reconfiguring his self and his life to deal with his new circumstance. John had a difficult childhood. His father was a life-long alcoholic who thought he was 'the world's biggest victim.' John downloaded his father's worldview and became a copy of him. John had not been taught any skills regarding coping, adjusting or accepting situations. He was only taught how to live as a victim.

Effective, long-lasting psychotherapy and real problem solving are about getting to the source of the problem and not getting lost in trying to fix the symptoms. It is rarely useful to drag out the disclosure of the real source of pain in therapy. This only prevents healing and solutions that confront the root of the hurtful matter. Delaying the process of working through pain, in most cases, will only intensify the pain.

Exploring Your Downloads

The following section consists of many questions to help you understand the beliefs, values, and attitudes that you absorbed from your childhood.

Take your time. Write your answers down on a separate piece of paper, rather than just answering them in your mind.

When you have finished, you will better understand what you have absorbed and retained from your childhood.

These questions will help you start developing an understanding of how much of you is made up of what you downloaded. The good news is that once you see it, accept it and understand it, you have a choice to keep that download or discard it.

Some of your answers might be surprising and some will be obvious. Whichever your response, be kind to yourself. Just take the time to feel through the awareness and see where it takes you.

Are there some questions and answers that you have never thought about before? Are there some questions where giving the answer feels weird or even upsetting? Those will help you understand the beliefs, values, attitudes and more that you absorbed from your childhood that may be causing problems for you now.

How many of these answers are directly taken from your family's beliefs? Have you ever questioned your family's beliefs? How many answers have come from your own explorations of belief?

DOWNLOADS ABOUT RELIGION

- What religion, if any, did your family practice when you were growing up?
- If there was no religious instruction, were you part of a religious community or religious culture? For example, did you grow up in a Catholic country, or within a Jewish or Mormon community?
- What were your earliest impressions about God or religion?
- In your family's religion, did God have a gender?
- How did God treat people?
- Why was God important?
- Why was God necessary?
- What messages did you get about the purpose of life?
- What messages did you get about death and dying?
- What messages did you get about what happens after you die?
- How did your religion feel about:

- Other sects of your religion?
- Other religions?
- Other Gods?
- Agnostics?
- Atheists?

- Were you encouraged to question your religions precepts and beliefs?
- What would happen if you did question them?
- Is participation in your family's religion essential to remaining part of the family?
- Did your parents love you more than God?
- More than their religion?
- What was the role of the church or religion in your family?
- If you did not get any religious training from your family:
- Do you wish you had?
- What is your current belief about:
  - God?
  - The meaning of life?
  - An afterlife?
- How do you feel about people who consider themselves religious?
- What is the difference between spirituality and religion?
- How have your views on spirituality changed since you became an adult? Or not?

DOWNLOADS ABOUT FAMILY

- What was the configuration of your family? Parents, siblings, and extended family who were an intimate part if it
- What made your family **different** from the others you knew?
- What made your family the **same** as the others you knew?
- In what ways was your family the **same** and **different** from the ones you saw on TV and in the movies?

- What part did you play in keeping your family together?
- Which parent were you closest to? Why?
- How did your other parent feel about that?
- How did you feel about the other parent?
- If you are a parent, how did that impact your parenting?
- If you had two parents:
  - What was their relationship like?
  - Did you know if they had an ongoing sexual relationship?
  - Did either parent talk to you directly about sex?
  - If so, what message about sex did you absorb from that conversation?
  - What did you learn about sex, love and marriage from observing your parents and their relationship?
- If you had a single parent:
  - Did they date or have sexual relationships during your childhood?
  - How did this impact how you saw relationships?
- If they did not date:
  - Did you notice at the time?
  - How do you think that they got their emotional and sexual needs met?
  - What did this teach you about relationships?
- If you are in a relationship:
  - How does your relationship look like the one your parents had?
  - How is your relationship different?
  - Did you intend to have a relationship different from your parents'?
- What messages did you get about having children?
  - Are they "required," "optional," "more is better?"
  - Do you believe that if you did not have children you would have failed?

- What did you learn was the reason to have children?
- Did/Do you want children?
  - Why?
- If you want children:
  - How many?
  - Is this the same or different from your parents?
  - What would you do differently from your parents about child rearing? Why?

DOWNLOADS ABOUT WORK & CAREER

- What was the highest educational level achieved by each parent?
- What messages about education did you get from your family?
  - Were there expectations that you would have a more successful or prosperous life than your parents? Or not?
  - Did you fulfill them?
- Did your mother work outside of the home?
- Did your father work outside of the home?
- What were their professions?
- Did they like what they did for a living?
- Was their job/career what they had always wanted to be?
- Did your parents talk about their work, dreams, or aspirations?
- Was having money, or a lack of money an issue in your family home?
- What role did money play in your family?
- Did you feel you got everything you needed?
- Did you feel you got everything you wanted?
- Did you have enough food, clothing, and shelter as a child?
- If not, how did that impact your school, social, or educational lives?
- When did you learn that money was finite?
- How did that change your view of your parents and how the world worked?

- How did it impact how you felt about your family's status in the world?
- Did you play team sports?
- How was being on that team different from how being in your family worked?
- What was your childhood fantasy about what you wanted to be when you grew up?
  - What age were you?
  - Did that fantasy come to fruition?
  - Do you still want to do that?
  - If not, when did it change?
  - What happened that changed your mind?
- Do you know what your ideal work job/goal is now?
- Are you doing what you feel is your ideal job?
  - If not, what should you be doing?
  - If not, how does that impact your worldview?
  - If not, how does that impact your work life?
- What is the purpose of work that you learned from your family?
- Is your own sense of the purpose of work different from what the family believed?
- If it is different, how is it different?

Going Inside Exercises

The brain is an input/output device. If we want our hand to move, the brain sends the proper signals and it happens. If we have a pain in our stomach, our brain processes the information. Our brain is the central computer. But thoughts are not all that we are. We exist and who we are is deep in the body.

Moving out of the mind, and not identifying with your thoughts, is key to finding yourself. Fritz Perls, the co-founder of Gestalt Therapy said, "*Lose your mind and come to your senses*," and it is still as true today as it was then.

These types of exercises provide the foundation for accessing your intuition. The deeper the relationship with yourself, the more likely you will know when to trust your gut feelings and when not to. That whispering voice inside you can become a body sensation, not just something in your head.

EXERCISE ONE

Here is a starting exercise often recommended to clients who have little to no idea what is going on inside them.

Stop three times a day and ask yourself:
- "What am I feeling right now?" (Physically, emotionally)
- "What do I want right now?"
- "What do I need right now?"

Keep a record, if you can. At the beginning, it is common to find you have no answers. Do not force it. Do not panic. These three questions add up to the first step. It may take some time for you to begin to get some clues about what is going on inside yourself.

Once you are tuning into your feelings, the next question to ask yourself: "Where do I experience that feeling in my body?" "Is it a gut feeling? Is it all in my head or is it in my feet or legs?"

Begin to understand where in your body your emotions and feelings occur. This is the next step toward making sense of them. You may feel fear in the chest. Some feel intuition in the stomach or solar plexus. You may feel love in the heart or even throughout the entire body. There is an old wives' tale that when your ears burn, someone is talking about you. True or not, it is information that something is happening inside of you. With practice and increased observation, you will start to make sense of the information you are gathering.

EXERCISE TWO

Close your eyes and focus on your eyeballs. Imagine rolling them back into your head and then down to the center of your body. Now, take a moment and see and feel what is going on, literally inside of you. Some people are more visual and some more sensation-oriented, try whatever works best for you.

Just breathe into your core and focus all of your attention there. What happens? Do you feel tension? Do you feel sad? Do you see a big empty place? Do you see a dark spot or place? Do you see light? Do you feel light or heavy? Do you see your internal organs? Do you see color? There are no right or wrong answers. This is the first step in getting curious about what is happening inside you and how those feelings are connected to your thoughts and your life.

Akio was a personal trainer. His therapist, Gill, had him close his eyes and focus all of his attention into his eyes.[8] Next, he had Akio roll his eyes back into his head and imagine them going down his throat and down into his stomach. Akio was asked to just stay there and see what happened. What did he see? He said that he saw his lunch. Gill laughed at him being so literal and encouraged him to stay with the process. Much to Akio's surprise, he found he was relaxing. It was a much deeper relaxation than he was used to, and he had no idea why.

Gill asked him what he was feeling. Again, Akio had no idea, but he clearly felt better. Gill encouraged him to ask himself the three questions about what he is feeling, needing and wanting, right now, so he could begin the process of discovering more about himself.

Over the course of the day that followed, he talked about the experience of being in the world differently. It was as if things had magically changed for Akio. He was seeing through new eyes, and he liked what he was experiencing. Before this, he had no idea there was another way of being in his body and in the world.

Meditation

Meditation is popular as a means of going beneath the surface and having a mechanism to do that exploration inside. A degree of detachment from your thoughts is essential to look at yourself. In psychology, this healthy detachment is called the *observing ego* — the ability to say, "Wow that was a curious feeling or thought. I wonder what that was about." When you are awash in your present experience and have no distance, it is impossible to see what is happening within you. If that occurs, someone outside is needed to reflect back the experience and help teach the skill to navigate the interior landscape and build those tools and awareness. A reflection is best received if one wants more knowledge about oneself and can trust the source offering the reflection. In modern society, this is the role of the psychotherapist. Some, but not all ministers, rabbis, and priests are trained to do this as well.

When people think of meditation, they usually think of a sitting meditation. But many people will need to start with a moving meditation before trying to sit. Attempting a sitting meditation before there is an awareness of the inner self can be difficult because of the patience and peace it requires. As a result, trying to sit and meditate too soon stops many people from continuing with the practice. A moving meditation is a superb method to quiet a speeding or busy mind. It is the beginning of deepening into your body. Qigong, Tai

Chi, or a spiritually based yoga provide excellent starting points. There are many types and styles of meditation and many books and websites offering information on the different types of meditation. Check them out and find the ones that work for you.

A SIMPLE MEDITATION FROM TIBETAN BUDDHISM

Sit with your back straight. Close your eyes and mouth. Relax your jaw and face. Put all of your attention on the air entering and exiting your nose. Continue to focus on the movement of air through your nostrils as you inhale and exhale naturally. You might have random thoughts come up: just notice them and let them go, returning your attention to your breath and the sensations of the air entering and leaving your body.

You can make this meditation as brief as one minute when you first start, and increase the time as you feel comfortable. Just notice what happens in your body and mind as you allow yourself to slow down and just have your attention on you.

Time Alone

Being in a long-term relationship can make the journey both easier and harder. Having the immediacy of another to reflect back how we are can be helpful, but also a distraction. We can get into a bad mood or feel unhappy about a partner or something they did or did not do.

There is also benefit to being alone when you want or need to focus on yourself and your process. Being with yourself, fully in relationship with your needs and having the freedom of addressing them, is a true vacation. It is like coming home, and practice for living fully inside you. Living with others or traveling with others is great in its place, but *it is important to find some time in your life that is devoted to your inner journey.*

Couples should take separate vacations regularly; parents especially need to take turns taking a weekend off from the family, by themselves. We all need time to be self-oriented, to be healthily self-centered. This means that if you are over-extended, you have to say no to some requests. Taking care of yourself and having the energy to fulfill your major commitments is your first priority. To be constantly focused on others is to be out of focus with your 'self' and your needs for too long. It will be necessary to shuttle back and forth between your needs and other's needs for you to stay in touch with your 'self.' This has to happen in little ways if you are in constant, direct contact with a child, partner, boss, employee, etc. but you do need downtime with no distractions from your 'self.'

It is important that kids leave the nest and have time on their own, alone, before marriage or a serious relationship. In many cultures, children live with their parents until they get married, then they may move out. But having time alone in early adulthood is crucial for creating the space for introspection and developing self-awareness. It is a key time to figure out what is "you" and what is "your parents." Without separation, the young adult stays merged and submerged in the family paradigms. This period of separation helps young adults gain self-reliance by allowing them to see their parents as separate individuals. The ability to enjoy being alone can strengthen the ability to be in a healthy relationship.

Parenting

Many people have children before they know whether they want them. They are parents before they know if they are really willing to sacrifice a major part of their lives to nurture and take care of little beings. They do it because they think they are supposed to. They do it because they were trained to believe this is what makes you happy. Parenting is a massive undertaking and huge responsibility, and should never be approached lightly.

There are two things that will make a big difference in developing a child into a solid, competent adult. The first is the parent doing as much as possible, before they have children and certainly afterward, to clean up their own pain and deficits from their childhood. Children imitate their parents. It is how they form. The more that parents resolve trauma and wounds from their own childhoods, the less the child has to download and transfer yet again to the next generation.

The second task is for the parent to have some knowledge of child development. Understanding what tasks the child is trying to complete at each age will assist the parent in meeting the child's needs. They should not have unrealistic expectations about what a child is ready to do.

When a child's needs are met, they continue on an uninterrupted line of development and are encouraged to explore feelings and responses. They have the opportunity to be aware of who they are inside and carry less negative programming from childhood. If the parents have the skills to navigate and process their own feelings, they can teach their children how to do it as well.

Kim was a very bright baby. His parents always encouraged his learning. He was constantly praised for his abilities. From an early age, he started to read and was well in advance of his classmates by the time he was ready to enter kindergarten. He was bored at school and had an increasingly difficult time relating to his peers. His cognitive abilities were limited by his brain development. Kim's parents continued to support and encourage his learning, but were missing his social and emotional developmental needs.

Kim was lonely. He felt his entire value was in how much he could learn. That is what made his parents happy. Also, with his advanced knowledge, he could not relate to his peers. He did not feel loved by his parents for being himself and he did not have a path to being social with his peers.

By the time Kim was 12, he felt like a freak. He neither really fit in at school, as he had skipped several grades to attempt to keep him challenged, but he now had even less in common with kids that were so much older than himself.

His parents were lost in their excitement about having such a bright child and took a lot of pride in his abilities, but completely missed his emotional needs. Kim had no roadmap for understanding or processing his feelings, as his parents did not provide that information or training. He did not really understand what feelings were, other than he felt bad all the time. Only by distracting himself with learning, was he able to function.

If parents attempt to shelter their children from every kind of pain, the children are ill-prepared for the inevitable pain that life brings. Loss, death, disappointment, hurt and shame are all things we must learn to process. Ideally, as children, we are taught how to handle these feelings and experiences. A parent's job is to guide their children through disquieting experiences, and not shield them completely. Children need to learn to respond and manage their experiences in both the big world outside of themselves and the even bigger world inside world inside their psyches.

Ten-year-old Eve had a project due in class. As usual, she was not interested, nor did she have the skills to complete the physical project. Following previous patterns, her mother stepped in and did the project for her. Eve was not even in the room, so she learned nothing. Instead of helping her daughter think through the process and learn problem-solving, Mom did it for her. Being taught that she should never fail or have any pain or discomfort was infantilizing Eve. Neither Eve nor her mother learned anything from this lesson. Eve will pay the higher price.

If parents fail to adequately parent a child, or simply do not try, the adult child will have the job of either parenting themselves or finding a good-enough parent substitute (therapist, coach, boss, extended family, etc.) to help them heal themselves. This is the role of the psychotherapist for many people. Long-term therapy is about re-parenting and meeting the needs of the client, needs that were not met by the client's parents.

There is nothing more valuable or important, other than protecting children, than knowing who you are as a parent and assisting your children in finding out who they are.

A Relationship With Yourself

How can you know your truth if you do not know *you*? Truth comes from deep inside. It is not a surface experience. If humanity is to grow and to mature as a civilization, it is important that people know what is inside of the individual self and not just mechanically respond to constant stimulus from outside the human shell.

There is no coming to consciousness without pain. People will do
anything, no matter how absurd, in order to avoid facing their
own Soul. One does not become enlightened by imagining figures
of light, but by making the darkness conscious.

—Carl G. Jung, M.D. (b. 1875) Swiss Psychiatrist

As we move further into a technology-driven, externalized world, it is more important than ever that we put increased effort into exploring our inner worlds. John Nesbitt, in his 1984 book *Megatrends*,[9] talked about the need for "High Touch" to counter all the "High Tech" that was coming into our world. High Touch is remembering that we are dealing with people: remembering it is both people that are inventing this High Tech, and people that are using it. We must not forget that we, as people, need to be heard, seen and valued. Nesbitt's argument was prophetic. But the real "High Touch" is to go inside yourself and not lose *touch* with your real self. If you surrender yourself to the technology, you lose the possibility for relationships and intimacy, which starts inside our self.

— 4 —

Rethinking Happiness

Happiness is when what you think, what you say,
and what you do are in harmony.

—Mahatma Gandhi (b. 1869)
Indian Civil Rights Leader

HAPPINESS IS ONE OF those words that has too many meanings. We all have our own definition of happiness. It could be as simple as enjoying an ice cream cone on a hot summer day, lying in the arms of a loved one, or sleeping until waking up peacefully.

There are the immediate physical level, relationship level, emotional level and the existential level being addressed here.

Having good sex, a sense of accomplishment, a great meal, a favorite dessert, time with a friend, the thrill of excitement, the quiet and peace of no demands, letting go, a good night's sleep, a baby sleeping peacefully — each is a form of happiness, but all are temporary forms. These are all things that happen and pass. We like instant happiness and excitement, but few of us seem to have a deep contentment and stillness inside. How are those qualities found? What are they? Can anyone have them?

Happiness should come from a place of being okay with yourself — a place where you know that you are doing what you think you should. Or where you are at least striving for that place. All those other things like work, friends, church and community can still be external and temporary. There are moments when you might be doing something as simple as eating dinner and taking a stroll with a partner, and you are overcome with a moment of absolute ecstasy and contentment. That moment aligns with your being present in the here and now and where life has led you. In the simplest moments, we can have the feeling we are doing what we were supposed to be doing.

If we are observant of these moments, they can bring a simple understanding of a profound level of happiness. These experiences transcend words. If we are lucky, we can stay in those moments of peace for some time, untroubled by normal daily annoyances. Rather than being focused on that favorite dessert or watching your favorite TV program, which are fine experiences and not to be shunned or avoided, there is something deeper inside of us that shows up when we are truly aligned with who we are and doing what we know we should be doing. It is then that our body and our experience will tell us we are in the right place. Those moments validate that we are on the right path. They encourage us to continue forward, even when it would seem that nothing is going right. To journey inside, to know who you really are allows you to find a deeper, more sustainable happiness.

People use many paths to find a moment of happiness. For most parents, the arrival of a child — assuming the child is wanted and desired — is when that special feeling can emerge. Tragically enough, not all parents have that feeling. For other people, it can happen in prayer or meditation. When people have learned to quiet their minds in meditation, they are aware of their thoughts but not lost or consumed by them. They are living in the present moment. Perhaps it is awareness of gratitude or of coming fully into one's immediate present that sparks a feeling of peaceful contentment. Happiness does not have to be a moment of profundity that manifests itself with an external physical show of emotion. Genuine joy is an internal, private interlude that need not involve anyone else.

The pursuit of pleasure is a path that many take in their quest for happiness. It could be the excitement of the roller coaster ride that takes us safely to the edge of danger or the endless pursuit of the next exciting thing that will distract us from what bothers us in our lives. While these experiences are fun and enjoyable, they are not happiness in a long-term, fulfilling way. Fun can enhance life, but fun is fleeting and the search for the next wave of elation can become a compulsion if taken too seriously, as a source of happiness.

Doing

Many people get lost in doing: staying busy in the endless pursuit of sensation and experience, focused on the external. Doing can be wonderful. It can make us feel alive. But it is just more of that short-term distraction or validation. It does not deepen your relationship with yourself or give you insight into you. It keeps you focused on "what is next?" instead of "who am I?" Some of both is great, but all things in balance. The real contentment and peace come from a place deep inside of you, not the next experience or rush that makes you feel alive. Being surpasses doing when it comes to happiness.

Pride

We should have pride in our accomplishments and celebrate life's milestones. Experiences like graduations, bar mitzvahs, etc., should leave us happy and with a sense of accomplishment. Getting a degree or promotion can bring significant happiness in the moment, but each simply becomes another facet of your life, rather than becoming a continual source of happiness. New challenges will emerge with the next phase of earned achievements.

Too much pride is often the result of attempting to hide shame. Pride is wonderful, necessary and useful in small and moderate amounts, but too much pride is often about pushing away deep feelings of not being good enough. No amount of accomplishments or the pride they produce will bury the shame underneath and make you happy.

Let's not make happiness about collecting external validations, but rather about walking down life's path and about deepening to find your *self*, letting the universe gift you with indescribable moments of ecstasy. That is not to deny joy or wonderful experiences, but just accepting them for what they are — finite moments.

— 5 —

Compassion and
Empathy for Others

*Our uniqueness, our individuality, and our life experience molds us
into fascinating beings. I hope we can embrace that. I pray we may all
challenge ourselves to delve into the deepest resources of our hearts to
cultivate an atmosphere of understanding, acceptance, tolerance, and
compassion. We are all in this life together.*

—Linda Thompson (b. 1950)
Author and Songwriter

THE ABILITY TO PUT yourself in someone else's shoes and to feel compassion and empathy for that person is one of the hallmarks of growing up and being an adult. Most people know what it feels like to have been a target of hurt, whether emotional or physical, and will have compassion for another's distress. Consequently, they will feel the impact from another person having a bad experience.

Bad luck, mental illness, being victimized by violence or circumstance — none of us is immune from bad things happening. Most of us have some reserves, financially and/or emotionally, to weather these storms. Some people may not. Accepting that each of us is vulnerable and deserving of sympathy and understanding is key to being part of the human race.

Getting outside their own experience or perspective is still very difficult for some people. They can see the world only from their individuated perspective and expect that everyone else can and should share this perspective as well. Communication with people who wear blinders is difficult, if not impossible, and compromise is unlikely. Narcissists and sociopaths do not feel empathy or compassion. They may 'get it' theoretically, but do not feel it emotionally. Other psychological disorders and structures can reduce the ability to feel empathy as well.

If you walk through any major city today, you will encounter homeless people. Some of them will have obvious disabilities. Some will not. They may be dirty or smell bad. They might be on their knees begging, prostrate in their helplessness and need, totally humiliating themselves in the quest for help. Their despair can be both heartbreaking and guilt-inducing for most of us. Some people look for reasons to criticize them as a means of blocking any compassionate response. Some give money or help. Others simply look away from the homeless people's obvious pain and discomfort to prevent their own pain and discomfort from surfacing. For all of us non-homeless onlookers, a chord is struck inside. For most, a discordant chord — "there but for the grace of God go I." To touch another person's suffering, even for a few minutes, may simply be too overwhelming when their own emotional state is already heavy.

Boundaries

Most of us have the ability to be empathic, to feel as if we have touched the seed of another's pain. There is a concept associated with compassion called 'merging', but they are not the same. Merging means fully absorbing the pain of others. It feels like taking a swan dive into another person, getting lost in their being and subsequently their emotions. Merging involves being meta-phorically outside of your body and inside the body of another.

Establishing boundaries in all relationships is important. There is a differ-ence between tapping into what you would feel in a situation — compassion — and completely taking on the other's actual feelings — merging. Compas-sion is an emotional approach that involves your internal self. Therapists obviously need to develop more durable empathic abilities than most. How-ever, to survive emotionally as a therapist, minister, healer or a professional compassionate person of any kind, it is key to stay inside yourself and not take on the pain of the other. You have enough of your own pain; it is not necessary or desirable to take on another's. Feel the pain of the other from the perspective of knowing what pain feels like and how horrible it can be, but not while taking on the actual pain of the other person. There is no pay-off and there are significant downsides. To acknowledge, but not absorb the other's pain requires practice.

Beginning therapists are often taught to shuttle back and forth between their experience and the experience of their client. Over time, they learn that the way to have an awareness of what is happening in their client is to stay aware of what is happening inside of themselves while sitting with clients. The be-ginning therapist must learn to distinguish between what is them and what they are picking up from the client. This is very useful for non-professionals and other caring professionals as well.

We have all had someone confide in us about something troubling them. If it happens frequently, practice shuttling and be aware. Notice when you become aware of someone else's feelings. How does it show up inside of you? Where is it happening in your body? Can you tell if it is yours, or are you being empathic and noticing what you are experiencing in response to what you are feeling from the other person? Your body is an amazing tool of information about what is going on outside of you, but only if you pay attention and learn to understand what it is telling you. Practice paying attention to what is going on inside you. At an appropriate time and situation, ask the other person how they are experiencing their emotions in their body as they are talking. This is an invaluable tool to help you learn to know which feelings are yours and which belong to the other person.

Having boundaries to not take on another's pain is not unkind; it is key to emotional balance. Deflecting another person's pain by being critical or angry, however, means you are probably too sensitive to allow yourself to have empathy and are trying to run away from your own pain. Anger at people in pain is usually, but not always, a defensive mechanism for the person who is angry, and not about what is happening in the moment.

Attachment is the great fabricator of illusions;
reality can be obtained only by someone who is detached.

— Simone Weil (b. 1943) French Philosopher, Christian Mystic

Detached

To be detached is not about removing yourself from your present situation. It is not about ignoring the pain of another. Being detached means holding your space in the here-and-now, offering compassion and moving towards others by making efforts to alleviate their suffering, if possible. The effective therapist's job is to witness to some else's pain but not to absorb it — to see the bigger picture and empathize with the client's pain and situation. Then there is the possibility of assisting the client in finding a road out of that pain. That is healing. That is compassion. And just being there as a witness is enough for most. It is not about doing something.

It can take a long time to learn how to hold boundaries between you and another's pain. Meditation can help let go of identifying with one's thoughts, and allow you to step back and watch yourself interact. Once that is achieved, then the observations of sensations in the body and what they signify can become invaluable information. Our bodies are highly sensitive instruments. Learning to understand what they are telling us can mean the difference between hearing something and actually understanding it. Empathy is felt in the body. Not just in thought.

Limits on Giving

To be a successful adult member of a community, you must possess empathy and compassion. But there are limits. This is where religion or some form of morality can play a role. It can teach boundaries and encourage an outlet for assisting the less fortunate. There are people who are truly victims of circumstance, whether it is by birth, personality or because of other people. We, as members of the human community, need to do what we can to assist.

Our intellect and intuition have to be in play. We are not to divorce ourselves from bringing all of us into any situation. Always ask yourself the following questions...

Is what I am going to do going to be really helpful?
Am I doing it to just make myself feel better?
What are my limits?
What is my goal?
What is my intention?
What am I getting out of it, if anything?
If I am getting little or nothing, is that okay?
Do I wish to continue giving?
Is this simply compassion and doing what helps another?

The healthy way to give is to remain conscious of what and why you are giving, but know your limits going in.

It is not always possible to understand what the limits might be or even what exactly is going to happen when we help someone. For example, imagine you are driving along when a car wreck happens in front of you. The car is upside down and the person is trapped. There is smoke coming from the car. Do you wait and have a conversation about what your limits are? Do you attempt to get them out of the car before it is engulfed in flames? Do you decide it is too risky for you to get involved? Do you just watch to see what happens, or do you drive on?

Many people would simply stop and do whatever they could in that moment to assist. They would put themselves at risk helping another. I think this kind of action expresses the best aspect of humanity — concern for others with no reward in sight. Without a thought for themselves, they are simply engaged in the process of life and face what is in front of them fearlessly. That is being alive. The situation might kill you. Yet to live means to have no guaranteed outcomes. Each day is a crapshoot, not knowing when we walk out the front door whether we will return later on in that same form, emotionally, physically, or spiritually.

Why Are You Giving?

Religions generally promote being kind to others and helping those less fortunate. That is admirable. But if the desire to help others is motivated by doing it for an outside entity in return for the reward of a happy afterlife, do those performing the acts genuinely feel the acts of compassion? The religion's followers are instructed to perform compassionate acts and, perhaps enjoy performing them, but telling someone to enjoy and feel fulfilled by a generous act does not mean the person performing the act *will*

feel fulfilled. The motivation to perform compassionate acts must origi-
nate from the person's internal sense of compassion and concern for other
people — altruism. Otherwise, the directive to perform compassionate acts
to ensure a luxurious afterlife seems like telling a dog to roll over to get a
biscuit. We are in this life for the now. Being the best we can be here and
now, genuinely feeling for others in pain or less fortunate is simply being
a good person. This is part of the path to having compassion and empathy
for our self.

Ashton was walking in Mexico one day. He was coming down a hill
on the side of a highway. In the distance, he saw a man in a red shirt
sitting on the side of the road on a railing. The red-shirted man was
some distance from him when he first noticed. Ashton was lost in his
thoughts about the day and not really focusing on his surroundings.

The man's face was unshaven and his clothes appeared clean. As
Ashton got closer, the man stood up and started walking up the
hill. Ashton happened to look down at the ground as the two men
passed. On the other man's feet were two flat white pieces of rect-
angular cardboard, with string holding them in place. Ashton was
shocked, stunned and appalled that someone would be walking
with only cardboard to protect his feet from the sun-baked gravel
beneath them.

Ashton's heart felt so sad for this man. He kept thinking: What
could I have done for him? If I gave him money; how much? Why
was he in this position?

The man in the red shirt did not ask for money, he did not even
look at Ashton, as his head was bowed. Ashton felt so bad for him
and even hours later his heart still went out to him. For days he felt
bad that he hadn't offered to help the man in some way.

I've learned that people will forget what you said, people will forget what you did, but people will never forget how you made them feel.

—Maya Angelou (b.1928) American Poet

Compassion Exercise

Practice this daily. As you go through your day, when you come across a person, look at them and say to yourself:

I am you and you are me. We are the same person.

Practice this for an hour, for a day for a lifetime, it will profoundly change you. It is especially important to do this exercise with people that are not like you. The homeless person on the street and the person of a different race or class are important to include in this exercise. There is a profound truth here, that when discovered and rediscovered each time you do it, will allow your compassion to become accessible and real. And consequently, you will become more real as well.

Conclusion

The key to being engaged and helpful is compassion and empathy but also non-attachment in a Buddhist sense. It means doing what you can do to help, but not getting lost in their pain. We were all moved by the tragedy of 9/11, but it would have served our health to avoid the repetitive TV clip of the plane flying into the towers. Understanding what happened, at least at the most basic level, but not getting lost in overwhelming emotion and pain, is important in such moments. It may sound heartless to some, but staying open to the entirety of the experience and not being lost in the pain allows therapists to help others out of pain. Watching a traumatic event on TV, over and over and over, can give people secondary Post Traumatic Stress Disorder (PTSD). It is served to us as if there is a need to absorb the pain.

From a psychological perspective, watching the trauma over and over might be an expression of survival guilt on a massive scale, which was first experienced as despair, and then turned to anger. Not getting lost in pain, yours or others, is the point of non-attachment. Empathize and understand the emotions of others, but pay attention to your response to their pain while processing and managing your own.

Feelings — emotions — connect us to others. Empathy and compassion are not thoughts. Someone might have an intellectual understanding of emotional pain, but it is through the 'walking in another's shoes' and acknowledging that person's emotions that we can genuinely understand another's suffering (and also their elation and pleasure, but here the focus is on painful emotions). It is by empathizing with the fragility or emptiness of another that we find our own humanity and acknowledge our own frailties and weaknesses.

— 6 —

To Love or Not to Love Myself

Because true belonging only happens when we present our
authentic, imperfect selves to the world, our sense of belonging
can never be greater than our level of self-acceptance.

—Brené Brown (b. 1965) *Daring Greatly*

Self-Love

Self-love, at its best, is empathy for yourself. It comforts you when there is no one else to give support. It can also be an awakening to one's true self-worth and an opening to being loved. Self-love is a first stepping stone to a deeper relationship with the public self. Because of our popular conception of self-love, it is important to understand its role and limitations in development and growth.

Self-comforting is a worthy goal and necessary for all of us, but self-love is not the destination itself. It is a building block that creates a stronger self, so that a deeper meta-awareness of being can be the basis for being alive. In accepting ourselves without judgment, we must also understand that we are constant work in progress. No one is without flaws. Through the process of accepting yourself, you have the opportunity to change how you choose to be in the world, in a fundamental way.

An old saying goes that you cannot be loved until you love yourself. There are people who are loved without loving themselves, let alone liking themselves. There are also many people who love themselves too much, and they are alone as the result. To love oneself, in theory, would close out others. Some people take love, and others give it. Burrowing down into a vat of self-love is not sufficient. Love is energy and it is exchanged. Love is something we give to others and receive from others. It might be romantic, platonic or parental, but love is a gift for all.

Like fear, anger or many other emotions, all of which have value, self-love can become a distraction or the end of the road, which misses the opportunity to reach a deep level of embodiment and comfort through self-acceptance. Carl Jung said, *"The most terrifying thing is to accept oneself completely."* This is a core fear some people have. However, it is required to truly know yourself and be fully present in the world.

The highest kind of love is unconditional love. It is best defined as seeing beyond another person's deficits. "I see you and love you anyway." When it comes to accepting yourself, it is about acknowledging your deficits or faults and deciding to do something about them or not. That is how unconditional love differs from self-acceptance. The deficits do not stop you from loving someone: I love you regardless of your faults; I just love you, good or bad. Self-acceptance means you have a personal responsibility to make a choice about what action you are willing to take or not take when you own something in yourself that is less than it could be. We must accept our faults, but we do not and should not accept them as the end product of who we are. What are you willing to do about it is the next step of self-acceptance. Self-love does not require that you do anything about your faults.

The same process happens with spouses, parents, co-workers, siblings and friends. It is possible to like or love all of these people, yet not like them or their behavior at a given moment. Once you get that concept and its universal application, you are well on your way to a much more peaceful existence and deeper connection to the world.

Self-love, or the pathological lack of love, can be used as blanket amnesty. "I killed twenty people, but I am working on loving myself." "I cheated on my boyfriend, but love myself." This is an abuse of both the word and process of love as well as a cop-out on self-healing. Loving yourself can mean not taking responsibility for your actions. Loving yourself is generally not a path to reassessment and corrective action. Self-love in these situations is largely giving yourself a pass in hopes that it will solve a problem you are unwilling to take responsibility for and solve.

It would seem logical that self-love is the opposite of wanting to kill yourself to escape shame and pain. But the real opposite of self-destruction is accepting yourself, defects and all, knowing that you can do something about them. People who want to kill themselves might very well have a good reason to do so. Perhaps they are in constant pain with no apparent escape. For most, suicide is an escape from the reality of who they are. Many gay and lesbian youths kill themselves because they think they are better off dead. That is tragic. The programming they downloaded from their families and communities tortures them until they choose death rather than to accept who they are. While self-love might be a stepping-stone, it is self-acceptance that will save lives.

Self-respect, self-worth and self-acceptance are the goals of maturity. "I am." "I exist." From a Buddhist perspective: "I chose to be here, on this planet as a human and have this life." "I have created the circumstances of my life." As an adult, "I am responsible for my choices and my responses."

A person has a long bout with drugs. They have abused their body, mind and soul for a long time. Will self-love cure them? Will it put them on the road to recovery? No, it is not a magical cure. Self-love could be used to self-soothe, self-comfort and self-empathize, but in the end, it is self-acceptance that will promote change.

Self-*acceptance* is the opposite of self-hatred. We learn to accept ourselves and not hate ourselves by taking in love from our parents and by owning who we are. Taking in unconditional love initiates self-acceptance.

Without unconditional love, when love is always conditional with an "if," self-hatred and shame are bred — none of which will lead to self-worth or self-respect. Self-hatred blocks you from knowing yourself and prevents you from being truly known by others. Accepting who you are can release the blocks to progress in your life.

Like a balloon, self-love can inflate the ego, but with nothing of tangible substance. Without forming and solidifying your public self, you miss the first step toward interdependence with the world. The single-minded pursuit of self-love is a distraction. Our root self is about our connections to the world — how we recognize everyone as our self. At the level of the root self, we do love everyone because we recognize that we are all the same person, drawing from the same universal energy. By extension, we do genuinely love ourselves. But this is a much higher level of functioning that few people reach. Universal love is the ultimate goal of many religions and spiritual traditions. It requires a lot of effort and patience to arrive at that level of enlightenment.

To focus on self-love is to ignore the deficits in the love we did not get from our parents. To accept yourself is to accept your flaws, but it does not assume you are content with your flaws and shortcomings. Owning the shortcomings is a primary step in changing them.

The exception to avoiding the pursuit of self-love is when you do inner-child work and you need to self-parent. The task in that situation is to love that child part of you and then to integrate the child into the wholeness of the rest of you. Accepting the wounded part and filling it with self-parenting or parent-like input from another mature source is how that wounded part is healed.

No child makes it through childhood completely unscathed. At best, we receive both conditional and unconditional love. Our job as adults is to sort it out, accept who we are, process and change the downloaded messages and beliefs we are not comfortable with. That includes the messages about conditional love.

Love is given and received. We can offer unconditional love to another person. They can offer it back to us. When a child takes in a parent's love and is secure in that love, they will know for the rest of their lives that they are loved. Even when the parent passes away, it is there. That is the feeling that sustains us in difficult times and gives us a model to recognize being loved and how to give love in a healthy way. A parent is not the only source of this gift, but it is one that ideally happens in childhood. Self-acceptance usually comes from being truly accepted by another. It only takes one person providing unconditional love, accepted and integrated in the right way, to change the life of another forever.

Self-love is not equivalent to self-acceptance. Self-acceptance is seeing what is good, owning the bad, and acknowledging that some parts of yourself need work. Recognizing your shortcomings is not about self-abuse or condemnation, but it is about knowing that you can be better. Hopefully, on some level, we can commit to making that happen. But to create a foundation for change, it is necessary to see and own those parts of ourselves we consider unacceptable.

Full acceptance of one's self takes you to a place of connectedness that has love for everything and everyone: accepting everyone's character faults in their fullness, just as you have your own.

Ultimately, you are here in this life to work on yourself and to love others.

SELF-ACCEPTANCE EXERCISE

Make a list of six of your faults.

These are examples of statements you might make about yourself:

I drink too much.

I am critical of others.

I do not trust myself.

I am fat.

I am incompetent.

I cheat on tests.

With your list in hand, find a mirror, perhaps your bathroom mirror. It should be one that you can see your entire face and preferably your entire upper body.

First Time

Look in the mirror and say to yourself each fault and say I love you.

I drink too much,	I love you.
I am critical of others,	I love you.
I do not trust myself,	I love you.
I am fat,	I love you.
I am incompetent,	I love you.
I cheat on tests,	I love you.

Second Time

Look in the mirror and say to yourself I accept that: and say each fault.

I accept that I drink too much.

I accept that I am critical of others.

I accept that I do not trust myself.

I accept that I am fat.

I accept that I am incompetent.

I accept that I cheat on tests.

How did you feel different after each exercise?

What happened in your body?

How did it impact how you feel about yourself afterward?

What were you compelled to do after the exercise?

Take some time to allow this experience to wash over you. Some people may feel out of sorts. That is a great beginning. The point of this chapter and exercise is not to take away love, but to increase and empower your self-acceptance.

PART TWO

Digging In

7

Selfish, Selfless or Self-Full[10]

Many parents use shame and humiliation to discipline their children rather than patience, teaching, and empathy.

FROM THE MESSAGES WE downloaded as children, there seem to be two ways of being in the world either you are *selfless* or *selfish*. They are the opposite ends of the spectrum. Selfish is bad and selfless is good. However, neither is good in excess. Can you be simultaneously selfish and selfless? Is there a middle ground? Is there a healthy selfish? Is there an unhealthy selfless? From the examples above, unquestionably, yes to all these questions.

Selfish is a pejorative that needs to be re-conceptualized in our consciousness. If you look up antonyms and synonyms for selfish, all of the synonyms are negative. Looking at the antonyms about being selfless, the only options appear to be 1) you are either completely self-obsessed and are oblivious to other people's needs or 2) you disappear and have no needs of your own. There appears to be no possibility for a middle ground.

Selfishness

What is *selfishness?* Selfishness means putting yourself before others. That is not always bad. Of course, the issue is, when is this type of behavior appropriate and when it is not?

Most kids download the "I am selfish" belief. How much they download has to do with their personality and how their personality style was used or abused by their parents. Accusations of "selfishness" are blunt tools that shame a child to the core. If a child downloads enough of the selfish shame, they risk functioning with little confidence. They will end up full of self-doubt, plagued by self-questioning, never able to step back and see if their actions are truly selfish.

If people do not develop a healthy public self, they will either be primarily selfish or selfless. Neither is desirable as a single way of operating. Truly selfish people come across as stingy and self-centered. There is never enough love, or anything else so they must get everything available, anyway they can. The problem is that whatever they seek, in this case love, will never be enough to fill the longing and need inside. The worst part is they will not be able to see the pattern. They are out of touch with how they are perceived and experienced by others. Their actions result from what they are feeling inside. If they are angry, they cause pain. When they feel happy, it is because they have something that others do not. Trust in others is not possible because no one else is on their side and other people just think about their own best interests. The selfish person is operating from a place of feeling unloved. Even though they were loved in some way, they are filled with a greedy yearning for the acquisition of things or experiences, to smother the pain of that elusive love being nonexistent or suffocated in childhood. They are too afraid to try and touch that pain, thus it cannot be changed. They attempt to use money, fame, etc., to replace that most essential of human experiences, feeling loved.

We all tend to have opinions about when people are selfish. It is easier to be understanding of them when it does not affect us. We, as well as others, judge each of us about how selfish we are behaving at any given moment, and whether that selfishness is justified or not.

Selflessness

What is *selflessness?* It's putting yourself last, being unwilling to show any obvious need at all. For the selfless, other people's needs are greater than their own, and they themselves are the least important people in any situation. The purely selfless person apologizes for existing and taking up space. Their only value is what they can give to others. We have idolized martyrs as being selfless. Their devotion to others has made them admired and even revered. A mother that eats less to make sure her children get enough food is appropriately selfless. An example of a bad kind of selflessness is an employee who works day and night while others take advantage by leaving their work for the selfless person. Perhaps for the other employees, it is good, but not for the selfless one that cannot stand up for themself.

There are few beliefs more important and in need of confrontation as the concept of *selfish*. Children are shamed, humiliated, beaten and battered while being told they're 'selfish' throughout their childhoods. The wound begins, often from external assaults and children turn it inward into a perpetuating self-abuse by the time they are adults. For many victims, it is hard to make decisions because their every activity gets filtered through the question, "Am I being selfish?" The question stops action, requiring a pause for self-analysis and self-reproach, which can circle back upon itself and become endless. Some people become so afraid of self-promotion that they sabotage their careers and never move forward professionally. Others work themselves to death for others and get next to nothing in return.

Fear of selfishness kills the spirit and stifles creativity when there is no way to be 'okay' to do something for yourself. It is similar to kids who are programmed by their parents and churches with hellfire-and-brimstone religious beliefs and subsequently become frozen in fear. They can believe that no matter what they do, they are going to hell, so why try? If there is not a path that will allow an unpunished life and no matter what you do is selfish, then, to prevent selfish behavior, you either collapse or give up.

Parenting

Kids are naturally narcissistic because they are in the process of forming a sense of self. Children's sense of being comes from having their external experience reflected back to them by parents, teachers and other authority figures — as well as peers — throughout childhood. Rather than explaining to kids that there is another way of handling a situation or helping them see the bigger picture to learn the social skill to be aware of others, some children are shamed into submission. When humiliation is used as a primary technique by the parent, the child can collapse emotionally and never recover. If a child has no other way to see itself, then selfishness is the only lens through which to understand their behavior. Children that have been parented with such negativity will usually parent their children the same way.

Parents give kids both positive and negative programming. This is the result of being parented by imperfect people. In other words, it is part of being perfectly human. Until others challenge our faulty programming or it is exposed through social failures out in the world, the programming will continue unchanged. Even after numerous failures, some people never question their basic programming because they cannot conceive of doing things a different way.

Selfless People

People burdened with selflessness are often burdened with codependency. They give up their own needs and want to fulfill that hope of being loved by others. We tend to applaud this behavior, despite the fact that there is nothing admirable in codependency. It can be justified as being giving and deeply spiritual; however, it is neither because of the motivation behind the acts. Selfless people are just as empty of love as the selfish person, but they respond differently: by constantly giving of themselves as an imitation of being loved or being needed. Being needed is the love substitute. As a child, the selfless person probably felt compelled, through parental physical or emotional hostage-taking, to constantly meet the needs of their parents. Since they were not allowed to have their own needs, focusing on other's needs evolved to be their primary way of functioning in the adult world. Selfless people stay busy to feel necessary and have little to no idea what emotions are roiling inside them. They are oblivious to internal messages about what they want or need. To have one's own wants or needs, to be aware that they even exist, would be reverting to "selfishness." By tuning out their internal voices and focusing on the needs of others, they stifle the pain of not being good enough: they are on autopilot.

Selfless people are overly concerned about what others think about them. Selfless actions are used to make people enjoy and approve of their company or simply not notice them. To be noticed, in their minds, is to be judged or criticized. Logically, it is better to remain invisible. For the selfless, decision-making can be incredibly stressful. There is no way to make a decision that is best for all involved, including themselves. Someone will always lose out. It is a self-abusing way to exist in the world. It means to make yourself inconsequential, to disappear, to disintegrate into a void. For the singularly selfless, to be visible or to take up space is being selfish.

The selfless person will not let love in. An individual who loves the selfless person in time will come to see the selfless person as selfish. But the selfless people do not think they matter, so it is not within their reality to believe that people want to touch or connect with them. For the selfless adult, the love offered in childhood was, at best, highly conditional and, most likely, negative — *you are selfish, you are bad, you are a disappointment, you embarrass me.* The selfless adult, when a child, felt their existence validated only when they received acknowledgment for performing acceptable behavior that met the needs of the parent. As a result, the child developed a negative internal sense of self. They can only be acceptable through giving and doing. Being loved for existing is not reality. A selfless person cannot risk having the love or caring taken away, so love is not let it in because it is not real or permanent.

As for selflessness, there are times when it is appropriate. Perhaps a parent stays in a painful job to support a child, or a spouse forgoes a sex life for some time to allow the partner to heal from childhood abuse or a rape. There are times for sacrifice. Some sacrifice is always necessary when living a life. Part of being a mature adult is knowing when and how long to be selfless.

Being Both Selfish and Selfless

Some people bounce between the poles of selfish and selfless and all people have some degree of this. This can be crazy making for the people close to them as they never know when the selfless or selfish personality is going to respond. Alternating between these extremes would suggest conflicts in the downloaded programming from the parents and that these people are still unconsciously disoriented by it. Emotional wounds from childhood are ruling their lives, and dwelling in the selfless/selfish extremes is an attempt to gain approval from others. To them, it makes sense to be both ways. They have all their bases covered. To others, it can appear to be inconsistent and exasperating. Because the mixed-programmed person is not consistent, pointing out their behaviors can be harder; holding them accountable can feel impossible.

Relationships between a selfish and a selfless person are common. They have made a bargain ensuring their life perspectives will not be challenged. They co-habit in a bubble that prevents the fickle outside world's changing realities from intruding and challenging their co-dependent union. Their future, a lifetime dance of pain and unmet needs, includes the hope, in vain, that somehow the other's love will fill their emptiness.

Self-fullness

The healthy path is *self-fullness*. A person with a well-formed public self will find the balance between self-promotion, self-care, and care for others.

Self-fullness is necessary for self-care. When choosing a place to live, a job, a partner or a friend, good self-care is required to make a healthy decision. Being self-full is about having clear boundaries and knowing when to be visible, when to self-promote, when to say "yes" and when to say "no." Taking care of yourself can be upsetting, even offensive, to other people. But we are ultimately responsible for our self-care, and that is being self-full.

Parents can go years taking care of children without considering their own needs first. In theory, this seems fundamental, ideal and proper. In practice, to the parents, it is exhausting, stressful, and damaging. Parents need to take time to remember, refresh and re-establish themselves. Parents — one of them at a time, in fact — should occasionally take time off for a weekend, at the least, to be selfish and self-indulgent. Time spent alone where one is the center of the world is a necessary part of remaining sane.

Some enlightened companies offer sabbaticals and require employees to take time off. These companies understand burnout and recognize that employees do their best work after rest and time to rejuvenate. It is much easier to be creative and productive when you have taken care of yourself.

The more you own/possess of yourself, the more you have available to give to others.

So much of life is a balancing act between what we *must* do, or at least, think we must do and doing what we *want* to do or what is good for us. Work, parenting, friends, and relationships — all these societal elements require constant consideration, evaluation and reprioritizing for us to stay sane and genuinely take care of ourselves. As in the physics of magnetism, opposing poles are drawn together. Selfish and selfless are the opposite poles of the ego. Too far in one direction and it will cause anxiety in a person's psychological makeup, and a rebalance will be needed.

Selfish people externalize anger. Selfless people internalize anger. While not all people that externalize anger are selfish, just as not all people that internalize anger are selfless, these patterns are consistent in these two personality types. The self-full person will do both and have the awareness to look at the situation, respond and evaluate if the anger was appropriate or not and where to go from there. Self-fulfilled people will endeavor to observe their inner workings and how they interact in the world. Self-awareness and self-evaluation lead to personal growth. For those stuck exclusively at one or the other poles, self-analysis can feel agonizing. Both types of people are already in pain, unconscious as to why, and are defensive against any additional pain coming into consciousness. Exploring the source of pain can be overwhelming; it can inhibit the necessary process of working *through* and *out of* pain. The 'devil you know is less scary than the devil you do not know' is all too often how many people go through life. But we *must* find a path through the depths of the pain to be free and able to live our own lives.

Self-fullness is about celebrating our separation from others and recognizing our essential aloneness in the world while remaining aware that we are still

Selfish—a judgment readily passed by those who have never tested their own power of sacrifice.

—George Eliot (b. 1819) Mary Ann Evens,
Author from *Romola*, pt. 2 *Silas Marner*

part of the world and not different from anyone else. Self-respect, self-worth and self-acceptance are at the core of creating acceptance, compassion and caring for everyone as you do for yourself.

Healing

The most important step in healing the selfish or selfless perspective is developing an *observing ego*.[11] Selfish and selfless people over-identify their existence with their thoughts. They do not have perspective to stop their behaviors and ask themselves:

Is this good for me?
What do I really need?
Why am I acting this way?
Where did this critical voice I hear inside my head come from?
Who told me these things? Are they right?
If I am not my thoughts, who am I?
What is this emptiness I feel in my body about?
What is missing?

An observing ego is essential to be able to ask these questions. Without it, you will be lost in a turbulent sea of thoughts, with no perspective on where they came from or what they might mean.

The key to healing for both of these polar opposites is to let in *caring*. Rejection of caring is at the core of the self-protection. *Caring,* to the adult who was abused as a child, is like the bogeyman — something that will control them and compel them into proper behavior. To allow someone to care for them is to allow oneself to be touched, emotionally. Even if it is a positive emotion, it is an emotion nonetheless and, therefore, as dangerous as radioactivity. A strong emotion that can surface is *hope,* and for this person, *hope* died a long time ago. To defend against caring sounds counter-intuitive, but doing that is what allowed them to survive childhood. The personality formed around this defense creates a negative sense of self. The key to undoing a negative sense of self is to open the gates to caring. As the gates open, the negative self will begin to erode. It will be scary, painful and even terrifying at first, but it is a required step to get to the real person underneath. Once that person is revealed, it is possible to move through and out of the belief of being unlovable.

The process of healing requires building and strengthening a solid sense of public self and repairing emotional wounds.

Because of past trauma and pain, we tend to shy away from situations that might bring up the hurt of those wounds. The only way out of past pain is to encourage yourself to take risks that challenge those beliefs, starting with small ones at first and seeing if the world ends. (It won't.) Create a support system to get reality checks. When distressed by confronting the pain of the past, getting other perspectives from people you can trust will be necessary. This is one of the central jobs of a coach or therapist. When you've made some attempts to process past feelings, pay attention to your interactions and see how it changes your relationships with others. Learn from your experiences, do not just look for the usual, familiar validation that has kept you stuck, recycling your past.

It is not possible to be loved by everyone. The only way to have almost everyone like you is to essentially be a non-entity. Selfless people feel loved only when they are giving, not for being who they are. The selfless person needs to risk not being liked. It will be excruciating at first. But once they have survived not feeling liked, or simply not needed, life will miraculously continue, and new possibilities will emerge. There is a difference between not having your actions liked and not being liked at all as a person. The selfless person has a difficult time distinguishing the difference. Selfishness in the selfless person can be reflected in an unwillingness to let love in or to be touched by others. To allow in caring or love may seem too treacherous, because it would require inhabiting trust and potentially open the door to hurt. If people are always hurting or using you, then you know what to expect: to be used — so you hide behind the drapes and stay available only to service, not dealing with the bogeyman of real emotion.

The selfish person is closed off to caring as well as to love. From the outside, it looks like it is about taking or getting what the selfish person feels they deserve, but inside they still do not feel loved and cared for. Selfish people believe other people always want something from them so they do not believe that caring is just caring. To them, it is manipulation. It has a price, just as it did in childhood. To defend themselves from paying that price, they make sure they get their share of whatever will make them feel better at the moment — temporary respite if at all, to believe that the money or some object will distract from the inward aloneness. This salve for their wound is all they have unless they take the risk of letting in caring. Healing requires them to begin to see the world from the adult perspective of 'give and take' and share with others, instead of the child's perspective of, "It is all about me."

EXERCISE ONE

There is an exercise done in therapy with children who have not formed a solid attachment to at least one of their parents. They are asked to visualize a jar in their heart.[12] The jar has a lid. When they receive a moment of caring or love, their job is to put that in the jar and put the lid back on. This experience of being loved is for them to keep forever. Adults can do this exercise as well. Too many adults have never felt loved or cared for. This heart-jar exercise is one way that can help people feel loved. Practice putting others' care in your jar often! When the selfish or selfless person truly takes in the love offered them and captures it in their heart-jar and owns it, then the path to self-fullness can begin.

EXERCISE TWO

Another exercise used in therapy is to adopt a "good parent."[13] It is not necessary to divorce one's parents to do this, though some may need to. The objective is adding a nurturing parent-figure who could be there for all the times that the real parent was not. I would recommend finding a figure in film, literature or TV who has the qualities that you would want in a parent. It is tempting to choose someone we know, but it is very important they are consistent in their behavior so you cannot be betrayed or abandoned by them. That is why I prefer the figure to be fictional — their personalities are well-defined and unchanging. Star Trek characters are popular surrogate parents. A grandparent who is in a nursing home or dying, or a neighbor can still abandon or hurt you, and that can counteract the benefit of the exercise. Living people are flawed. They make mistakes. Fictional characters can be perfect parents for the child inside of us. The parent of a childhood friend, or a favorite schoolteacher can be used if you need a more tangible figure, someone from the distant past that you would trust to love you if they could.

It is best to do this exercise for one parent at a time, rather than both. Once you have a mental picture of the figure, go into your mind and ask this person if he will be your adopted parent. Assume they say yes: most do. A no would suggest your intuition believes this is not a good choice for you. After a lifetime of bad parents being your only role model(s), it can be difficult to imagine what a good parent might look like, but your intuition might very well be much more realistic about your needs. Once the adopted parent has agreed, begin a tour of your childhood and let your unconscious bring to mind, one incident at a time, places where you needed a good parent to be there. Allow this good parent to give you what you needed in that situation. There might be tears, but at the very least, if you are taking in the caring and love, your body will respond, and you will feel lighter and loved. You are in the process of rewiring your brain to accept caring and to feel safe and loved. This is powerful and can shift your entire perspective of being in the world.

Allowing a therapist to hold a space safe while you do the exercise can enhance the experience and provide you with someone to process and reflect the experience afterward. Having our emotions witnessed in therapy validates them and keeps us from diminishing the experience later.

Healing Continues

You need to know how and where you fit into the world. Otherwise, you get lost in making others meet your needs instead of seeing the bigger picture of life and people.

Interdependence creates compassion and empathy. Codependence does not. If you are giving up yourself to make others like you, it is not love. It is a Faustian bargain — you sell your soul. My shorthand for codependence is *"giving me up to be loved by you."*

Finding out where you belong is an endless quest for some people, but it is worth it to embark on the journey and explore why you may not feel you fit in or belong. As the observing ego becomes aware of a repeated pattern that is not working, it is a signal you need to try something different.

For the selfish person to achieve healthy interdependence with others, a hint is to stop seeing others as competition for resources — love, money or anything else. One step at a time, the selfish person has to realize that others' needs are as important as their own, generally speaking. It is not necessary to get all the stuff or all the attention, as it will never bring love to fill that empty place inside. A selfish person has to face and feel the pain inside and stay with the pain of not feeling loved, rather than externalizing it and beating down the other person. Not everyone is trying to victimize the selfish person, even though their internal universe is saying this is how the world works. It is hard, very hard to move out of this place. As with the selfless, the selfish see themselves as victims. The difference is that the selfish victimize others, whereas the selfless unconsciously set themselves up to be victims to validate their own perceptions of the world.

The central task for both the selfish and the selfless is to stop identifying with their circular thought patterns of victimization. Both are suffocated by their self-abuse and simply do their best to survive. With one painful step at a time and beginning to recognize that thoughts are simply thoughts, instead of defining who they are, the outside world will begin to come into focus.

Laura is in her late 50's, married, but not really. She and her husband have not lived together for years and barely speak to each other.
Laura begins an imaginary conversation with her deceased father:
Dad, you taught me to be selfless. I gave you everything you asked for, but you never thought it was enough. You did everything possible to prevent me from being me. It was like you tried to make my breath yours.

I was just a little girl. It was your job to love me, it was not my job to love you, or you make you look good or make you proud or any of the other things that were about you. My childhood, my life was supposed to be about me, and you never let it be about me. I felt I was never good enough for you to love me. No matter what I did, you told me it was wrong, and that I was not good enough.

You see, a child is supposed to be loved by their parents just because that child exists. But since I never felt that, I never learned that. At 59, I must learn it now, or I won't survive. I still work to make everyone love me and still it is never enough because they do not. And if they do, I cannot take it in.

I'm in a lifeboat afloat in an ocean of love, but I'm not able to let it touch me, because if I do, I will be burned alive. Because of you, love is death. I believed the price of your love was giving up being me. I could not hope to be loved if I was myself, so I had to die.

I worked for others to get love and I also learned to deflect love when offered freely. To finally let love in, I have to say goodbye to you. I think you are the most selfish man I have ever known. Thanks to you, I believed that all men were selfish. That was all I knew.

Now I choose me. I choose to move on. I choose to let you go. I choose to retire your voice, a voice in my head that makes nothing ever good enough, especially me. I choose to open my heart if only a crack and risk the pain of love and see if my fear of it being death is really true. You see, I cannot go on any longer being selfless as you taught me to be. If taking in love means death, which I do not believe anymore, I would rather risk dying to feel love in the hope that I will live my life and not yours.

— 8 —

Redefining Forgiveness

Saying "I forgive you" is about taking care of the other, instead of yourself.

AS A YOUNG BOY, I watched an episode of *Gunsmoke* — a 1960's TV western. In the episode, a man shoots a priest and, as the priest lies dying, he lifts up his blood-covered fingers and anoints the forehead of his killer and offers absolution. The killer is startled and unsure what to make of the priest's forgiveness. The killer had never before experienced compassion, and this tenderness shakes him to his core. The killer feels so guilt-ridden that he kills himself. He could not find a way to live with the pain of having killed someone who was kind to him.

Gunsmoke's writers made a compelling case for religious forgiveness. Inspiringly, the priest lives out his beliefs to his last seconds of life. This one-hour of melodrama has stayed in my memory for over 50 years. Young children can more easily learn other languages because their minds so readily absorb information. Consequently, we are deeply receptive to and influenced by messages received in our youth. Back then I thought the priest's forgiveness was admirable. But now as an adult, a psychotherapist, former Christian and now Buddhist, I have a different perspective of that TV episode.

Forgiveness is a subject about which most people have an opinion. Due to the childhood religious upbringing or immediate family's particular beliefs, forgiving or not forgiving is usually a settled question in most people's minds. Forgiveness is a religious concept. In the West, forgiveness is deeply ingrained in the culture and consciousness whether we are religious or not.

The kinds of transgressive acts referred to in this chapter are violations in which you were an innocent victim. You did not voluntarily play a role in what happened. Your child is killed by someone, or paralyzed in a car accident that was not your fault. These are examples of those kinds of victimizations.

Small and Medium Hurts require a different path to healing. Those hurts were when you had a role in what had happened. The other person may have the bulk of responsibility, but you participated by making a choice to be there in some way. Those situations will be discussed in the Small Hurts chapter.

Overview

It is important that we look at our beliefs about forgiveness and see them in a larger context about life, healing, and as an aspect of why we are alive.

Forgiveness is one of those over-used words that can be made meaningless like *friend* or *love*. We use these words because they are powerful, and we think they will convey a positive meaning. I think forgiveness has no place in psychotherapy. Offering absolution is not good for the victim or the abuser. People have their own process of healing. Forgiveness can derail that process.

Back in the time when the TV show *Gunsmoke* was set, traveling salesmen touted tonics, elixirs and magical cures for every ailment you might suffer, mostly to uneducated country folk, who believed simple solutions worked. Forgiveness is used as today's cure-all elixir. It makes everything ok, and everyone feel better as if bad feelings are not necessary and should be avoided. Say the magic words, "I forgive you" and we believe that we will now be whisked away from the pain of the experience. It might give a short-term reprieve, but you cannot escape the necessary healing process that is required to truly release the pain.

Forgiveness

It is important to differentiate forgiveness from acceptance. A dictionary definition of forgiveness is "offering absolution." Others think forgiveness is letting go of the anger at the one that hurt you. Acceptance is the process of clearing all the pain of the victimization and reclaiming your life and power.

Too often, people appear on TV whose child has been murdered or abused and immediately proclaim forgiveness for the perpetrator. Forgiveness is used as a bypass to try and avoid the pain that must be worked through to let go of victimization and heal. People frequently say, "I forgave them, but I am still angry." The victim did what they were supposed to do, as a product of their religious beliefs, but it did not heal the wound or resolve the victimization.

Forgiveness is about catering to others — the person who hurt you and the people who have witnessed the hurt or its aftereffects. It is a gesture to re-assure others that you are in control of your victimhood, more so than your antagonist. If your perpetrator asks for forgiveness, it is something you may or may not choose to give. The perpetrator has taken enough from you. You need not give more. If forgiveness is requested, it is not required on your part to grant it, and should only be given honestly, if at all. Giving forgiveness too soon or even ever may mean the perpetrator has no real opportunity to own their responsibility and consequently, they avoid their healing. Forgiveness is a central religious concept, and as part of a person's religion, this might be part of their healing process and the path to acceptance. Forgiveness, whatever it means to them, would be the last step in their own healing.

Forgiveness is the wrong goal and absolving someone of their injury to you is neither helpful to you nor the other person. The real goal should be acceptance. Acceptance is admitting that something happened to you and that it hurt. It possibly altered your life forever. Your survival is part of the reason you are the person you are now. Pain is what makes us who we are. How we learn to deal with pain will define how we are in the world. Not having some way to cope with, transform or transcend pain means to live as a victim. Being a victim means remaining angry. Staying angry keeps us trapped in the past. Living in the past prevents us from being able to sincerely love and be loved.

Too many people have gotten stuck in a **victim identity**, meaning their entire identity becomes lost in being a victim. While it is crucial to accept that you may have once been a victim, it can become a deadly trap for some people. Multiple traumas, especially from childhood, can make it very difficult to move out of the victim mindset. However, there is no winning in remaining a victim. It is a black hole of pain. It is the "get out of jail free card" that means, **"I never have to move on. I have a permanent excuse to 'wallow in pain.' "My life will not move forward; it is over already."**

Rather than consciously feeling like a victim, they rush to forgive. However, the trap of avoidance is the same as being a victim. Neither are healing nor freeing. When people feel like a victim, they have to remind themselves that they already forgave the perpetrator. They are stuck in a loop, which as long as they stay in avoidance of being a victim, they cannot get out of.

Some parents make careers out of the loss of their child, through lawsuits, starting organizations and movements, whether they were close to their

Freedom is what you do with what's been done to you.

—Jean-Paul Sartre (b. 1905)
French existentialist philosopher, writer

child or not. A child who loses a parent feels abandoned and fears they will never be loved again. Either loss is tragic, but life goes on.

Healing the pain means: accepting the loss, grieving the 'might have beens,' and knowing that it has changed who you are and will color your world for the rest of your life.

Loss does not mean having to re-live the experience every day. It is a part of the past where it belongs. Pain shapes us and hopefully makes us stronger and better able to survive the small stuff. If we smother ourselves in being a victim, there is no hope, and there can be no life left to enjoy.

Acceptance

Acceptance is acknowledging you are a victim. Acceptance is about completely processing the trauma, grief, and rage of being victimized. Acceptance is about moving being "a victim" to the past where you were victimized. Acceptance is about taking back all of your power from the person who victimized you.

Acceptance requires that you process the pain. *All of it.*

Acceptance requires that you own the anger. *All of it.*

Acceptance means that you have come to a place where the experience no longer controls you; you can look the abuser in the face and not give them your power anymore.

Acceptance means that the pain and the transgressor are part of your past.

Owning your anger is an essential step in acceptance and healing. It is a necessary step to take to reclaim one's power over the transgression before moving toward acceptance. Too many people emotionally collapse under their victimization and never try again, or realize they can get back up. They are lost. They need to find a way to own the pain, feel the anger, express pent-up volatile emotions — write, yell, break something (safely). It is important to move through these stages and realize life will continue; healing can happen. Staying too long in misery does not honor or help the loss. The task is to reach acceptance.

Healing Requires:

- Owning that you were a victim.
- Feeling the anger of being victimized
  - Grieving the loss, the 'might have beens' (the marriage or children that will not happen, the last I love you, etc.)
- Reconsolidation of your life
  - Letting go of being a victim. You were victimized, but you are no longer a victim
  - Accepting that you and your life are different
  - Liking who you are
- Honoring the loss
- Taking back your power from the perpetrator

This process can take several rounds and will not necessarily occur in the listed order.

There is a difference between victimhood and being victimized. One is an identity, the other is something that happened to you. One will lead to healing, the other will not. It is necessary to own that you were a victim and then to process the pain, anger, etc., so you can move into a place of accepting that

You either get bitter or you get better. It's that simple. You either take what has been dealt to you and allow it to make you a better person, or you allow it to tear you down. The choice does not belong to fate, it belongs to you.

—Josh Shipp (b. 1985)
Author, Speaker, Youth Advocate

you were victimized, but that you are *no longer a victim*. Having been victimized is something that happened to you in your past. It is not who you are. Getting to acceptance is crucial in healing and getting on with your life. You still have a life to live. So, what are you going to do with the rest of your life?

Asking for Forgiveness

The forgiveness dance has two partners. One is the act of forgiving — the other is the act of asking for forgiveness.

Polite culture and most religions suggest that when we hurt another, we should ask for forgiveness. It is supposed to show contrition and ownership of the wrong or injury. There is a world of difference between asking for forgiveness and offering an apology. For a perpetrator to ask for forgiveness is narcissistic, because the focus shifts to the aggressor, not the victim. To ask for forgiveness is an attempt by the offender to bypass the shame of having committed the offense and to receive absolution for the egregious act. This is not healing, either to the victim or the victimizer. If a perpetrator really wants to heal, forgiveness should not be sought.

The first healing step for the transgressor is to acknowledge to themself, and ideally to the injured party, that the act was unpardonable. Accepting responsibility is the key to begin healing. Only then can any process of amends begin. Letting the injured party know you are taking full responsibility, and not asking to be let off the hook, shows a real understanding of the violation and pain that was caused.

The next step is to face the guilt and shame of having committed the offense. Every concept has good and bad aspects: love, guilt, shame, even killing. The task here is to acknowledge the guilt and shame. Working through these feelings can be exhausting and agonizing.

Guilt
Feeling bad about something you did or did not do or wanted to do.

Shame
Feeling bad about who you are.
Thoughts like:
I am bad. I am evil. I am sick.

It is often necessary to get help from someone to hold you emotionally so that you can surrender to the pain: a therapist, a sponsor, a minister, or a close friend. Having our pain witnessed compassionately is usually necessary for healing. The other person provides a mirror, not only for your actions, but also for your responses and emotions.

The gun-toting killer in *Gunsmoke* could not hold the pain accumulated in his life that had led him to kill. He had no one to help him in the moments of despair after realizing what he had done. He killed himself because that realization was intolerable. It can be hard, if not impossible, to remember and access the good parts of ourselves when we are deep in the agony of guilt or shame. Part of the job of the witness is to remind you of your humanity and your innate goodness.

Shame and guilt can be millstones when they are not shaped, honed and utilized to deepen and strengthen the evolving self, both emotionally and spiritually.

Owning the unpardonable act teaches us compassion. If we acknowledge our limitations and failures and have compassion for ourselves as just human, we can empathize more easily with another's shortcomings and failures. If you punish yourself, you are more likely to punish others for their shortcomings. This can lead to more isolation, loneliness and victimizing others. Tragedy should bring us closer, and reveal our shared vulnerability, not build walls to make us feel more alone.

Mistakes can be our greatest teachers. Trying to bypass the pain resulting from the mistake by asking for forgiveness misses the **value of the lesson**. Owning, accepting, atoning and feeling the burden of the act are all part of the healing and growth that can come from having made a mistake.

We all have regrets about something, whether we admit it or not. Living with regrets and finding compassion for ourselves is part of finding compassion for others. Finding empathy for others' failures is the benefit that comes along with owning and accepting our own unpardonable acts. This is the key reason why those who commit these kinds of acts should not be let off the hook.

The task for us in our lives is to look inside. Too much of our society is about looking outside ourselves for validation. Or, we spend our time distracting ourselves with the excessive consumption of food, sex, drugs, or alcohol. We may even find a compulsion to collect records, DVDs, dolls, comic books, or graduate degrees, obsessively immersing ourselves into the impersonal — anything to avoid and push the pain out of immediate consciousness.

In Buddhist terms, the task of this and every life is to remember who we are. From a Christian perspective, life is about learning to love others unconditionally. To accomplish either of these, we are required to go inside ourselves to find, understand and own who we are. By not turning away from any ugliness we might find, we can transform ourselves into something beautiful.

The common metaphor is the metamorphosis of the caterpillar into the butterfly. Trite, sentimental and overused. Yes, sure. But accurate. What does the caterpillar see inside the chrysalis? Does it dream about its former life as a caterpillar? Or does it dream of what will be? The period of self-reflection and transformation contains no shortcuts so that the beauty of the healed self can emerge in all its glory.

Reconciliation

How could we expect someone whose child has been killed to forgive the person that killed their child? There is another possible path. A few people who have been innocent victims go through a reconciliation process with the people that victimized them. This means that the two or more people that are forever joined by tragedy have decided to heal through owning and acknowledging the process of their own journey and pain with the other.

Coming together as equal human beings, completely vulnerable, expresses both the pain of the loss and the pain of regret and remorse. Through witnessing another's pain, we come to a place of understanding. The perpetrator is seeing and holding the pain of the victim. The victim is taking in and witnessing the acknowledgment and ownership of the wrong and the consequences of the actions. In the end, the victim acknowledges and/or accepts the apology and the amends offered for those actions. Ultimately, each eventually discovers compassion and humanity in the other. This allows for the deepest healing. It is not a short process, and it takes the willingness of both sides to walk through fire to find peace on the other side. This is about the transformation of horror into solace.

This is not about forgiveness, nor is it about diminishing the loss. This is about fully accepting another person and reclaiming life.

The Missing Piece

When talking about forgiveness or specifically, not forgiving someone, it can be uncomfortable for some people. The concern is that if you do not forgive people, then there is the possibility that you are not going to be forgiven for hurting someone else. In Christianity, forgiveness gets you into heaven and if you do not forgive someone for hurting you, you might not be forgiven for hurting someone else.

At one time, given the development of people and society, it made perfect sense to find a way to de-escalate conflict and make peace so that people in small communities could continue to live together. We now have a deeper understanding of development and spirituality. If we are to support each other in maximizing our growth, then forgiveness is not the path. If done too soon, forgiveness stops the process of the victim healing themselves, and it prevents the perpetrator(s) from healing themselves. That is neither kind nor humane to either party.

The concern here is the fear of punishment or retribution for not forgiving someone. If the goal is growth and possibly reconciliation, how could this not be seen as a higher purpose? The goal is to love everyone. You can love them and not forgive them. You can want them to grow and come to terms with their actions by taking responsibility for them and yet not let them off the hook. While this might seem incompatible on the surface, love transcends forgiveness. Can you love someone enough, to allow them to stay in pain?

Offering someone forgiveness might give a temporary relief, but underneath, they know they hurt someone, badly, and it will not just magically disappear by saying, "I forgive you." And you must still come to terms with the pain of the loss or injury and process the hurt, anger, and sadness of it.

Expressing kindness and compassion is far more profound than forgiveness. You want the other to heal. You really want what is best for them — then you want them to come to terms with what they have done and process it, so they can get on with their lives and not consciously or unconsciously carry the guilt of having so severely harmed someone.

As you take back your power, after processing your pain, loss, anger, rage and sadness, you have an opportunity to be the bigger person. You no longer have to treat them with contempt nor shun them. You can be polite and understand their discomfort without having to rescue them from their pain and guilt. It is the job of the perpetrator to heal themselves. They must own their actions, make amends and apologize. You have the choice and opportunity to accept that apology if you feel it is sincere. If you are in a place to do that, great. Then there is healing, and reconciliation can begin.

Simply giving the other forgiveness is about giving your power away and taking away theirs. It is a lose-lose proposition. It might make things smoother and easier on the surface, but you cannot forgive them and yet still be okay with the level of relationship that existed before.

Conclusion

Words matter, and how they are used matters; words can hurt and they can heal. It is part of our current culture to believe that no one should ever feel bad. Being conscious of our words and actions is essential to being in *community*. Most of the time, deliberately setting out to hurt someone and/or make them feel bad is wrong, not to mention being unkind. However, protecting people from the consequences of their words and actions blocks emotional growth and maturation. It creates generations of narcissists. Feeling bad *is* part of being alive; it tells us something is wrong, brings clarity and creates boundaries that are necessary for real communication and honesty in relationships of all kinds.

The active and passive sides of a human-initiated tragedy are important. Each has to heal, and both have a role to play in the process. Healing together is not necessary, nor does each have to acknowledge the other in the process. But profound healing can and has occurred when both engage the other equally. We are the product of our pasts. Denying our past, trying to avoid it, or trying to leap over the pain is not useful. In the long run, it is disabling.

Let's not talk about forgiveness. Let's explore acceptance and healing.

Compassion is not about forgiveness or absolution, it is about seeing the humanity in a person that hurt you badly, knowing it is their responsibility to heal themselves, apologize and offer amends. That is healing.

Unspeakable loss, unspeakable guilt, and shame can tie people together forever in a dance of remembrance and healing. A tragedy experienced is a key to the door of transformation.

The primary objective is to stay with your pain, whatever that pain is, to work through the process from each side of the injury until it becomes a gift on the journey to remembering who you are and to love others.

Acceptance means healing. And healing requires acceptance.

— 9 —

Victim Identity Disorder

We cannot simply sit and stare at our wounds forever. We must stand up and move on to the next action.

—Haruki Murakami (b. 1949)
Japanese writer, from 1Q84

SOME PEOPLE MAY FIND this chapter harsh and painful. This was written in the style of the DSM, the Diagnostic and Statistical Manual of Mental Disorders, which is the standard work that psychotherapists use to classify behaviors and disorders. This concept, the Victim Identity Disorder, is not in the DSM. This diagnostic structure is used to both emphasize how serious a problem it is and to give an organized description so that it can be more easily understood.

Description

People suffering from Victim Identity Disorder (VID) will see themselves as powerless and unable to overcome the pain of the past while projecting a victim self-perception into a universal view of the world. This new perception is then attached to how religion, government, health and personal relationships operate.

Here are some of their core beliefs:

> The world is an unfair place and there is no hope for something better.
> Life is painful and unfair.
> Everyone else has it easier.
> Others get help I never received.

Often, people suffering from VID are generous and giving in presentation, but underneath their facades, they are resentful and envious of other people's success and happiness.

This personality disorder can be caused by early and, pervasive trauma throughout childhood. The trauma can be physical, psychological and/or emotional, but the key feature is that there was no escape from the situation and/or the pain. The cause of the pain is often the primary caregiver, usually the parents. It can also result from not being rescued from the abuse whether perpetrated by the parents or others. Sexual, physical, and psychological abuse victims can all develop a Victim Identity Disorder.

This view of the world, developed and validated in childhood, is projected onto the adult world. Everyone is suspected or guilty of treating the person just like the abuser did. If the abuser was a parent, then every boss or landlord is perceived as the parent, out to harm them and treat them unfairly or with disrespect. *It is difficult to see authority figures as anything other than perpetrators.*

A converse reaction to the authority figure is the endless search for a savior. The person with VID is always in search of the good parent; the person who will rescue them from this terrible, unfair world. This rescuer might be a religious figure, deity, politician, a rich relative or acquaintance. The greater distance of a potential savior from the VID person, the greater the projection of being rescued by the authority figure can be. Politicians, cult leaders, even CEO's can often be the objects of this rescue fantasy.

Children of the VID sufferer are typically indoctrinated into this perception of the world, as it is passed on from generation to generation. The parent's insistence on this single view of life is abusive and can deny the children other perspectives, causing them to be underdeveloped psychologically. The children are not taught problem solving or how to take responsibility for their actions and life. The family system will replicate and validate this perspective.

Not everyone with a childhood of extreme abuse develops a VID. Two children raised the same way and in the same family can turn out completely different. Some children are more resilient than others, and this makes a difference. Some children also get positive validation and reflection from other people they do not get from their parents. A minister, teacher, coach, or someone in the extended family who makes them feel loved can change and save a child's life.

Five Types of Victim Identity Disorder

TYPE ONE will emotionally and even physically collapse when triggered by trauma and move into dependency on someone else, such as a spouse, therapist, teacher, coach, a religious body or the government. They are unable to care for themselves. They need assistance, and yet resent other people getting assistance, seeing the others are fakers and leeches on the system. They often somaticize[14] their victimization. Somatization is turning emotional distress into physical symptoms or even illnesses, rather than feeling and expressing the emotions being experienced. An example would be when someone feels angry; they get an upset stomach or a headache instead of expressing the anger. This is just one example. Not everyone has this experience of anger.

TYPE TWO is distrustful of society. This type will tend to live a marginal life since there is no ability to trust, and little to no ability to take a stand for self-care or advancement. They are surviving but not thriving. Unable to take the stand or risks that could pay off, like getting more education or advanced training, they go along, surviving between poverty and just making it. School or advancement in a company requires self-confidence and trust that is absent in them. They are resistant to obtaining degrees or working within a system, as it feels as if they are giving in to authority and they will be controlled. They exist on the edges of society, often semi-homeless, often transient, not staying in one place very long, trying to exist invisibly. They often do not trust that the affection they are offered is real or that it will be sustained.

TYPE THREE may be able to obtain wealth and/or substantial resources and yet they will still feel like everyone else had it easier than they did. No one else has it as hard or has worked as hard for their success. In their view, anyone else with success had it handed to them or were helped by family, friends, the government or religion. Those others "got a free ride," while the person with VID had to work extra hard to get anything at all.

TYPE FOUR is the eroticized victim, which is characterized by the pursuit of degradation, humiliation, even annihilation as punishment or retribution for existing. This behavior is prevalent in race play, cuckolding, voluntary slavery and other sexual fantasies. This type of VID actively seeks out situations and encounters that validate and reinforce their lesser status and encourage others to seek the same life. While this has a lot of overlap with a masochistic structure, this is more purpose driven. This type of VID wants to be erased and objectified. Eroticizing the desire is the way they make sense of it and keeps them removed from thinking about their lives by being focused on the other. Their goal is to end their misery by surrendering responsibility for decision making to people with real power, who they feel are superior to them. It is staying in the powerlessness of childhood through limiting their choices and responsibilities.

TYPE FIVE is the rigid religious type. These people were often born into a closed religious environment and were programmed to accept very narrow religious concepts without question. Any information that would challenge that belief system is rejected outright, without any possibility of consideration. Anything that threatens their worldview is an assault on their world and they are victimized. The belief system is the most important thing in their world and is the glue that holds them together. Without it, they fear they would disintegrate and very bad things would happen to them. Defending against any other perspective or reality is paramount to surviving. The rest of the world is victimizing them and trying to harm them by destroying their life and world. People coming to religion later in life, as well, can adopt this worldview.

General Comments about Types

Each type is not rigid; people with VID can be a mix of two or more types. The five types are simply an overview of the broader categories.

The VID person can be prone to paranoia, follow conspiracy theories and are afraid of authority to the point of phobia. They have a hard time believing that anyone can be on their side and are always on the lookout for betrayal or dishonesty. Trust is very hard to give, and often when they do, the person they give their trust to is a replica of the abuser from their childhood.

Any trauma or tragedy in their adult lives only serves to validate their belief that life is unfair, they will always be a victim, and nothing will ever work out for them. The VID person chooses unconsciously to stay in pain. It is how they feel normal. They are drawn to situations and relationships that keep them victimized.

Appendix is a Differential Diagnosis for VID Note: This is for therapists or people with a substantial background in psychology, or those who are just curious.

How they cope

People with VID are prone to looking for white knights or saviors: the bully or saint that is on their side and is going to correct all wrongs and make everything right. They are susceptible to scams and disingenuous spokesmen. When they think they have found someone who understands them, they are willing to sacrifice anything for their flimflam man to succeed. It can be a politician, religious figure or motivational speaker. They fuse their identity and their hopes onto this figure. They are finally able to hope, because help is just around the corner, ensured by the transfer of an appropriate amount of power or money.

They perceive the pain of the past as unsolvable, because it is too much to bear and overwhelming in size and weight. They must not face the monster, as it will consume them. It is to be avoided at all costs. Their victimhood can be worn as a badge of honor or shame. They are not interested in processing the pain and moving on, it would rob them of their identity. The victimization is not something left back in their pasts; it is always with them, just beneath the surface.

Drug, alcohol, sex, and gambling abuses are common for the person with VID. The goal is to bury the pain or at least keep it at a distance.

Resentment and envy roiling at the surface of the person with VID can turn inward and be manifested in self-abuse, somatization and inaction towards helping themselves. It can also be expressed externally through abusing and bullying others with mild to extreme violence. When they become violent, they are attempting to stop what they perceive as more wrongs and can act with extreme self-righteousness and arrogance. Everyone else is wrong except themselves. There is no ability to see or understand logic or reason; the world is a black and white existence. They have a child's view of the world as their principal perspective. Emotionally, they have been unable to grow beyond the onset of their childhood abuse.

Relationship-wise, the person with VID is either going to look for a fellow victim or a rescuer. If they couple with a similar victim, they will validate their shared skewed perspectives. They validate and support each other's observations, and will not challenge the logic of their responses to their perceptions.

If the person with VID partners with a rescuer, the rescuer becomes responsible for ensuring the person with VID feels happy and takes on the job of being the primary caretaker. This might show up emotionally, financially or physically. Unfortunately, it is likely that nothing the rescuer can do will be enough to make the victim feel continually happy, safe or truly loved.

Prognosis and Treatment

Many people with Victim Identity Disorder are resistant to psychotherapy because they expect the cure to happen instantly, without pain or suffering. They are already in constant pain, consciously or not, and do not wish to invite more. Their pain can be experienced as comforting, a reassurance that they're alive, that they can feel. It is difficult, if not impossible, for them to imagine their lives without their victimized identity, their victimhood.

People with Victim Identity Disorder rarely commit suicide. They are unwilling and/or unable to take self-responsibility, and suicide is perceived as a form of taking back power. If they are expressing anger externally, they can force others to kill them: for instance, performing acts that compel police to shoot them or wanting to be on the front line in a war. Mass killers are often victims who want to punish the people they feel victimized them. They have VID, and after externalizing their rage, they either end up killing themselves or are killed by the police.

Their contentious relationship with authority figures makes psychotherapy challenging and sometimes impossible. They are suspicious of every action and refuse to trust even the simplest interaction. It takes a long time to establish trust and to be able to assist the client more directly.

The first step in a shift from victim to having been victimized is to acknowledge that you are a victim. This can be very painful. In therapy I would ask someone to look me in the eye and say: "I am a victim and I always will be." They would be strongly encouraged not to look away, up or down but to maintain eye contact as they were speaking. Then they could close their eyes and allow the feeling to go through them. This is crucial. Owning, deeply owning the original feeling allows the change process to begin. There is a difference between knowing it intellectually and owning the feeling in your body.

Owning being a victim is about taking responsibility for your life. Once that happens, you can begin to change your life. As long as your focus is on being a victim, nothing can change. People with VID are experts at explaining how much of a victim they are. Being a victim is a child's mindset. If the VID person is going to shift, they need to find the most adult part to take charge and make the necessary life changes.

The second step is to figure out what needs to change. If you are a diabetic, perhaps your diet needs to change. If you are sure other people have it easier: ask them how they got to where they did. This process is called a reality check. It is easy to make assumptions about other people that have nothing to do with reality. Everyone makes choices every day. When nothing is working, it is imperative to try something different each day. Success can come from the most surprising places and from unusual choices. Ceasing to be a victim will not happen overnight, but a commitment to the process of finding your most adult self and taking responsibility in whatever way you can, will produce progress. Not changing, not trying and giving up at each roadblock are guaranteed to keep everything the same.

There is some place in each of us where our most competent adult self shows up. Perhaps it is at work, perhaps while parenting, perhaps when exercising or doing a favorite hobby. It is possible to draw on that part of you throughout all the other areas of your life.

Jen was a super manager. When she was at work she was on top of the world. Her success and rise in the company validated her abilities. But when she was at home, she made bad choices. One boyfriend after another was physically and emotionally abusive and she struggled to move on. She could not figure out why she was drawn to the same kind of man, over and over. Her therapist asked where in her life she was the most adult. She replied, "At work." She felt competent and clear-headed in her choices and vision. So the therapist asked her to get in touch in that moment with her manager self. Jen took a few deep breaths and closed her eyes. Her body changed positions. She started to sit up straighter, her chin came back up so she could make direct eye contact and a strong capable woman appeared in the room. Her therapist then asked Manager Jen to look at her relationship and tell her what she wanted to do.

It was clear to Manager Jen that it was time for her current boyfriend to go, because he was only one of the father substitutes in her life. Jen realized she was still trying to get Dad's love. While she had not brought that need into her work, she had in her personal life. It was the most clarity she had ever felt. She was taking responsibility for her choices and getting clarity about what she needed to do differently.

Another key is building on successes. People with VID tend to diminish successes and to make failure the most important part of their life. It is the over-identification of being a victim. Everyone has failures. Everyone. People who dwell on failures or do not learn from them repeat failures. Each one is provides important information about what works and what does not. Learning that lesson and navigating around those obstacles in the future is the way to work toward success. Seeing a failure as a learning situation instead of as confirmation of who you are is essential to moving forward and having a next time to try.

For most people in this situation, some kind of therapy may be necessary. There are deep wounds of childhood that need to be addressed, processed and healed. A successful outcome in therapy requires establishing trust with the therapist, as the VID clients must download a new perspective and grieve the loss of original beliefs. They must process the anger at their parents or caretakers that programmed them to be victims. The client with VID must come to trust the therapist and accept the therapist's point of view. The therapist's task is to help the client build ego strength so that they can tolerate the

It has always been much easier (because it has always seemed much safer) to give a name to the evil without than to locate the terror within. And yet, the terror within is far truer and far more powerful than any of our labels: the labels change, the terror is constant. And this terror has something to do with that irreducible gap between the self one invents — the self one takes oneself as being, which is, however, and by definition, a provisional self — and the undiscoverable self which always has the power to blow the provisional self to bits.

—James Baldwin (b. 1924) American Writer,
The Price of the Ticket: Collected Nonfiction

pain of processing the past and move forward. As clients gain self-confidence that they can handle pain from the past, they can face being in the 'here and now' as something not only survivable but also welcome. One other component of treatment is that children who are victimized are often not taught how to problem solve. They are not tutored in how to think through a process or figuring out the steps to solve life's ongoing dilemmas, both big and small. The therapist teaches the client to solve problems by creating processes to do so. This allows the client a sense of mastery and self-empowerment in the world that is missing from the current purview. The right therapist, paired with the right client, can give a hopeful outcome.

Commentary

The concept of VID is not researched-based, nor is it intended to be a scholarly work. VID is not an actual disorder in the Diagnostic and Statistical Manual of Mental Disorders (DSM) used by psychotherapists to classify mental illnesses. While there has been no discussion about creating this disorder classification, based on a substantial body of private practice experience and consultation, it is very real.

A person with VID can change, if the desire is there. For some, a shift from that perspective will require effort, courage and determination. The style we learned in order to survive childhood is deeply ingrained in our adult minds. Making ourselves conscious of our childhood style of being in the world is the first step in healing and shifting to a more mature way of being in the world.

VID is very painful and it prevents most people afflicted with this perspective from enjoying their life. It is easy, but painful, to see one's self as a victim all the time. There is never a win. While most things in life have a good and bad side, if the bad side is the only one seen or experienced, it sucks out any possible joy of life.

This dynamic is played out in families, workplaces, politics, religions and most definitely relationships. We do create our own reality. In his South African prison cell, Nelson Mandela could have turned bitter and wallowed in being a victim. He *was* a victim, physically and politically, as well as emotionally and intellectually. But he chose to see a bigger picture. He saw his jailers as victims as well, trapped in a prison of their own making.

As long as our focus is exclusively on ourselves, there is no hope for compassion or empathy, because our gaze remains fixed on our dilemma, completely missing the bigger picture of life and the world going on around us.

The brickwork of the prisons we create in our minds is laid in our childhood from our childhood experiences. We have a responsibility to our adult and child selves to dismantle our faulty perspectives, brick by brick, until we can see ourselves as part of all humanity. That is when we can be fully alive. That is when we are uniquely ourselves instead of a robot endlessly regurgitating the programming from our childhoods.

We all have obstacles to overcome. Some are more difficult than others. Lacking money can make the task harder to find time or assistance in healing. Too much money can make you think there is no need to heal, because you can buy yourself distractions and avoidances. While some are hyper-focused on the next life, it is largely a distraction from being here and now. Be here now, focus on who you are, rather than who you think you are. That is worthy of your time and effort. Being subsumed by victimhood is a waste of your limited time. Heal. Process. Move on. There is no honor, wisdom or glory in being a victim. It is a task to complete so you can get on with the rest of your life.

This book, this chapter, this moment is a petition for you to find out who you are. It is a plea for you to take the risk of self-discovery by putting aside the fantasies of childhood and coming out into the world as your true *you*.

——10——

Small Hurts

If you are irritated by every rub, how will you be polished?

—Rumi (b. 1207) Poet

WHEN WE ARE EMOTIONALLY hurt, it is difficult to distinguish between trivial, everyday misunderstandings (what I call 'small hurts') and malicious life-altering tragedies ('big hurts'). If we are to successfully handle what life throws at us, it is crucial to recognize the distinction; otherwise, time, energy and effort are wasted when a discordant incident is blown up into a monstrosity. Others may be subject to hurt by the incident's inflated significance.

Big Hurts: A sexually, physically, or emotionally abused child is a victim. A person sold or forced into a marriage is a victim. A loved one killed by a drunk driver, or killed in a mass shooting — all are big hurts. These unfortunate people were in the wrong place at the right time, mere objects in the tragedy. The experience is life changing. Nothing will be the same after again.

Small Hurts: You get bad service at a store, someone said something mean to you, everyone forgot your birthday — all are small hurts. They may seem like personal attacks on you, but they stem entirely from the perpetrator's temporary emotional state. You have power in the relationship or situation, and while you were wounded, this small hurt requires looking at your part in the interaction before you can address or repair what is happening to the other person. These experiences may cause distress or (temporarily) compromise your daily life, but they do not alter your universe unless you choose for them to do so.

Some of the small hurts can be called 'medium hurts,' but they are processed the same way as small hurts; thus their inclusion in this chapter. These medium hurts, such as an affair, betrayal by a friend or business colleague, *can* change your life and you will certainly feel like a victim, which you were in part. The difference is that you played some role in what happened, rather than being a non-participant in the experience.

Big and small hurts are processed differently. Big hurts require you to go through the process of working through your despair and recovering your power; this process is covered in the chapter *Rethinking Forgiveness*. Small hurts require you to go through the process of looking at your role and choices in the problematic relationship and either change the situation or make new choices.

In modern society, at some point, to some degree, everyone becomes a victim. Because of victimhood's universality, victimization is a major excuse for not taking responsibility. Using victimhood as a scapegoat is another way of bypassing self-reflection and self-analysis — an excuse to avoid dealing with our shortcomings and poor choices. Being a victim too often diminishes the validity of people who were undeniably the objects of a transgression of irreparable magnitude. You might think of someone in your life who "cries wolf" too many times.

We need better terms to distinguish those who have suffered from absolute tragedy and those who have been compromised by lesser interactions, since they can both be called "victims." In this chapter, the words 'small hurts' are used to represent the emotional bruises and major wounds that do not truly rise to the level of victimhood. Referring to them as 'small hurts', keeps the experience in perspective.

A husband has an affair. His wife is enraged that he would cheat on her. She goes into "I-am-a-victim" mode about what he has done to her. What hasn't been discussed is that the two of them have not had sex in years or at best, once or twice a year. They do not talk about sex, they do not talk about what has happened to their marriage or whether they even want to be married. Instead, he is the evil cheater, and she is the victim.

He is not blameless. Instead of confronting his partner about their lack of intimacy or whatever justification he uses, he has looked elsewhere. Instead of ending the marriage or changing the agreements about sex outside the relationship, he bolts ahead and rewrites the contract. Both have contributed to the situation, and both would be better served by looking their own selves, instead of attacking the other. Self-reflection would lead to healing and growth. The relationship might survive and, if so, might certainly be stronger and healthier. Is not making the relationship stronger the real goal? If the relationship did not survive, wouldn't they better off to create something with someone more compatible? This is a stereotypical example from a male/female marriage but the same thing does happen in same sex relationships.

Yes, finding out your partner has cheated on you will hurt. However, getting lost in the hurt is not useful to you. Acknowledging the hurt and processing it is important, but to begin the process of healing and more importantly, to grow from it, requires looking at yourself.

What was my contribution to making them look elsewhere?

Why did I pick this person?

What are my expectations in a relationship and why?

Are they realistic, and where did they come from?

Are my expectations still working for me? What do my partner's actions say about me, as a partner?

Asking these questions and pondering the answers is useful. Focusing on being a victim is not.

All too often, people talk about 'forgiving' a spouse for saying something mean to them. It is perplexing as to what the spouse could have said that rises to the level of needing absolution. In a relationship, as often as possible, emotional bruises need to be processed together. If that is not possible, it needs to be done alone or with someone else. It is necessary to vent the 'hurt' and come to some level of understanding about what happened, why it happened and what will keep it from happening again, if possible. Acknowledging you were hurt or that you hurt someone, intentionally or not, is important. An apology is often necessary and accepting the apology is appropriate. Working through it and letting it go, rather than escalating and holding on to the small stuff, is the key to keeping the connection between the couple alive.

Keeping Perspective

Not all transgressions are created equal. Often the meaning of a remark is completely mistaken and someone feels hurt. Should the person who makes the remark apologize? After it is processed to whatever degree, an apology might be order, but after the processing, it may not be. It is more important for the person who felt hurt to inquire as to the meaning of what the other person, the transgressor, said or ask why the other said that. Information is our friend. Asking questions helps avoid misunderstandings.

Making assumptions can get us into trouble. Sometimes assumptions will be proven accurate. But all too often, emotional bruises that turn into victimizations begin with a misunderstanding coming out of an assumption. Not being curious, not taking the time to develop perspective and doing a reality check, can let bruises go unhealed and damage or end relationships.

If you misunderstood what another person said or why it was said, how is that the other person's fault? They are not responsible for your feelings, you are.

Your job is to take care of yourself. Ask questions. Get clarifications. Accept responsibility for believing something incorrect that was never was intended to be hurtful.

People are imperfect. We often say things that hurt someone else's feelings. We do it before we think, or sometimes with completed thought but with a desire to hurt. And then the damage is done. Words can be as hurtful as they can be healing. But while words are potential weapons, there needs to be some distinction between being physically attacked and violated and being upset by the exchange of words between peers.

Words in a relationship of "non-equals," however, can be as damaging as physical or sexual abuse. A boss or parent who intentionally uses words to bully, humiliate or abusively dominate a subordinate is committing an unpardonable act, because the object of the verbal abuse is not in a position to defend themselves or fight back.

Words between equals, except on rare occasions, are just words. They are part of communication and interaction. Words should not be elevated to the point of being as painful as inflicting physical violence. We should not allow our rage to be so heightened that the words we chose in an emotional outburst will require us to apologize and make amends later.

We bring our best and our worst to every intimate relationship. Far too often, what surfaces is our worst. We often filter our interactions with co-workers, classmates and colleagues. Because there is a stronger bond in an intimate relationship, we may feel those filters are no longer necessary. We may feel the other will overlook our need to be our natural, uncensored selves. We may expect that no matter how much of a shit we are, it will all work out. Too often, people use others in intimate relationships this way, as punching bags. While this may all be "training" from our parents and society, it does not make it right or excusable.

Not all families love or even like each other. If someone is emotionally abusive, it is important, no matter what the relationship is, to stop the behavior or exit the relationship. The fact that they are biologically your family is not an excuse to stay connected. Family members often treat each other abusively. There is an unwritten rule that "you have to stay connected to family, no matter what." Not true. Insecure people created that myth so they could manipulate and control other people. You are not required to give abusive people power over you — whether your biological family, your chosen family (i.e. spouse, lover, cohorts or close friends), your work associates or your neighbors.

Are you sure that what is making you angry is what you think it is?

So often in arguments with friends and especially with partners, the issue being dissected in an argument is not the real one. Arguing about the unfinished laundry could actually be about the lack of sex, or a missed signal about needing tenderness. The lack of sex or the tenderness may be too sensitive an issue to bring up, so the laundry becomes the surrogate.

Bill joined the Army and was transferred with his wife and two children to a base in Asia. They soon found their relationship in trouble and entered counseling. Bill's wife, June, told the counselor they had come in because the husband had resumed smoking while at work, and the she was ready to divorce him because of it. That response immediately seemed out of proportion to the counselor, so she was curious as to what was really going on. They spoke for a while, and it quickly became apparent that the issue was June's depression.

Bill and June had only been at the new post for about three months. She was home alone, with full-time responsibility caring for two boys in a country where she felt isolated, because she did not speak the language. June demanded more of Bill's time and attention, or she would go back to the USA. She wanted him to cure her depression by spending more time at home as her medication. Bill smoked at work to maintain sociability with his colleagues, but also to deal with own anxiety resulting from June's depression. His smoking was not as much a threat to their marriage as her depression was. June's attack on Bill's smoking was what she used to distract herself from her depression.

The counselor focused them on the real issue, and looked at what opportunities there were on the military base that would help June get some assistance with child care and help her end her isolation. They also explored reasonable steps Bill could take to relieve some of the pressure his wife was feeling.

If an argument seems to be out of proportion to the supposed subject, it is time to stop, look through the layers and see what the real hurt is about. The surface argument will just dissipate into nothing. But it requires one of the partners to recognize what is happening beneath, interrupt the progression, and change the focus to find the root. You need to look at the context and put what is happening into perspective.

It is not always easy to change how you are perceiving things, particularly if the two of you are both tired or there is a backlog of unspoken or unresolved issues. The small arguments about less significant things may be the way a couple releases pent-up anger together. It is not the best solution, but it is common. Talking about the big stuff might threaten the relationship, so blow up over the small stuff and keep the status quo. Not a good long-term solution. Generally, if you stick to that method, it will lead to resentment and can be a good recipe for a divorce.

Recreating Our Parents

We are formed in the container that is our parents' relationship, however that relationship might have been configured. If we have a single parent family, the absence of the other parent is still part of the universe that the child downloads. We download elements of our parents' personalities and absorb their organizational-psychological structures. It is common that we take on more aspects of one parent than the other. Part of the reason that parents have trouble with children is that children often download, and then mirror, the less desirable parts of their own personalities. When a parent is not capable of seeing themselves in the child's behavior, they will punish the child for embodying what the child is reflecting. That is why it is crucially important for parents to have worked on themselves and to have some consciousness about how child development works. Otherwise, the parents might just abuse the child for reflecting back their own shortcomings and insecurities.

Jaxon was a typical Southern man, not really a redneck but educated and highly verbal. His and his wife Crystal had three boys. Jaxon was very sarcastic. He was incredibly amusing to talk and listen to. He enjoyed his use of language and it was a defining part of his personality. As his boys grew up, they naturally imitated dad's engaging and florid way of speaking. When the boys turned that sarcasm back toward Dad, he was not amused. While Jaxon enjoyed his impact on others, he did not like being on the receiving end of sarcasm from his sons.

Crystal, who was not without her own verbal skills, pointed out the boys were talking just like their Dad. Jaxon looked in the mirror at how his own behavior came across. Suddenly, he felt it from the perspective of another, and it gave him pause. He was both proud of his boy's imitation and grew more aware of the impact of his own verbal style. He tried to moderate his behavior and educate his boys about the costs of this style of interaction.

"Children begin by loving their parents; as they grow older they judge them; sometimes they forgive them."

—Oscar Wilde, *The Picture of Dorian Gray*

We learn to deal with conflicts and relationships through watching our parents. We mimic their personal style. They are our role models and our "God" at birth, all-powerful and all wise. As we grow up, hopefully, we gain insight into who they are, rather than who we thought they were. Since we had downloaded so much of our parents, it can be very difficult to see ourselves in them. Like the physical features defined in our DNA, it is just who we are.

The Enneagram,[15] (created by the Sufis and brought to the West by George Gurdjieff) is a wonderful tool for looking at how we formed in the container of our parent's relationship. In describing some of the personality patterns we inhabit, it gives both awareness and a path to break out of those patterns and free ourselves. I recommend the study of it. Two highly recommended authors of books about the Enneagram are Helen Palmer[16] and Donald Riso.[17] For a deep psychological/spiritual version read Palmer; for something straightforward and accessible, Riso is the choice.

Elements of your sensitivity, conflict avoidance or conflict obliviousness may have likely been learned from your parents. The old adage that "we tend to marry our parents," either one or both of them, is accurate. So is "I'm becoming my mother/father." In our own relationships, we also tend to recreate our parents' relationship. In childhood we learn a dance of intimacy, watching how our parents interact on all levels. It is the language of vulnerability, anger, sex and all the ways that two people in a relationship interact. When we became adults and first went out into the world, we unconsciously looked for that familiar and comforting way to dance even if it was an awkward, labored or violent one. Hopefully, the dance of intimacy that you learned is an elegant, reciprocating, life-affirming one. It takes a life long journey of increasing self-awareness to let go of the bad footwork we absorbed from our parents. Once we do that, we have a much easier time figuring out who we are and how we choose to be in the world.

Insecurities

Each parent or parent 'stand-in' — if we do not have our original parent, from tragedy or choice — teaches us about our relationship with their gender. It might be a grandparent who makes us feel loved, or it might be a coach who provided the strength and role model in place of a missing or abusive parent. If you have a bad relationship with your father or were too close to your mother, those relationships will inform how you perform in relationships with men or women. We are *not doomed* to recreate the relationship with each of our parents, but if you did not feel loved by Dad, then you are going to have complicated or stressful relationships with men. If you felt consumed by Mom, then the suffocation you felt under her will taint your relationships with women. Your sexual orientation is a separate issue. Gay men as well as straight men will have complicated relationships with all kinds of men if their relationship with Dad was difficult. The same happens in the case of a difficult relationship with Mom. Recognizing and freeing yourself from the lessons learned from your family on how to be in the world is usually needed. Living your life, instead of re-living your family's life, is true freedom and real maturity.

As you gain insight and learn more and gain momentum toward change, it is easier to see what you actually downloaded, instead of being blind to the dynamics. For some, who are badly damaged by their parents, healing can feel like an interminable road. But each step forward is about re-claiming yourself, emotionally separating, breathing your own air and making your own choices. The pain of emotionally separating from your parents and increasing insight about yourself is the price of growing toward emotional maturity and secure adulthood.

It is very rare for kids to grow up with two parents who are completely healthy emotionally. Some parents are much better than others, but as mentioned before, childhood is not intended to be pain-free. Some parents were well-parented themselves, so they were better equipped to help their children through the rough spots. These kids grew up with fewer issues and were emotionally much more advanced than others their age because they were supported in working through the trauma and pain of childhood resulting in healthy adulthood. We all have our issues, some of us much more than others. Parents who are emotionally well-developed are nicer, have fewer outbursts and are really able to set aside their needs in an appropriate way to assist and be there for their children. Being a parent means putting your child's needs first — most of the time.

If a guy's close to you, you can't slight 'em. You can't slight that guy. A real grievance can be resolved; differences can be resolved. But an imaginary hurt, a slight—that motherf***er gonna hate you 'til the day he dies.

—Jimmy Hoffa, as played by Jack Nicholson in "Hoffa"

Are you too sensitive?

Does it seem like you feel emotionally hurt every day, or even every hour? Do you perceive everyone in your life as abusive? Do you think other people should be responsible for being cautious around your feelings? Do you frequently take offense at something negative that happened to you without consideration for the context to objectively understand what just occurred? Does it matter what really happened? Is all that so important that you feel like sulking?

There are many reasons that some of these questions might be answered in the affirmative. But they all mean there is work to do on your sense of self. Almost all people are sensitive in some way. However, too much sensitivity is not only painful for the person who is too sensitive, the over-response to situations and statements can make relationships difficult with others, if not impossible. Excessive sensitivity is not normal nor is it reasonable.

Over-sensitivity suggests a person's perspective is primarily focused outside of themself. What that means is that the experience of their public self comes from the reflection others give back whether in the form of praise, criticism, or just attention. This type of person finds it very difficult, if not impossible, to step back and observe their own behaviors. This lack of ability to self-observe suggests an underdevelopment of the public self that would allow more perspective. If there is no awareness of one's public self, the hypersensitive person comes to crave and depend on that feedback. With either, an underdeveloped public self or the non-existence of a solid public self is a recipe for continual disappointment and a painful life.

What is the solution? Psychotherapy, meditation, yoga and being single for a long time are all good starts. Such activities will assist in developing an observing ego that will support the building or solidifying a solid public self. Meditation, yoga, and psychotherapy are all tools for slowing down, going inside and tuning to the world inside rather than being focused on the external experience. Until a person is able to sort out what is really hurtful and what is or is not about them, every day will seem impossible to survive. Having someone there to listen and to gently reflect a different perspective is an invaluable asset to both the solidifying of the public self as well as having a calmer, stable life.

Are you oblivious to how you impact others?

Do you care about how you impact others? Just as you feel an impact from others people's words, deeds, presence or absence, your own words, actions, presence or absence have an impact on others as well. Cause and effect, action and reaction is the primary law of the universe. It is a two-way street. The oblivious person in particular, may believe this law does not apply to them, but in time, the consequences will show up.

The oblivious person is the flipside of the too-sensitive person. The origin of the problem is same as with over-sensitive people, and the solution is also the same. Both the over-sensitive type and the oblivious are lost in their own universe and do not have a way of seeing their own behavior as a negative trait. Each takes their thoughts very seriously and has no real ability to understand or take in another person's perspective. Each has a deeply damaged public self and is underdeveloped emotionally. The elephant in the china shop must begin to get a glimmer that their own actions are causing most of the problems in life. The consequences will continue to escalate until they are either totally isolated or they begin to get a clue that their actions are what create the problem.

Living lost in your own universe only emphasizes the isolation we all feel, but isolation does not have to be our constant companion — you can change that. It takes effort, facing purposeful self-evaluation and finding a way to see other perspectives. This is not without stress, turmoil and discomfort, but the reward is a greater connection to the human family. While a custodian of your body, part of the journey is to explore and heal the wounds that we brought in to the world and those we experienced here.

We exist in various communities, not in individual vacuums. Feedback from others is pertinent. The key to discovering who you are is finding a balance. Believing everything people tell you without analysis is lazy and valueless. Yet, ignoring all the feedback reinforces isolation, not independence. Feedback from others is information. Figuring out what feedback to accept, and what to reject is a big part of growing up and developing confidence in the world of relationships. A therapist is there to help you sort out the useful information and to support you in rejecting what is not really about you. The goal is to download new tools and perspectives so that you no longer need the therapist. Building a solid public self, with introspection and useful self-criticism is invaluable to you, your friends, co-workers and other relationships.

All relationships are ultimately about discovering ourselves

There are three stages to go through in beginning a relationship. Stage one is what is referred to as *limerence*. This is the time when you are so infatuated that you cannot get enough of the other person. They are all you think about and you want to spend every moment with them. They can do no wrong, and for now, perfect in every way.

Stage two is when you start to lose your illusions about the other person so it is fair to call this stage *disillusionment*. Suddenly, they are not perfect. They use too much cologne or they talk too loud in a restaurant. You are starting to see them more clearly, both the good and the bad of their personality, their actions and behaviors.

Many new relationships end at this point. If there is enough perceived good to continue, stage three, *the mirror* will emerge. The other person becomes a reflection for you to see yourself. This can be startling to many people. While up to now most of your focus has been on the other, now you are beginning to see your own behaviors.

Jim and Jerry had been dating for about two months. Everything was going well. They met at a party and had instant attraction. The initial sex was good and they continued to connect a few times a week until it was clear there was something more here. The initial sexual connection was very hot and a big part of their getting to know each other. They liked many of the same things and had overlaps in their social networks.

After about the four weeks of dating, the sexual heat was calming down. Jim began to see that Jerry, who was a diabetic, did not eat very well. Jim really liked Jerry and was excited about the possibility of something long term and saw Jerry's not taking care of himself as a potential problem. Jim also recognized that Jerry had a much smaller social network than he did and in some ways what they brought to the relationship was unbalanced. He wondered how it would turn out in the long run.

By the time the eighth week came around, Jim had several concerns about the viability of a long-term relationship. But something else began to happen. Jerry had expressed no concerns to Jim about his behaviors and seemed very happy in the relationship they were developing, Jim began to see how he was treating Jerry.

Jim was becoming aware of a pattern in their sex life. He said "no" much more often than Jerry when it came to initiating sex. Also, he was beginning to realize that he was always in control. Jerry was happy, or it seemed so, to let him take the lead. Jim could see it had been a pattern his previous relationships as well. Jim both appreciated Jerry's willingness to go along and not fight to be in charge. By recognizing his own behaviors, Jim could more appreciate what he had with Jerry. Jim also wondered if he really wanted to be in charge all the time, and if it was even good for him. Would Jerry be able to take the lead, if necessary?

All of these questions were unanswerable in the short run, but as Jim was less merged with Jerry and the initial sexual excitement, waned, he was better able to see the both of them. More importantly, as he saw himself, he recognized he had the power to change those parts of himself he felt were not in the best interest of himself or the potential relationship. Or he could move on.

The relationship becomes a very close up view of who you are and to a larger extent, how you are in the world. For some people, this is painful and too much to handle, so they run away. For the ones who stay, no matter how long they stay, they have an opportunity to learn about themselves and grow into a better person.

This process of learning about ourselves in relationships is not limited to intimate ones. How we find out about ourselves rests primarily in all of our relationships with others. The more communicative relationships — friendships, work colleagues, club memberships, and romantic pursuits — we engage with, the more opportunities we open ourselves to learn who we are, provided we are willing to pay attention to what is happening. Many families, churches and other like communities teach what *they think of you* is more important than what *you think of yourself*. This is not true.

Closed communities are usually damaging, whether a sect, a cult, an exclusive group or an isolated family unit. The norms of behavior can be too narrow, and thus the emphasis is on strict conformity. That allows too small of a measure to see our real self. It is necessary to expose ourselves to other communities, families, races, cultures and the world at large, if we are to truly get a bigger perspective. In world history, the most intelligent, progressive, enlightened, tolerant and scholarly societies have been in cities or regions where a great diversity of people lived and interacted daily. It helps us see and understand our impact on others and our self in the world. Information about how we show up in the world is invaluable to our growth and healing.

Finding our limitations

Knowing what we do well and what we do not is useful. Part of maturing is learning what works for us and what does not. As we get older, we tend to narrow our world more and more, until we exist in a very small sphere. There may be fewer and fewer friends, or we choose to live alone. It is important, however, to continually push ourselves out and not lose the desire to expand and grow. Geriatric studies show that as people age, they often become more fearful of change and the world. Being present in a larger world, rather than a small one, will help to keep perspective.

Get some distance

To cure yourself of being too sensitive to the small stuff is to become curious about yourself. Look at who you are, your reaction to people's behaviors and figure out where you might have learned your repertoire of responses. The cure involves developing accuracy and clear-sightedness of your observing ego so that you can step back from your habits and see what you do and why you do it. As long as you are lost in your thoughts and not get they are just thoughts, you are not fully part of the conversation that occurs between people. Being aware of your stuff, while remaining engaged with others will assist you in strengthening your public self and will improve your relationship with yourself and others.

Next, get curious about why other people act the way they do. Think like an anthropologist and try to make sense out of the other person's perspective and why they are doing or saying whatever they are putting out in the world:

> *How do you think they are feeling at the moment?*
> *What do you think is their primary motivation in making that remark or performing that behavior?*
> *How does their action fit into their worldview?*
> *What rules would their community have that would make those actions normal or acceptable?*

Maturing means developing a compassionate and empathetic honesty with our self so as to have more compassion and empathy for others. No one is perfect. By being in dialogue with others, truly engaged in what is happening with others and willing to learn, we grow and become more rational, intelligent, mindful and responsible people.

Do not lean back in anger. Lean forward in curiosity. Attempt to understand and be clear. Ask questions.

People run amok with assumptions about things that have been said to them. Especially what they *think* was meant by what was said to them. They are setting themselves up for misunderstanding, insecurity, bruising and conflict.

Just asking: "What do you mean?" or "Would you repeat that?" or the therapist's response: "Say more about that," is the road to communication and understanding.

Once our defensive instincts are triggered, it can be hard to step back. Take a breath. Replay in your mind what happened. Assess the circumstances. This saves time, drama and potentially the unnecessary escalation of conflict.

Throughout any given day, anyone can trip across plenty of intentional and unintentionally mean things said around and directly to them. You get to choose how or even if you respond. Not taking things personally, or really understanding where someone is coming from, will make your life much easier. If you have to escalate an interaction, it should be for the right reasons and not because of a misunderstanding.

Pause to review your response

- What is your response?
- Are you reacting?
- Is your reaction an irrational, mechanical, knee-jerk reflex?
- Could it be out of proportion to what was said?
- Is your response really about *this* person and *this* moment?
- Was your reaction triggered by something from your past, or from your shared past with the other person?
- Did someone actually just trip over an old wound; are they now about to pay the price for someone else who had done or said the same thing to you previously?

- What are the consequences of becoming emotionally volatile in this situation?
  - Do you risk creating even more conflict and hurt?
- Is this a pattern?
- Do you want to handle this differently, so that you can create a less antagonistic outcome?

But Pause

Before you are ready to address what happened in an incident in which you felt hurt, the necessary pause to analyze the encounter may be five seconds, or more than a month of self-reflection, perhaps with assistance. Usually, you are under no obligation to address what is happening in the immediate aftermath. And often, you are better off allowing yourself time to view all the facets of the episode and how it felt to you. This enables you to confront your emotional bruise in an empathetic, clear-eyed manner. A reaction in the moment to a tense situation might sometimes be required; most of the time it is not necessary. If not, taking the time to reflect, understand and respond will produce an honest answer to what was happening in the moment, without any inflation of emotion. You are in control of you and that will dramatically increase the likelihood of a good outcome for all involved.

By pausing, someone might get by with humiliating you or hurting you. But if there is a pattern that is happening over and over with this person, it is worth the embarrassment of not defending yourself in the moment. Most conflicts or disagreements can be readdressed later. Whether to react or to walk away and deal with the conflict later is always a judgment call. Healing is not always easy, and we make mistakes. Do not abuse yourself because you did not come back with the perfect retort at that moment. Accept that learning and growing does not happen in an instant and that you are still doing both. The question is, "Which is more important, making sure they are punished or pushed back against at that very moment, or healing yourself?" You get to choose and know what is best for you.

If the blow up or incident is connected to some old wound, process the earlier experience(s) and begin to separate the present experience from the past one.

Eddie, an older peer at the office, called Tomas stupid, or at least that is what he heard. Tomas walks away and does not reply. He is enraged and wants to tear Eddie apart. But Tomas controls himself and takes time to pause. After calming down and reflecting on the experience, Tomas recalls that as a child, when an older brother, Jeremy taunted him for "being stupid." Tomas could not defend himself back then, physically or verbally as Jeremy was able to both confuse and humiliate him at will. Once Tomas made the connection to the childhood experience, he could separate the two experiences.

The next task is to process the childhood experience. Tomas could write a letter to his brother, expressing his anger at him for his abuse and how it had both hurt and damaged relations with older men. Tomas needs to get angry, cry, use whatever means to express the feelings he could not as a child. Tomas would then engage in a conversation with his child self. He would tell him that is safe now and Jeremy cannot hurt him anymore. Tomas would tell his child self that he has done a great job protecting him, but Tomas can handle these situations now. And then, Tomas would invite his child self to come home to his heart, and be safe forever.

After that process is complete, it is time to address the current situation:

When Eddie accused Tomas of making a mistake, what was he really saying?

Was it true?

If so, what can Tomas do to correct it, assuming it can be corrected.

If Tomas was not wrong, what did Eddie see that made him think Tomas was wrong?

How should Tomas correct Eddie about what thought he knew?

Having a conversation about this will allow for clarity on both parts. Blowing up would just make the situation worse and there would be no clarity and very likely no positive resolution.

To address a hurt with someone, it is important you be present with just the current event, unless the current event is a repeated pattern from the same person. If it is a repeated pattern it has probably escalated to a medium hurt. It is helpful, if possible, to separate the past from the present. This way you will have a much better chance of clearing the hurt.

Compose a response about what occurred. If it is related to a past experience, you can own that, but only if necessary. For now, it is or was obstructing your path to the present. If this is nerve-wracking to consider, practice what you want to say several times before discussing the episode with the antagonistic person. The key is that you know what you want to say and that you stay in an alert and responsive mindset. Pay attention to the response, instead of tripping over words you want to say as you confront the person face-to-face. Write it out if necessary, but certainly practice so it feels natural to express your feelings and thoughts.

Kim was really sensitive. She felt that all her mother ever said to her was critical. Kim grew to believe she was only worthy of being considered inadequate and in need of correction. Because of her lack of self-worth, going to college was really tough. Being around so many new people and seeing the world through a lens of feeling like a terminal liability was debilitating to her confidence. That was Kim's reality. She didn't think her anxiety and melancholy was cause for alarm. She thought other people must feel this way as well. It was just how the world was.

With one wounding conversation after another with professors and bosses, if you had asked her how the meetings went, she'd say her interrogators were maliciously critical. But was this description accurate, or was it merely her perception? Kim floundered in depression and thought she would not be able to have a successful career or fulfilling life.

Kim's friends saw how unhappy she was and after learning some of her story, encouraged her to seek out professional help. While it was difficult for Kim to ask for help and trusting an authority figure, she felt so bad, she was willing to try anything. Kim decided to see a counselor at the college she was attending. He helped her see that each time she had an interaction with a teacher or her boss that didn't feel positive, her self-confidence collapsed, just as it did when she talked with her mother. Her mother was never pleased with her behaviors and not shy about expressing her disappointment and lack of hope for Kim. When Kim became an adult, she perceived all authority figures as her mother.

Kim and her therapist started to look at some of these conversations and explore what was really said, versus what Kim heard. She was amazed to realize they were trying to be helpful and not hurt her. She learned that not everyone was going to treat her like her mother, and that it was possible to have good, supportive relationships with authority figures. Now she could hear what was actually being said, instead of just hearing her mother criticizing her over and over.

What if it is about them?

Is what happened really about you at all? What if you were just a convenient target for some else's outburst of upset or rage? Is there an advantage in your taking what happened personally? Was it random or unusual behavior — we all have bad days — perhaps an external expression of compassion is the proper response, rather than personalizing and internalizing the offense and feeling hurt. If the abuse is a recurring pattern, you need to rethink the relationship. People who are unaware of how they hurt others will continue to hurt them. You are welcome to try and bring this to their attention, but all too often, the messenger gets punished. Just know that your feedback might not be welcome and you might encounter more hostility and denial. We should certainly try to work things out if there is an investment in the relationship, but there is no assurance of success.

WORKING IT THROUGH

The Questions:
- Is my response proportionate to what happened?
- Do I care if this person likes me?
- What is my investment: with this person? This relationship?
- What do I really want out of this interaction? This person?
- What did it touch in me that hurt so much?
- Is there truth in what this person said?
- Is the conversation a relationship-ender?
- What do I need to do to clear up the interaction?
- Do I want to clean up the interaction?
- Do I need to clean up the interaction?
- What do I really need them to hear from me?
- What is the best possible outcome?
- What is the worst possible outcome?

- Am I willing to risk either of those?
- What is the cost of saying nothing?
- Can I find a way to let it go?
- Was this really about me?
- Does it matter this person sees me negatively?
- How does that make me feel about myself, if they see me negatively?
- How does it change how I see this person?
- Is the situation worth this much effort?
- What is my next step?
- Do I need to talk to someone else to help me get clarity?
- What is needed for me to see this interaction as complete?

If you are uncomfortable with confrontation or possible conflict:

Practice, Practice, Practice

Place two chairs facing each other, no more than five feet apart. Sit in one chair and in the other visualize the person with whom you will be interacting. Take a moment to observe your emotional and physical responses to sitting across from that person. Consider the issues that need to be addressed. Prepare your words. A pillow or stuffed animal can be put in the chair if an object is helpful for you to visualize the person there.

Begin the conversation about the incident in question. You will be giving voice to both sides of the conversation. It is common to switch chairs so you will be in the chair of the person talking. You can also have a different person, someone you trust, sit in the chair and role-play with you. Be sure to practice not only your questions and accusations, but also the answers and defenses the person who had hurt you might respond with.

If sitting and facing the other is overwhelming, start by standing up and as you grow more confident and safe, sit in the chair. Continue practicing until you can have the conversation with the two of you sitting face to face and you are comfortable and confident in what you want to say.

Another way to practice is write down what you want to say and read it out loud. Reading something aloud often makes you aware of changes in the meaning or tone of your carefully chosen words. How it sounds in your head can be very different from what you are actually trying to say. When and if you decide to read it to them, be very comfortable with the material and it will seem more natural. It will allow you to be alert to their responses and yours in the moment. You might also record yourself reading it, and then listen to it. Would you listen to someone saying that? Did it make sense when you heard it being played back?

Expectations

Going into a potentially confrontational conversation and *needing* a particular response from the other person is a set-up to fail. You will likely not get what you want. You are confronting your antagonist to clarify your experience and reaction to their behavior, to take back your power, clear the air, and hopefully, move forward toward mutual respect. They do not have to agree with you. You are not doing this for them; you are doing it for you. You should certainly consider anything they say back to you, particularly if it is not abusive or escalating the tension. But in the end the conversation is about you. You are the one who has to live with you.

Monica's brother sexually abused her for many years when they were kids. He was four years older than her. This was their childhood secret. Like most kids, she felt shameful about sex and confused by what was happening. She loved her brother and did not want to get him into trouble, but still felt bad about the experience. She carried their secret into adulthood and didn't reveal her brother's abuse to her husband when she got married. The burden of her hidden victimhood overwhelmed her. She was chronically depressed, morbidly overweight and had many physical health issues. After a lot of therapy, she decided she needed to confront her brother and tell her family. She could no longer keep their secret and fantasy of the happy home life they all had.

After much practice she wrote a letter to her brother and told the rest of her family. They were very angry and not believe her. They told her she was making it up to hurt her brother and family and should be ashamed of herself for telling such awful lies. Her brother of course, denied the accusations. She had long been the scapegoat of the family, and this was continuation of that family tradition. No matter what she did, it was never good enough or as good as her siblings, so Monica deeply internalized not being good enough. In some ways, the attention she got from her brother made her feel special and liked, a feeling she never got from the rest of the family.

Sadly, being abused for reporting abuse is not an uncommon result. If Monica had gone into the situation needing and expecting the family's affirmation, support and love, being on her side, believing her and sharing her anger at her brother, she would have been even more wounded and hurt. But having prepared for both the negative response from her family and denial of her brother, she was largely unfazed by their response. She broke the silence, stated her truth, there was nothing they could do to her.

Not taking perceived jabs personally

What advantage can there be in taking most things personally? Being attached to how others see us is a set-up for suffering. In our most personal relationships, we let down our defenses. Those we are close to are the ones with the opportunity to hurt us the most deeply. But we also know the tendencies and motivations of those we're close to better than anyone else. The more intimate the relationship, the more essential it is to maintain perspective. No one is able to stay above the fray all the time. We all get lost in our own anxieties and pent-up anger on occasion, and that emotional chaos can emerge as aggression to be thrown at others. When someone antagonizes us, are we really the root of the attack? Stepping back, looking at the situation through a broad lens to figure out what is really happening is always the initial step toward self-care.

Just reverting to a knee-jerk victim response is not rational for our everyday lives. We need to comprehend the context and find the seed of the aggressive behavior. Be in your aggressor's shoes. Look from within their perspective before choosing to respond.

A now largely forgotten psychological theory was called *Psychology of Mind*. It employed an inventive accurate metaphor for thought and mood. A ship's anchor is used to symbolize your low mood. Grab the anchor and drop it into deep water. If you start a conversation by wrapping your arms around the anchor, around that down mood, you will stay underwater, drowning. If you let go of that anchor, you will naturally come back to the surface. The same applies to your mood. If you stop conversing with the low mood, or a situation that is bothering you, your mood will naturally come back up. Only then, will you be able to see it from another perspective and probably be able to resolve it and move on. As much as possible, do not make important decisions in a low mood. When you are underwater "talking with your anchor," you are lost in your perception, and will be compromised by the water and lack of oxygen. You will not make your best choices.

Processing is useful. But wallowing in the process or just going in circles is not productive. You need to be able to obtain perspective to change things, sooner rather than later.

Accepting others for who they are

In our most intimate relationships, we need to accept people for who they are, just as we expect them to accept us for who we are. If you fall in love with the packaging instead of the package, you will eventually be very disappointed. Each of us has our quirks and foibles. It is important to recognize them as a part of our self and others. In intimate relationships, they have to be seen in an amusing way that endears the other to you. If they are seen as irritating, the relationship has a good chance of failure.

People tell you who they are. Believe them. The task is to pay attention to what they are really saying. A man or woman who cheats on their partner to be with you is telling you they do not have integrity or understand commitment. They will cheat on you as well. Either you can accept them as they are, or move on. There is no requirement to like everyone. Love them as part of the human race, sure, but like them? No. Have them in your life? Not necessarily. We have choices. We create our own miniature communities of choice. Be conscious and selective of who you include, and life will be much more enjoyable. All relationships involve compromises. It can be said that an accurate definition for 'relationship' is 'compromise.' Knowing this and being clear about the compromises you are willing to accept makes it easier.

In an old joke, a woman marries a man to make him into the man she wants him to be; she divorces him because he is not the man she married. We all change as we age, because we all live through new experiences. Accommodating change in others and in yourself is part of maturation. When you are in a long-term relationship, hopefully, as you mature together physically, you also mature emotionally and intellectually and live happily ever after. If this does not seem possible, or clearly will not happen, wish the other person well and move on. Accept who that person is, and what that person believes. Accept who you are, believe in yourself. Do what is best for both of you.

Expanding our caring

In most religious and spiritual practices, the goal is to love everyone. This does not mean you have to like them. Caring may mean letting others hurt themselves, because that is what they need to do in order to learn. With children, as in children considered legally underage, we still need to intervene in their behaviors with the hope of putting them on the best track to maturity. But, once we are adults, we usually have to learn our lessons the hard way. Adults do stupid things. Friends and family sometimes intervene for better or worse, but as adults, we are ultimately responsible for ourselves.

Part of compassion and empathy is seeing other people's pain. Even when they attack or act stupidly, understanding they are hurting can change our response and shift our perception of what is happening. There are people so lost in their hurt that they literally see nothing but their own anguish. A conflict with them will have little to do with you. You still have permission, if not the requirement, to get out of the firing line and not allow them to damage you. Your retreat does not have to be due to your own anger.

Striving for compassion in each person's individual journey will help reduce hostilities, diminish defensive responses and stop the interpretation of everyday conflicts as personal attacks. If you care about someone, there is always the possibility of 'giving them the benefit of a doubt.' You want what is best for them and you do not want them to endure unnecessary anguish. You are concerned about what is going on with them and have perspective and compassion for what might be hurting them. Bad behaviors and acting out in various ways may go on and on, but seeing the humanity and connectedness in the other person is what is really important. It helps to reduce stress, isolation and keeps us in contact with the other, even in bad times.

One day, someone stops talking to you. You have no idea why. You could get upset. You could confront them. You could ignore them. You can ruminate as to why. If the person is not a particularly close friend, you have more choices about how to deal with the situation if at all. But in any case, seeing them on their journey and wishing them well is mature, compassionate and not invested in how they see you. Choices make us powerful. Not having choices means we're in a weak position. If your employment or home is dependent on making someone feel better about themselves, about them, at your expense, you are in a weak position. It might be necessary in the short term, but in the long term it will take toll on your self-esteem and self-worth.

Personal power lies in the ability to choose. We have the choice to be upset or to have compassion. We also have the choice to stay or move on. Jesus called this turning the other cheek. Buddha advises us not to be attached. That applies whether the other person likes you or not. Each of these is about stepping back and not engaging. That leaves you all the choices. If you confront, engage or lash back out of being hurt, it limits the possible options of how you might respond more thoughtfully.

We all need to be reminded from time to time that it is not "all about us." And to be reminded that most, if not all, people are lost in the painful experiences of their own lives. How much, varies, but we all have trauma. Frustration and disappointment are part of the human condition. A pet dies. An adult child refuses to let relatives see their grandchildren. They have no work. They have too much work. The possibilities are endless and we cannot know what it is all the time.

Placing things in perspective; looking at the context

Part of growing up is developing the ability, when caught in a situation of conflict, to look beyond one's self and see the bigger picture. Conflicts are rarely only about us. An antagonist is definitely involved, journeying through their individual lives. They have hurts, needs and wants. Those get in the way of our needs, hurts and wants. Keeping perspective will save you from endless hurt and no-win situations.

*Did the person who is behaving poorly towards you have
    a recent loss in their life?*
Did they think you did something you did not?
Do they act badly most of the time?
Do they talk before they think?
Do they always think the worst about everything?
Did they just have a fight with their spouse?
Did their boss just yell at them?

There are so many possibilities about what might have happened to the person who was being hostile toward you. The context is crucial to comprehend the entire picture. The most important perspective is **it is not all about you**. Often, *it has nothing to do with you.*

OVERVIEW OF THE PROCESS

1. Disengaging & Processing

Take your time. Step back. Look at the total picture. Be gentle with yourself. If you cannot do it alone, get help. With practice and awareness, this part will be reduced because so many things will just fall away like water off the back of a duck. Wisdom and experience are great teachers. The goal is to move through the unpleasant experience and let it go. With a little practice, steps become instinctual. Practice until they are part of you.

2. Letting go

Bruises can add up to big pain. Working though the steps outlined is about letting go of the small hurts so that you are free to move forward in your relationships. Whether it is your spouse, your coworker, your best friend, your sibling or parent, each person will hurt your feelings at some time. Being the bigger person, the more understanding person or a compassionate person is about letting go, not forgiving. Work through the hurt, if there is real hurt there, but let the conflict go. Understand the context and/or the motivation and let it go. Figure out what you are actually arguing about. Say what you need to say, hear what they have to say and let it go. Carrying pain around is harmful. Pack animals sometimes need to be unpacked or their strength and longevity suffer. This life is too short and there is too much to do to hang on to small stuff, which, in the bigger picture of life, does not matter.

3. Completions

It is important to put hurt feelings into perspective. Getting lost in a moment will make the situation much worse than it is and can distract you from the opportunity to learn about yourself and your antagonist. There are and will be many big wounds in your life, so do not waste time and energy on a trivial incident drawn from an avalanche of submerged emotions. Richard Carlson's title for his book, *Do not Sweat the Small Stuff* is accurate. The challenge for most people is to figure out what is small or large. It is on you, in that moment, to figure it out. It is not the other persons' responsibility to explain the moment. You felt slighted. You are the one in pain. You cannot determine what the other person is feeling or why. If you do not know if it is a big or small hurt, stop and do not do anything until you know.

If everything feels like a big wound you are much too sensitive or too wounded from the past. You should turn all of your attention to working on healing yourself, because there is clearly no observing ego, therefore no bigger awareness about what is happening. You can be lost in the pain of the current hurt until the next one comes along, and never see your role in creating, extending or even making up hurts that may not even exist.

In the end, our own selves are the only things over which we ever have unequivocal power and control. Use your power of self-ness wisely. Use it to guide and heal yourself. Use it to have stronger and more honest relationships with others and yourself. Use it to live a happier, more resonant life.

—— 11 ——

Being Different
is Not a Choice

*It's really important to share the idea that being different
might feel like a problem at the time, but ultimately,
diversity is a strength.*

—Carson Kressley (b. 1969)
Television personality, activist,
actor and designer

AS WE COME INTO a consciousness of others, more than anything, we
want to belong. Belonging to our family, school and community is part of
where we draw a sense of safety and of being. The baby is merged with the
parent and there is not yet a sense of separateness. But once the awareness
of the other becomes more real, the concept of being acceptable or normal
comes into play and suddenly, fitting in is one of the most important things
in life. Starting with play dates, eventually pre-school and kindergarten, these
are hot beds for making personal comparisons as an increasing awareness of
differences comes into consciousness. It can result in despair, as somehow,
they are not as good as what they perceive in others. If the desire is to blend

in, to feel a part of your environment and to figure out how to get along with people, being very much the same as other people has a lot of advantages.

As we continually try to create a safer community, by making being different okay, it becomes easier to be who you are. It is easier to come out about all sorts of things and own who you are. Having cancer, being transgender, an atheist or a member of a religion other than the local, dominant one, being psychic or vegan, having HIV or another STD — the list is endless. These are some examples of things people may need to or want to be open about. People today are more willing to risk being ostracized than ever before, to no longer hide who they are, and to live an authentic life.

Being Different

Being different is a set-up for ridicule and shaming. Being different means negotiating many potential pitfalls and landmines. For children to suddenly understand they are different in some way can be devastating. Children can be cruel and remorseless in their determination to belittle or destroy someone different.

> *I do not have the same skin color as you? How do I relate to you?*
> *I am really short and when I look up at you it makes me feel younger, less competent and powerless.*
> *I am fat and everyone else is skinny.*
> *I have braces on my teeth. I do not see anyone else with braces. Am I deformed in some way?*
> *I feel as if there is something wrong with me. I do not feel like one of the group.*

Some differences are obvious: race, ethnicity, age, looks, some developmental disabilities, deafness, blindness, birth defects, birthmarks, scars or missing body parts.

Some differences are less obvious: being gay, lesbian, bisexual, transgender, intersex, or having Klinefelter's syndrome.[18] This is just a short list of some of the many invisible differences people all around you have.

Inside, all minorities sense they are different. And if that difference is invisible, often people will go to great lengths to protect their secret because they know if they reveal it, they can be harassed, bullied, tortured and made to feel less than others. There is something inside that tells us from an early age that to fit in is the key to being safe. Kids who realize they are gay or transgendered at an early age somehow know it is not safe to tell people, especially their family, even if they do not yet understand their exact nature. They just know they feel different.

It is not possible to overstate the impact on how a person is formed growing up feeling and/or being different. Still, some thrive. Being different has a dramatic impact on how you feel about you, whether it is visible or not. The way a person responds to being different is found both in their genetic makeup and in how children are parented. If a child is assisted in developing a strong sense of self, they have a much better chance of succeeding even against incredible odds. It does not mean they were not damaged. That damage or pain may very well be the driving force underpinning their determination to succeed. One way people compensate for being different is to be better, more successful, better educated, to shine more brightly to compensate for their self-perception of being less than others.

Many give up, stop trying and never find their voice or place in the world. It is easy to be victimized and to get lost in being a victim. If you collapse and only see the world from the perspective of being a victim, there is no path out of the painful world of the shame, and a victim you will remain. Each slight, or perceived insult will wound you again and again, and validate the inner belief that you are bad or worthless.

A life spent living in fear of being rejected is no life at all. Fear can freeze us to the bone in the same way the wind goes through our clothes in the middle of a winter snowstorm. We can find it too easy to imagine the worst possible things happening. While there may be consequences, even severe ones, from being rejected, most of the time the torture inflicted by one's self-talk in fearful anticipation is generally worse than what actually happens. Wallowing in fear of what might happen is painful to go over and over in your head, instead of facing the reality about how people feel about you and where you actually stand with them. Once you establish your position, you can deal with facts, instead of a fear-plagued fantasy.

Everyone is different in some way. Everyone has parts other people either dislike or would find uncomfortable to be around, mostly out of ignorance or stupidity. But living your life just so that others are comfortable diminishes you. There is also the difference between forcing your difference on someone and being respectful. If you expect them to respect you, you need to respect them, but it all starts with self-respect and self-acceptance.

Socialization

In many families and religious communities, people are socialized or programmed to believe that the community's opinion is more important than their own perspective. There is a place for reality checks and community norms, but completely giving up one's own perspective for the group mentality is dangerous and contrary to a secure sense of public self and capacity for self-confidence. Enforcing sameness is counterproductive to building respectful, broad-minded communities.

Being some way that is not within your family paradigm can be perceived as simply your rejection of them, from their perspective, whether you intend that or not. Cases of children being killed, thrown out of the home or shipped off to be "cured" simply for being gay, are well documented and still common. But families and communities can have all sorts of different requirements for maintaining membership that the individual just cannot conform to. Shakespeare's *Romeo and Juliet* is a play famously about choosing one's own desires over the family's desires and the heartbreaking destructive consequences of deviation from group belief.

Part of being an adult, or becoming an adult, is to own who you are. Differentiating yourself from your family, community, and religion as well as acknowledging in what ways you are the same, is all part of that maturation. If you are raised Christian and you come to the conclusion you do not believe that particular religious perspective, your belief may or may not be well-received by your family or community. If the family or community places a high value on shared beliefs and actions, this could feel threatening to them. As we individuate from our families, come to terms with who we are and accept ourselves as okay, we have the capacity to accept others who are different from us, rather than persecute or fear them. Too often, we sacrifice ourselves for the approval and acceptance of others.

Actually, most children go through childhood wondering, from a little to a lot, if they are truly loved at all. The rebellion that many children display at adolescence is, in part, a test to see if their parents love them. But if feeling different means that you cannot risk exposing who you are, either to your family or the outside world, for fear of being rejected or harmed, the damage will be reflected in how a child sees themself for the rest of their life. If the difference is obvious, such as race, then the family might offer a refuge from the danger of the outside world, and teach the child to deal with being different, both externally and internally. That is the best possible outcome. Good parenting makes up for most of the problems children experience in the world.

We take the coping skills, the programming or socialization we learn in childhood, into adulthood. We can be trapped in hiding or protecting ourselves, or we can work through the programming we have downloaded from our families, communities or the world in general, and make our own choices about how we choose to be in the world.

Hector has been in the army for 18 years and dreamed of retiring from there and starting a new life. Hector is transgender. She knows deep inside she is a woman. She joined the Army right out of high school in an attempt to prove to herself that the feeling she was in the wrong body was not real. As her father and brothers taught her to do when she felt hurt or afraid, Hector only needed to toughen up. Then those confusing, terrifying thoughts and feelings would go away. But they did not.

Hector struggled to keep the feelings at bay through work and living the way her fellow soldiers did. But no amount of drinking, work, weekends away where, in fleeting moments of bliss, she could dress and glimpse herself as a woman, would take away her fear that if she revealed her real self, her life as she knew it would be over. And she was right. At that time in history, her military career would have been over, she risked the danger of being assaulted and even killed. And since she had stayed in the closet and the military so long, she was just a few short years from retirement and the possibility of creating a life that would allow her real self to come out and blossom.

Many years of playing a role and hiding had required much sacrifice and self-denial until her self-deceit was second nature. It would take a lot to learn how to let go and let her true self emerge. Staying in the closet had validated and solidified many layers of self-hatred and self-loathing. It would take lot of time and help to gain a new perspective and become vulnerable. Hector knew that most of her friends would go away if they knew she was a woman. Living in a hyper-masculine, conformist, military society left little room for any degree of individuality. But a real life often requires a new life. It is not a sacrifice, but a gift to come home to who you are. Hector would find home within herself and Sofia would emerge.

Shame

The shame of being different and the need for survival can drive people to hide parts of themselves out of fear of rejection and retribution. The antidote to shame is bringing whatever caused it into the light. Once the light is shown in these dark corners, there is a healing process that can happen. Give yourself time to go through that process. There may be more rooms to be opened and the light brought in.

We all have shame about something. Shame is feeling bad about who we are. Guilt is different. Guilt is about feeling bad about something we have done, want to do, or did not do. While there is overlap, the key here is facing the shame about who we are. Once we accept ourselves, others do not have the power to make us feel bad about ourselves.

You will know you have worked through the shame when you can come out to someone, receive a negative response and not be hurt, damaged, destroyed or made to feel less a person. Their response is not about you. Their response is about their ignorance, fear and insecurities. They have their issues to work through. Not being tied to how others see you, even accept you, is the foundation of being fully you.

Finding peace in being different and even joy is key to accepting who you are and in time others will as well. Coming out is no longer just for gays and lesbians.

Growing up, I just wanted to be like everyone else. I didn't value or understand the beauty in being different at the time in my life.

— Marisol Nichols (b. 1973) Actress

The Big Reveal

Coming out is the act of accepting yourself more than needing to be accepted by others. If you are hiding who you are, overtly or covertly, because something about you causes you to fear rejection, abandonment, or injury, you are in a closet. A diamond under a rock will not sparkle with all of its possibilities.

There is the act of coming out to others, and there is the act of coming out to yourself, fully accepting you as you are. That creates the opportunity for you to stop wasting energy on an internal war of self-hatred.

Come out, come out, wherever and whoever you are. Find out who really loves you for yourself. Most of all, accept yourself and bring out the person you really are. You have to value yourself enough to find people who will love you for who you are. Ideally, and hopefully, that is your biological family. If not, you get to create a family based on choice. These are people who love you for yourself and support you as you are.

There is one caveat. Safety is paramount. If coming out or being honest about who you are puts your life in danger, perhaps by depriving you of food and shelter or bringing threats of death, consider delaying your announcement about being different. Not coming out in that situation is understandable and necessary. But if that is true, the first and primary task is to create security and to remove yourself from the unsafe place. You cannot fully come into who you are while hiding. It is imperative that you find a safe place, where you are loved for who you are.

To reveal a hidden part of your life, coming out should be planned and rehearsed. Coming out is for *your* own benefit. It is not for your parents or family or community. Coming out is for you. If your self-acceptance is dependent on them accepting you, it is a set-up to be hurt, because you have no control over how the others will react. Too often when men who were sexually abused come out about their childhood abuse to their families or their perpetrators, they find themselves abused again — this time verbally, being called liars, tattletales and sometimes much worse. They are re-victimized by their perpetrator, their families or even the authorities who were supposed to protect them. If you decide to come out, do not have any expectations or requirements about how the information will be received. Coming out is your opportunity to take back your power, to reveal who you are on your terms and to begin life as a whole person.

How do you rehearse? Place an empty chair or couch in the room. Imagine the person or persons you are talking to, sitting in those seats before you. Verbally present to them who you are. Sense how you feel *as* you do. See how you feel *after* you have said your piece. Practice this over and over until you no longer have the need to hear their reaction to your coming out. What you are doing is expressing your feelings and truth. I repeat, practice this over and over until you no longer have the need to hear their reaction to your coming out. This is about you and for you; it is not about or for them.

When you come out to your family and friends, they will have their own kind of coming out after yours. They may need to keep the issue secret for a long time. Your family and friends must come to terms with who you are in their own way and time. You probably did not get to your happy place overnight and they probably will not either. Give them time.

If it is not geographically or emotionally possible to come out in person, it is completely okay to write a letter, send an email, talk on Skype or Facetime or even send a video. A letter, email or video can be very useful, especially if you suspect an extreme or negative response. This gives the receiver of your coming out time to process, adjust, research or just scream — hopefully not at you — as they digest the information and formulate a response. If there is the possibility of a violent response, do not do it in person. Make sure you are safe from physical harm.

If you come out and receive confirmation that you are not going to be loved for who you are, it may be necessary to leave your family, friends or community behind.

You are under no obligation to have a relationship with anyone in your family, or from your past, who is not healthy for you.

Anyone who cannot add positively to your life should not be in it.

For most people, after the initial coming out to oneself and perhaps to a friend or an understanding person, there can be a phase of wanting to share it with everyone and shout it from the mountaintops. This is common once gays and lesbians come out. Once the shame fades, they want to tell everyone. Telling people is normal and healthy. It is part of the normalization of your new visibility in the world. But it is possible to share too widely in the beginning, before you are prepared to deal with different responses. When you come out, not everyone will share in the happiness of your news. The first coming out conversations should be with people you reasonably expect to be supportive. Someone you thought would be open to who you really are might blindside you, but generally, on an intuitive level, we already know who really loves us and will support us.

After doing a lot of work in therapy about being sexually abused by his uncle in childhood, Chang decided to tell the family about his abuse. He was sure no one knew. He wrote his family a letter telling them about the abuse he suffered from his uncle and the healing he had undertaken and accomplished to put the harm behind him. He wanted his family to protect other family members.

Chang got mixed responses. His parents were in denial. Both accused him of lying and being a tattletale. His sister, Asa, was mad at him because he was bringing up her own memories of being sexually abused by the uncle as well. She claimed to have put it in the past and was angry he was dragging all the horrible memories up again.

One of his cousins was supportive and also revealed that the same uncle had sexually abused him. Because Chang had succeeded with his therapeutic work, he knew he was revealing the abuse only for himself so that he could release the pain and not for his family's acceptance, agreement and/or apology. He handled the emotional consequences of the disclosure with maturity. He did not dwell on the negative responses and was able to support his cousin with his own emotional issues.

Benefits

The *first* benefit of coming out about something in your life is finding out *who loves you for yourself, not for who they want you to be*. Life is so much easier when you absolutely know who loves you for you. This includes family, friends, religious, work and any group you might be a part of.

The *second* benefit is caring for others who are also different. For those who do not get stuck in being a victim, it brings compassion, empathy and a willingness

About all you can do in life is be who you are. Some people will love you for you. Most will love you for what you can do for them, and some won't like you at all...

— Rita Mae Brown (b. 1944) American writer

to face and deal with the world as it really is, rather than as a fantasy of everyone being the same. Everyone wants to be accepted for who they are. Accepting our differences and understanding others' differences makes us stronger.

The Curse of Being Like Everyone Else

The curse of being the same as everyone else around you is that you may likely end up going through life asleep. Most people do. It has never occurred to them they have been programmed. Why would it? Things in life seemed to work largely as they were told to expect. Most of their friends had the same experience. There was little or nothing to make them question their programming, so they grow up, go to school (or do not), get married, and have kids. Because that is what everyone does. The only reason to question it is when you do not get what you expect, or suddenly you are different.

A veteran returns home from war. An accident leaves them paralyzed or disfigured. Becoming different or unhappy is what causes people to look at their expectations (programming). Suddenly, life is not working out the way they were programmed to expect. With a new, visible difference, people treat them differently, as if they had a contagious disease. Suddenly, they are on the outside, wondering what happened to the world they knew.

Midlife crisis happens when many men wake up and realize they are unhappy. It usually occurs around age 40, when they have a wife, kids, and a career.

They have done all the things they were supposed to do, but are unhappy and do not know why. It is a shock. They feel trapped and rudderless about how to deal with this internal crisis and get to a happier position. It never occurred to them that they were programmed from childhood, or that this programming might take them to places unfulfilling. Some look outside of themselves and figure if they change the things in their life that are making them feel trapped, everything will be fine. While it is an internal crisis, they will likely attempt to solve it by changing the external parts of their life — thus the cliché of the fast car or a younger wife.

Surprise! The programming swallowed in childhood didn't lead to the happy ending that was promised. For the true believer who has never questioned the path or the goal, this can feel like the end of the world when it all falls apart. As that reality hits, it can be devastating and throw all his beliefs into chaos. Many are trapped financially with family or work obligations. They may get depressed and turn to alcohol, drugs, sex or any number of destructive and mostly unhealthy bypasses to distract from pain and unhappiness. 'If I do not think about it, it will go away,' is the game they are playing with themselves and their life.

Boys are not encouraged to have an expressive emotional life. Consequently, most men do not have a model for going inside or examining their feelings. This leaves them with few options to resolve this inner crisis. The superb book, *Raising Cain* by Kindlon and Thompson, has the subtitle, *Protecting the Emotional Life of Boys.* We are not doing that. For a healthy society, it is essential that we raise emotionally intelligent boys. It would transform their relationships with women and make the world a much better place.

Women raised in traditional life paths have their own version of the midlife crisis. Being a mother is not all they imagined it would be. Once the kids leave home, who are these women now? To decide not to have children is a break with the core of the programming. How do they reconcile being a woman, or even their continued existence? Deciding not to marry or have children is always an issue that brings the programming from childhood into question.

There are two major downsides to being like everyone else. The first is not realizing you have even been programmed. We have all been programmed. It is a normal part of growing up and learning to be in the world. It is also called being socialized. While not all programming is bad, it is still programming, and *if you want to be your authentic self, you need to choose to be you and not just the sum of your downloads.* The process of consciously accepting or rejecting your programming, piece by piece, is taking responsibility for how you show up in the world. The second downside is that you may have simply been and done whatever it was that your parents expected of you. You do not have an obvious test of finding out who loves you for you.

Just doing what you were programmed to do can cause you to stay in jobs or relationships that are not feeding you. It is like being on a treadmill that goes nowhere.

It is worth taking the risk of being you.
It is invaluable to know who loves you for yourself.
Break the spell and know who you really are.

Worlds Merge

People are now more aware of and willing to question their programming. The earlier they do this, the better the chance of living life on their own terms. With the advent of abortion, contraception, mobility and other benefits of modern society, people have more choices and they can often act on them, instead of just doing what they were programmed and fated to do. They have a much better chance of having a satisfying and fulfilling life. This way, when you arrive at a point where you are still not happy, you have the ultimate responsibility for your choices and no one else to blame. Life is easier when you are not a victim.

Resolution

Being different from an early age makes people see the world differently. That can be a huge advantage. It lets you know that not everyone is the same. It can create empathy for differences and understanding of people on the outside of the norms. It can also make you stronger and empower you to make your own choices. For most people, being the same means going through the steps they were trained to take. But at some point, it is likely that those steps will eventually lead to a place that does not work. When they encounter those moments and are wholly unprepared, it can be devastating. Neither being the same nor being different can guarantee success or failure. It all comes down to the individuals and how they deal with conflict and pain.

Good parenting is key to giving children what they need to survive being different. A person's personality type, being liked or ignored, or the parent's unequal preferences and treatment of the child, can all contribute to children turning out differently.

Life is too short to allow something about you that may not please other people, rob you of contentment with yourself. Their response is not about you. Their response is about their own ignorance and fears. They have their issues to work through. Each of us deserves to be happy. Find your path. Accept who you are, find your community, your family of choice, and enjoy life.

——12——

Spiritual vs. Religious

The religion of the future will be a cosmic religion. It should transcend a personal God and avoid dogmas and theology. Covering both the natural and the spiritual, it should be based on a religious sense arising from the experience of all things, natural and spiritual, as a meaningful unity. Buddhism answers this description.

—Albert Einstein (b. 1879)
Physicist and Philosopher

RELIGIONS ATTEMPT TO ANSWER humanity's universal questions about what happens after our body dies. Individualistic spirituality is an exploration of the possibilities of what is next and why you exist, so that you can reach your own conclusions about life and death. As we continue to explore our inner landscapes, answers will evolve with reevaluation of our previous experiences and the addition of new episodes. That is the key point of spirituality: continuing to push the boundary of what we think we know, in order to see what emerges from our progression into the unknown.

Some people are able to combine personal spirituality and organized religion. They are less defined by the rules of a religion, yet keep the superstructure of the religion. This gives them a framework as they explore more deeply into themselves, questioning and adding new experiences in an attempt to learn more about themselves and the world they live in.

Organized religions seem to revolve around controlling people's behaviors. The religion's directives attempt to establish social order by providing rules by which to structure their follower's lives. In *God is Not One,* Stephen Prothero asserts that each religion was started to solve a problem. For instance, Buddhism was started to end suffering. Christianity was started to end sin. Each had its own purpose and was designed to fulfill that end.

Sex seems to be an obsession for many religions. A large amount of time is spent talking about sex, how and when to have or not have it, and with whom. Perhaps this was important in a time when we did not have contraceptives. However, as we have evolved and have more choice and control over our reproduction, much of the obsession with procreation seems out of date and intrusive.

Being spiritual does not require that you believe in God. Living a spiritual life means being open to new experiences, new information and new understanding. Many people have spiritual experiences when they go out into nature. Most people would not refer to nature as God, but feeling both the connectedness and the smallness of one's self in nature is a profound experience.

'The Tao that can be described is not the eternal Tao."[19] That is to say, the God that can be described is not God. Religions seem to be overly concerned about materializing a defined God. They are determined to know what God is thinking. Such an activity is simplistic and unrealistic. If there is some force big enough to have created the universe, it would be beyond our limited minds. So much harm in the world is done in the name of fulfilling an individual human's interpretation of God's wishes. Over-defining God seems to limit, rather than expand, the possibilities of our existence.

This need to define God is an urge to anthropomorphize the Unknown. It is all done in the spirit of reducing anxiety about the unsolvable questions, and for most, putting those questions to rest. It is an attempt to stop or limit inquiry, so that other less troubling things can be focused on. It encourages a focus more on things that are tangible, comprehensible or controllable.

Personal spirituality manifests itself as an endless quest to explore the unknown, but not necessarily resolve the unanswerable. The goals are to be comfortable *not* being able to comprehend everything, and to embrace that nothingness. Why is an answer required? The unanswered question or undefined state of being is so much more powerful. For some people, to know the unknowable *is* the challenge and their reason for existing. The quest for those answers is the foundation of a personal spirituality.

People do get to answers. Zen Master Linji said, "If you meet the Buddha on the road, kill him." Linji is using the value of shock to instruct his followers to think, react and search inside of themselves for answers, not to seek enlightenment from a charismatic 'fearless leader,' not to give away the power inherent in all humans. Life is your teacher. A good spiritual teacher is a guide to ask you questions, to cause you to reflect or look at yourself in new ways. While Jesus did these things, his followers who created a religion were not as wise. Religions can become businesses, with the need to stay in business. The business of religion can undermine a spiritual pursuit.

We usually need an outside source to help us gain a better perspective of our journey and ourselves. The mentor's job is to push us further down the road, not to be the answer itself. The mentor is on a journey as well. Hopefully, they have been on it longer and are aware of traps along the way. The mentor's task is to assist us on our journey, not to stop it.

To be happy in the world, it is necessary to have a cosmology (or at least a working theory) that explains:

What happens after we die?
Why are we here?
What is the purpose or meaning of life?
Why are there differences between people?
Why are some born into wealth and some into poverty?
Why do bad things happen to good people?
Why do good things happen to bad people?
How do we all fit together?

The point of this exploration is to understand that a fear of dying — hand-in-hand with a fear of living — can be extinguished. When we release these fears, a large amount of our psychological energy is unleashed. A door is opened to a path that allows for our continued exploration and recovery of our deep interconnection and a discovery of our connection to something much bigger than ourselves. Humans instinctually have always known how to evolve into better humans, but our knowledge of 'what life is about' has been subsumed by society and religion.

Some religions do a better job than others at answering these questions. It is up to you to figure out what works for you and what doesn't. My personal path after being raised Southern Baptist was Buddhism. I call my journey Spiritual Buddhism. Buddhism is a path rather than a religion and it fits most definitions of what a religion is as well. In my experience, it is a path that simply gets richer and richer as you go further down the road. For me, it is not

There is no deeper pathos in the spiritual life of man than the cruelty of 'righteous' people. If any one idea dominates the teachings of Jesus, it is his opposition to the self-righteousness of the 'righteous.'

— Reinhold Niebuhr (b. 1892), American theologian and ethicist

about following a religion, but rather drawing from those concepts and truths discovered along the way, while using Buddhism as the frame for the journey.

Being fully alive means owning all of you, physically, emotionally, psychically, and accepting pleasure as well as pain. To deny either sensation is to miss the point of being human. People get to choose their own path. From a Buddhist perspective, this might be a lifetime of contemplation, but extending that to mean that this is how everyone should be is problematic.

It is easy to get obsessed with needing to know, or having the answers. Totally buying into others' answers denies your own intelligence, experiences, interpretations and perceptions. A minister, politician, psychic or tarot card reader claims to give you the answers to your questions. At best, they give you pieces of information. Your job is to make sense of it. For most, it seems answers are the end of the process, but on this journey, there is no end. There is only more information that you carry forward in an unending exploration of the meaning of life and existence. That is the gift and frustration of the spiritual path.

There is no absolute answer to what comes next after we die, only endless speculation. Evidence from Near Death Experiences may provide clues. There may have been communications from people who have passed. Different spiritual traditions, in particular Hinduism and Buddhism, have explored this part of the landscape and have come to some intriguing conclusions. What is most clear is that the concept of the afterlife is not an intellectual exploration. It requires moving beyond the intellect to explore what else is out there. Neither does it mean completely abandoning the intellect. This may sound impossible, but even when people are working with intuition, they have to rely on their intellect to sort out what is true intuition, and what is just a reflection of their own thoughts or unconscious.

Turning everything over to God to solve, or be responsible, is to abdicate the responsibility for being in charge of your life. It is a cop-out. Not all religion/ spirituality has to be about anthropomorphizing some imaginary being to be responsible for all the good and bad in our lives. While faith is important and can be a crucial personal support, it is a not a substitute for personal responsibility.

If you have a personality defect or an inability to emotionally connect with others, it is still your responsibility to address and find a way to resolve, to whatever degree possible. It is all part of being in the world and being an adult. Works of literature, art and music make us think, consider a bigger perspective, and understand other people's insights. These can be starting places to inquire about how others see the world.

We are responsible for coming to terms with our own moral code, not just adopting someone else's because it is convenient not to have to think things through. That awareness requires coming to terms with who you are on the inside. Too many people surrender who they are to something outside of them. It is a bad choice, because it does not let you off the hook; it only looks like it does.

Spirituality is about staying in the unknown. It is about being responsible for what you believe and always being willing to challenge and revise your beliefs with new insight and information. Traditional religion, as it is practiced in much of the world, is about giving you the answers, so that you do not have to think. The key is to find your truth and to stay open enough to consider new possibilities.

Finding one's connection to the divine or universal energy is great. Reducing it to something as small as a humanized definition of God defeats the purpose of the journey.

PART THREE

WALKING THROUGH THE DARKNESS

13

The Importance of Aloneness

The relationship with yourself is, by far,
the most important you will have in this lifetime.

A PERSON CAN BE alone and not be lonely. A person can be in a relationship and be lonely. Aloneness is not about physical isolation. Aloneness is a mental place.

Americans live in a culture of distraction. The purpose, in addition to getting you to buy things, is to help you avoid loneliness, despair, dejection, despondency, melancholy or the gloom we have been taught to have as a proper response when one is found to be marooned with one's self. It is also common in other cultures to focus on family and/or work as a means of avoiding any potentially negative feelings arising from aloneness.

Many people have never lived in a residence by themselves, and therefore never had the space to develop comfort with their aloneness. First, they lived with their parents and siblings, then with roommates, then in a live-in relationship or a marriage, and, now at 30 or even 60 years old, find themselves facing a sense of isolation. This pattern of never living alone can actually be stunting to personal development. It is malnutrition of the self. Having social connections is important, but the relationship we have with our self is still the most significant one to nurture.

Life is moving extremely fast. We have constant intrusions into our personal space. If we disconnect, we imagine we could be left behind, out of date, and out of touch. But we can also end up out of touch with ourselves, the biggest loss one can experience. All of life comes out of your experience. If you do not know what you are feeling, how can you possibly know what is going on? If you never had the awareness of your experience, how would you know what you are missing?

Embracing aloneness is probably one of the most valuable things that you can do for yourself. It helps you develop a strong public self and build a foundation for the journey to the core of the root self. Time alone, no matter at what stage of your life, is essential. It is necessary to know who you are in order to shut out the distractions and the intrusions of modern daily life. Whether you are a parent, student, doctor — no matter how important you are — it is necessary to have time alone. And at some point in your life, there needs to be *substantial* time alone. It is most valuable in your early 20's, but also useful after the end of a long-term relationship. Reflection, sorting out which is you and which is the other, clarifies behavior from your past to influence future behavior and actions.

Almost at the exact moment a gay man (heterosexually married) decides to come out later in life, he begins to think seriously about a relationship with a man. He is inclined to immediately jump into a relationship, even a live-in situation. He is terrified of spending time as an unattached, single, adult person. Even while he is busy hopping from bed to bed, going through adolescence again, it is just a way of interviewing candidates for a possible immediate relationship.

What he doesn't understand is that he needs extended time alone to recon-figure and discover who he is on the inside. He has spent a lifetime fulfilling the programming that he downloaded about what "success" is and about the "necessity" of a long-term relationship.

After this one significant insight into who he is, with coming out, he is ter-rified that looking any deeper would open a Pandora's box, and he will never get to be happy. Being in relationship with the wrong gender was only *part* of the reason for his unhappiness, and far from the core reason. If he had been honestly aligned with himself on the inside in the first place, he never would have married a woman and ultimately damaged the lives of others in that family. He has been dancing the whole time with the symptom, rather than the cause of his unhappiness.

The reason this kind of man was unhappy was because he did not know himself. By jumping right into another relationship, he will continue to have the distraction of another person, so that he does not have to know, or come to terms with, who he is. Caring for another can be less stressful than caring for yourself. When emotions run strong, the other person is convenient to blame and can be used as a distraction.

Being alone can bring clarity about what you want, what you need, what you care about and most of all, how you feel about yourself. Being alone can bring to consciousness any negative self-talk that can permeate the unconscious. "I am bad," "I am wrong," "No one loves me," "I am unlovable," with endless vari-ations of self-doubt and self-abuse. This is why distractions are so enticing and addictive. Even if you are not consciously aware of the negative self-talk, you may unconsciously act as if all of those negative messages are true, and those messages will then influence your choices and actions. Being alone allows you to reconfigure you, sorting out what is you, what is about them, and what you are not yet sure about, but need to learn more about to make a decision.

Blessed are those who do not fear solitude, who are not afraid
of their own company, who are not always desperately looking
for something to do, something to amuse themselves with,
something to judge.

— Paulo Coelho (b. 1947) Brazilian Lyricist and Novelist

Aloneness and Strengthening Self-Awareness

Meditation is the most common method, historically and contemporarily, for inhabiting your aloneness and strengthening your self-ness. It is a structured means of quieting the mind and tuning into the inner noises emanating from your inner gears. There are many forms, from sitting to moving. Find what works for you and enjoy your self-discovery.

Working with a competent therapist is an excellent means to help identify your distractions, learning how to detach from them and transforming those negative beliefs into something positive and useful in your life.

In Chapter Three, *Moving Beyond the Surface*, there is an exercise that describes rolling your eyes back into your head. This is an excellent first step in going inside and quieting the outside world. Review it and practice it. It is very effective.

Spending time in nature is an activity that helps many people quiet their minds and find themselves. Even if you do not meditate, just stop in a quiet place and sit for 5-15 minutes with no distractions and uncover what is going on inside of you. Here you can begin to stop identifying with your thoughts.

Start with that short amount of time and work on extending it. Whatever works for you to clear your mind of distractions and tune into yourself is a step in the right direction.

Silence

Whether in meditation or not, it is very important to have time in silence — to lose all the outside noise and just be with your thoughts and feelings. Silence is amazing. It allows so many things that have been pushed down to surface and to be heard. While much of what you hear may be painful, it is not possible to confront, challenge and change something that you are not willing to hear and face in the first place. Make time for silence. Contemplation is useful. Find time to hang out with your self and see who you are. Develop that relationship and it will change your life.

EXERCISE: ALONENESS

Imagine being alone on an island. There is no one to talk to, no books, TV or music to distract you. There is just you, alone with the voices inside of your head and feelings happening inside your body.

Walk around, take a swim, do anything you like. Build a sand castle, meditate, or masturbate. It is all up to you.

When you run out of things to do, then what happens?
Do the voices inside your head get louder?
What are the voices saying?
Do the feelings in your body demand your attention?
Where are they located?
What are the feelings telling you?

Do you feel at peace?
Do you feel empty inside?
Do you panic?

Who are you when you are all alone?
What is different?
What is the same?
Are you surprised by either response?

What is your body telling you about how you feel right now?
What do you need right now?
What do you want right now?

You are safe here on this island. There is no one to bother or hurt you.
You are free to do, say or think anything you want.

Is this a place you want to return to? If so, how often?
What are the benefits?
What are the downsides?

It is not necessary to go away to an isolated island to have time for yourself. It is a matter of choosing how to spend your time. Knowing yourself and knowing how to get back to you are invaluable skills that should be learned in childhood, but sadly, many never learn. Do not leave yourself out. Really knowing *you* will make your life much easier and enjoyable.

Conclusion

It is invaluable to live by yourself for an extended period, to learn to be alone, and to enjoy your own company. Only by letting go of the distractions, quieting the mind and inhabiting your body is it possible to get in touch with the foundational beliefs of who you think you are. This is beginning the process of healing early wounds, questioning and changing programming and subsequently changing how you fit into the world.

The *existential crisis* is coming to terms with the fact that we are inherently alone in the world. No matter how large our family or group of friends, at the end of the day, when we close our eyes, we are alone. Being alone needs to be a comfortable and comforting place that heals and restores us for the next day. If being alone is fearful and desolate, you cannot renew yourself.

Conor was in a 20-year relationship. He felt most alone when he was with his partner. While ending the relationship was the most painful thing he had ever done in his life, he knew he had to, for both himself and his partner. Love brought them together, but in spite of their best efforts to repair and make it better, the relationship was no longer what they both needed.

They found each other at 22. At 42, they were very different people. Life had changed both of them, and while the love was still there, it was not a good relationship. What they needed 20 years before, no longer applied to their current lives.

Conor moved on after a painful, but cooperative, ending. It was the first time he had been alone in a very long time. There was a necessary reorganization that happened; some of it very painful, but all of it useful in recreating himself and his life. Facing long nights of no one to come home to or sleep with, sex was now a process of searching out strangers and trying to make them into something more. In addition, learning how to date again at midlife was just another in a long list of new experiences. Once again, Conor needed to figure out who was.

Conor could not blame his partner for holding him back or keeping him from getting what he wanted. They were all his own choices, and only he got to feel the impact and fallout from them. It was like growing up all over again.

After five years of being alone, he was ready to consider going back into a relationship. There were people along the way who wanted to form a partnership, but Conor was aware enough to know that he was in the middle of an intense self-discovery process. This process would lead to his making the right choice for this time in his life, rather than trying to re-create the past, which would have seemed more familiar and comfortable. Conor set himself up to have a deeper and better relationship, based on who he had now discovered himself to be, rather than finding someone to distract him from himself.

Not mentioning a sexual orientation for Conor was deliberate, because this dynamic can happen in any relationship, regardless of the genders of the couple.

—— 14 ——

Facing Fear

I must not fear. Fear is the mind-killer. Fear is the little-death that brings total obliteration. I will face my fear. I will permit it to pass over me and through me. And when it has gone past I will turn the inner eye to see its path. Where the fear has gone there will be nothing. Only I will remain.

—from "The Litany Against Fear"
of the Bene Gesserit in Frank Herbert's *Dune*

THERE ARE LEGITIMATE REASONS to be afraid. Fear is real and often a useful thing when your life or safety is threatened. For instance, when you know your job is in peril with few options to replace it. You are awakened to someone breaking into your home. Being told that you have cancer. These are just a few examples of reasonable fear. This chapter is about the mostly irrational fears that torture you and make life miserable. The good news is that you can do something about it. Irrational fear is debilitating and robs you of having a life and being present in the world to the good things that happen to and around you each day.

If you perpetually experience the world as a scary place and fear is a long-time companion, there is no more important task for you than to understand your fear and find a way to a more peaceful place.

There are four general kinds of problematic fear:

The fear of getting in trouble
The fear of being wrong
The fear of bad things happening
The fear of being out of control

These four types of fear sound simplistic. But fear, irrational fear, usually comes from a child's perspective. To a child, the world is a very simple place and things are black and white, good and bad. When we get into regressed places and cannot get out of them, it is the child that is afraid. They are looking at an uncontrollable world, doing their best to survive.

Some people obsess about any and all negative possibilities, and it stops all their forward motion and productivity. Other people live their lives, keep an eye out for trouble, but still get on with life, believing themselves capable of handling whatever comes up and able to deal with the situation.

Jose was conflict-avoidant. When his boss would confront him about something, instead of hearing what was being said, Jose's inner 12-year-old would surface. He would suddenly feel humiliated, stupid and terrified of being fired.

It was his inner child's response. Like all children, Jose was dependent on his parents for his survival. Unfortunately for Jose, his parents never supported him in finding a path to self-reliance and he was stuck in this childhood perspective.

Each time Jose was confronted, his very survival was in question. Jose was convinced he would be fired and was powerless to do anything about it. Fortunately, he had a boss who took Jose's approach in stride. While Jose found work stressful, his coworkers were not the source of his anxiety. It was a good fit for him and an opportunity to learn self-reliance and let go of his fear.

The difference between the 'just obsess' and 'I can handle it' responses depends on how adult you feel inside. The un-integrated child parts desperate to survive, can surface and feel terror at any signs of trouble. They fear that any mistake will lead to their destruction. Some parts of the grown adult were unable to mature, so the wounded child part is running the life of the adult. As children, they never felt safe, for whatever reason, and are still making the attempt to feel safe. The younger child was not taught to problem-solve and does not have the skills and self-confidence to handle problems that confront every adult on a daily basis. This style of being in the world was typically absorbed from one or both of the parents, or the child was unable to download a sense of security growing up. When fear is the "getting in trouble" kind, a person tends to be more conflict-avoidant and collapses in the face of unavoidable conflict.

Layla was well educated but stuck in her life. She found it really hard to make decisions. When there were narrow parameters for making a decision, it was much easier for her, as there were fewer possibilities to consider.

One day Layla was driving in a part of town she did not often visit. She was trying to find an address while driving. Layla came upon an intersection and was unsure which way to go. All directions seemed possible and she was unable to make a snap decision. Instead she stopped in the middle of the intersection. The passengers in the car were astonished and baffled by this behavior. They asked Layla to make a choice but she was frozen, afraid to make the wrong decision and get in trouble for going the wrong way.

Fear of making a choice, any choice, had frozen Layla into making no choice at all, which was certainly the wrong choice for being in the middle of traffic. Layla got lost in the decision, and missed the bigger picture of what was happening in the moment and what would keep everyone safe.

Another piece of persistent fear is the downloaded critical parent, an adaptation of the fear of getting in trouble or the fear of being wrong. If you are never wrong, you will not get in trouble. The drive to be perfect becomes the obsession that attempts to override fear. At least part of love was conditional in the child's home. If they were wrong, they were not loved. If they got in trouble, they would not be loved. The person who is overwhelmed by fear of a critical parent has never felt completely loved. Even as an adult, perfection is the goal in order to be loved.

Fear can transform into anger. A cornered animal can be the most dangerous, since it may feel there is nothing to lose. Adrenaline takes over, and rational thought goes away. Just like fear, anger can be irrational. Being lost in fear (or anger) is being unable to experience the world realistically.

The perfectionist adult may be experienced as angry. But underneath that anger is the child's fear of being wrong and thus not being loved. Having too much fear is not being a part of the world; it can create separation and isolation. Yet, anger can push someone frozen from fear into action. However, in that respect, it can be useful and sometimes necessary. But if the actions driven by anger are irrational, they can backfire, invalidating the fearful person's self-belief that they are incompetent. It can lead to their return to being frozen in place.

No one is perfect; it is simply not possible. Some people seem to be perfect, but in their most honest moments, they would admit they are not. Humans are not designed to be perfect. But each of us needs to be loved. If the parent's love had been felt as conditional, the child would likely have developed a strategy to attempt to get that love. The other significant difference with this type of fear is that anger fuels it. A perfectionist can be explosive and demanding.

Adopting the perfectionist style is likely, when at least one of the child's parents was also a perfectionist and the child absorbed the parent's style. It is no more effective for the child or the adult, than it was for their parent. It is a very painful way of interacting with people.

Bad things happen. The fear of bad things happening is why people try to be in control of everything. But control is an illusion. The paradox is that you have to give up control to have it. The more we tighten our grip on life to make sure we are in control, the less in control we actually are. Pursuing total control means we are not flexible and thus cannot *respond* to a situation; instead, we *react*. The fear of being out of control is real. But as adults, we get to choose our response to that reality. It might take a moment to regroup and move forward, but it is possible once we find our way through the experience. The not-so-favorable alternative is to stop trying, and to stop living. These are foreign concepts to the unevolved child-part of the adult psyche that does not believe in the ability or power to choose as an adult. Other people have this ability to create change in their lives, but it is just beyond the capability of the unevolved child-part.

Tell your heart that the fear of suffering
is worse than the suffering itself.

— Paulo Coelho (b. 1947) *The Alchemist*

Handling Fear

The first step to addressing fear is to create an awareness of what is really happening. Without that, it is almost impossible to get perspective. Once again, developing an observing ego is essential.

Being able to step back and look at your thoughts from a detached place is life-changing. It is absolutely required to begin to heal and transform how you choose to be in the world.

Once you have the ability to see your thoughts and not get lost in them, you can begin to apply a reality check to those thoughts. Walk through a checklist of questions. Here are some examples of questions to ask yourself.

(While the following questions are not from *The Anxiety and Phobia Workbook* by Edmund Bourne, the book is an excellent resource for a more detailed process.)

Is there something real to be afraid of?
What am I thinking?
Have I thought this before?
Have I had this thought many times?
Is this thought always triggered by the same situation?
What has happened in the past when I had this fear?
What is the likely outcome this time?
When did I first learn to see this situation this way?
Did it work well for the people who taught me to feel this way?
What are the benefits of seeing this situation the way I see it?

Do others around me see it this way?

How are others responding to this situation?

What part of me is frightened?

Do I need to get angry about it?

Has anger worked in the past?

What is another way of taking care of myself rather than withdrawing in fear or turning to anger?

What can I do to stop this from happening next time?

What are the signals I should be aware of, the ones that tell me I am getting lost in this fear?

Sasha was an experienced and well-trained architect. He had excellent customer service skills and always went beyond what the client asked for. He wanted to be liked, but also stay out of trouble. He had trouble owning the quality of his work and having confidence in his decisions. His anxiety tormented him throughout his day and it continued when he went home for the night.

Because of Sasha's insecurities and fear of getting into trouble he would continually ask his boss for a second opinion. He wanted confirmation that he was doing everything right. His need for reassurance slowed down the process and was a continual interruption for his supervisor. Sasha would have to take work home most nights, because he was unable to finish on time, mainly because he was constantly in need of that reassurance.

Sasha's fears were his primary companion and ruled his life. In order to keep the voice of fear in his head tamed, he would do everything he could to short-circuit it. But he was in a constant dance with it, instead of just seeing that it was a program from his childhood that would continue to make his life miserable.

At the core of the fear is a lost child. They neither felt safe or loved. While the cognitive interventions are an essential starting point, once there is some perspective, it is necessary to address the underlying emotional defects and wounds. The next tasks should be re-parenting the child, rescuing the child, and healing the trauma. If the trauma can be identified, EMDR,[20] Eye Movement Desensitization Reprogramming Therapy, is by far the most effective means for addressing the trauma directly and can produce the fastest results. Phobias are often connected to trauma. See a qualified EMDR therapist to address this so that you need not expend energy dealing with the past. You can come into the present, and live your life.

*All important decisions must be made
on the basis of insufficient data.*

—Sheldon Kopp (b. 1929) Psychologist,
from *If You Meet the Buddha on the Road, Kill Him*

EXERCISE: WORKING WITH NEGATIVE BELIEFS

A classic exercise in psychotherapy is to write down what is bothering you. If there are negative thoughts, take a sheet of paper, and begin writing down the negative things you say to yourself. You can keep the list and add to it, as you recognize more of your internal dialogue.

The next step is to divide the sheet into two parts, and if possible, use a different hand for each voice, one the critical voice and the other the adult you. Have a conversation with yourself and those negative voices. It can be an enlightening and freeing exercise.

You might ask yourself

- Where did I learn this?
- Who said this to me originally?
- Was it true then?
- Is it true now?
- What do I want to say to that voice, that belief?
- What do I need to do, or say, to let that belief go?

The same principle applies to your fears and all the ways you have been a victim. Get everything out of your head and put it on paper. Once on paper, put it to the side for later. You will be shocked at what you have written and it is very likely you will see it from another perspective. Seeing it differently, from a different mindset, is the goal.

By accepting that you believe these things, you have the opportunity to decide, first, if they are true, and second, what, if anything, you want to do about them.

Some people create a ritual by burning the sheet of paper and disposing of the ashes. It is a representation of clearing those negative beliefs. Sometimes, it is necessary to read them to another person. Listen to yourself say them out loud and come to terms with how you have treated yourself. Having our most negative self witnessed in a compassionate way is very healing.

Another Possibility

Fear and excitement are felt nearly the same way in the body. It is quite possible that instead of being afraid, we are actually excited about what is about to happen. We do not know for sure whether we will win the prize or if we will do well or perform our best. Not knowing, and the anticipation of something good happening, feels a lot like the fear of something bad about to happen.

You gain strength, courage, and confidence by every experience in which you really stop to look fear in the face. You are able to say to yourself, 'I live through this horror. I can take the next thing that comes along.'

— Eleanor Roosevelt (b. 1884) American First Lady

Consider for a moment that you might really be excited instead of afraid. This simple shift in your perception could change your life.

Conclusion

For many, fear is the belief that people will validate your worst beliefs about yourself and others. The real enemy is negative beliefs about yourself.

There is only so much you can do to control how others see you and what they think of you. Accepting yourself and being content with who you are is the best recipe for having others think well of you. Actions also play a huge role in how you feel about yourself. If you feel good about your actions, the feelings will also carry through to how you feel about yourself.

Irrational fear is debilitating and exhausting for the person with it, as well as the people around them. Fear is a tunnel vision of a scary, and mostly unreal, world. Recognizing disruptive thoughts, facing the roots of fears, and healing them is necessary to reclaim your life. Gaining perspective, coming to terms with the trauma of the past and the abandoned child parts will allow for healing.

—— 15 ——

Oh, To Be Vulnerable!!

*Realizing that we've surrendered our self-esteem to others
and choosing to be accountable for our own self-worth
would mean absorbing the terrifying fact that we're always
vulnerable to pain and loss.*

—Martha Beck (b. 1962)
American sociologist, ex-Mormon and life coach

REVEALING OUR SEXUAL TASTES to one another, secrets becoming public, our perceived shortcomings becoming visible to others — these are examples of how we might experience vulnerability, voluntarily or not. Our response might just be blushing or may go as far as recoiling in fear of being attacked or abused. This chapter is about the emotional vulnerability we all experience, where we have some power or a choice about how we respond or reveal ourselves to others. This is not about adults and children who are indeed powerless or vulnerable and cannot protect themselves.

Allowing yourself to be vulnerable is, to most people, a negative thing to be avoided at all costs. The fantasy that we can go through life fully defended from all hurt and loss can also prevent us from the joys of human contact. Attacks happen daily. Someone gets angry with you. Someone blames you. There will always be difficult stuff. Someone betrays you, or is lost to circumstances or death. Loss is a part of life. To stop being emotionally available, in order to reduce or prevent hurt, can rob you of intimacy and connection, the best parts of life. Emotional vulnerability is absolutely required to create intimacy; it is not optional.

Brad and Susan had been dating for six months. It was increasingly clear they really liked each other and they were seriously considering a long-term commitment. Wisely, from experience, they had not introduced each other to their parents, understanding that is a big step in deepening a relationship.

Brad was nervous about meeting Susan's parents. This was not his first relationship. When his last one got to the point of meeting the girlfriend's parents, the relationship came apart. Brad really cared for Susan, so he felt extra pressure to be liked and was troubled by the prospect of another relationship being derailed by parents.

On that fateful day, Susan took Brad to her parents' home for dinner. She was excited to introduce him and felt confident they would like her handsome boyfriend. Brad, on the other hand, was bordering on a panic attack, trying to memorize dialogue for the conversations with her parents. He was lost in what might go wrong and more and more removed from what was actually happening in the moment.

To Susan's parents, Brad seemed uptight and unfriendly. Susan was concerned the Brad she knew was suddenly not there. She was not aware that this ritual meeting had once signaled the end of his previous relationship. Consequently, she did not know to intervene and reassure Brad it would be okay.

In an effort to relax and calm down, Brad started drinking, and kept at it until he was drunk. While the alcohol relaxed him, it also reduced any boundaries he had and now made him overly friendly, so Susan's parents experienced him as going from one extreme mood to another. Thus, between his anxiety about the meeting and his overmedicating to deal with that anxiety, he produced the very result he was attempting to prevent.

There are two types of emotional vulnerability:

Defenseless Vulnerability – This type of vulnerability is when you expose some protected or shame-infused part of you. When you do, you are completely vulnerable to others' responses and judgements. A negative response is devastating and there is no recovery. You have given your power to another to determine if you are acceptable, okay, or normal. Our negative perception of vulnerability comes from a feeling that we are unable to defend whatever we have revealed.

Defendable Vulnerability– When you choose to expose yourself and are willing to risk being ambushed, attacked, humiliated or perhaps loved, that is defendable vulnerability. For a visual correlation — in Star Trek terminology — the shields are down. You also have the power to raise them at any time you feel is necessary. This is the power from knowing you are able to take care of yourself. Defendable vulnerability creates intimacy — the ability to accommodate emotional connections and make contact with another person. Defendable vulnerability *does* require the knowledge and belief that you can take care of yourself. It is not the job of other people to make you feel more confident about yourself. In most situations, it is best to come in with 'shields down' and use the redirected energy to increase empathy and contact with another person.

What makes something feel un-defendable is when it carries the possibility of being shamed. If you feel shame about something, and take the risk of exposing that part of you to someone, it could feel un-defendable. If the other person rejects or directly shames you, it could expose a major wound inside, validating your fear of being bad, wrong, worthless, sick or whatever core belief is tied to the exposure.

During sex, our most intimate relationship, we can become defenseless with a partner. Deepening intimacy requires more and more exposure, risking hurt and rejection. This is why hookups have limited intimacy. There is little emotional risk. A hookup is primarily an act of projecting a fantasy onto the other of what you want them to be.

Intimacy takes knowledge of the other person and an investment in the relationship. The benefit of a long-term monogamous relationship is that when you take the risk of putting all your sexual energy into another person, you can go deeper and deeper into exposing who you are and what you truly desire. When two people commit to exclusively meeting the sexual needs of the other, that kind of focus has the potential of reaching transcendent states beyond words. But both partners have to want to go there and take the risks in order to get the potential payoff.

Bill and Jennifer had been together for five years. While they had some challenges in their relationship, they clearly liked each other. After five years, they were still having sex, but had not yet progressed to 'making love.' It turned out that neither had a road map to something deeper. Their emotional intimacy and willingness to be vulnerable were limited and therefore so was their sexual intimacy. They felt their sex life was okay, but routine. Through conversation with their therapist, they learned about these deeper states and what would be needed to create them in the relationship. First, it would require a degree of vulnerability with which neither was yet comfortable. For each to go deeper, they would have to work on their trust of each other. That meant looking at and exploring their perceptions of what it meant to be in a relationship.

In our world of instant gratification, people expect that when we commit to a relationship, a fairy will magically grant us instant intimacy, with no walls and total trust. A good example of this is when a stranger is sitting next to you on a plane. Because of the forced, unavoidable physical intimacy, an imagined instantaneous trust emerges in which one or both of you feels compelled to expose their pain to the other. You feel as if you've found a lost life-long friend. A life-long friendship can germinate under such circumstances, but it would be highly unusual. This is "faux intimacy." Exposing yourself emotionally on a plane also can be like a priest's confessional. Since you are on a plane, you will likely never see that person again, so you have no qualms about divulging your deepest feelings. Additionally, the other person is trapped. The same thing can happen on a first date. Too much is revealed too soon, and it destroys the possibility of something long term or deeper, right from the beginning. Real intimacy and real vulnerability come from developing trust through experience and accumulation of knowledge. It deepens through taking small risks by exposing yourself to another, then taking bigger risks as you develop more confidence. Revealing too much of yourself too soon, before the other person has a bigger picture of who you are, and has developed a deep caring, is likely a set-up for failure.

There are times you go into an encounter with someone, and it is necessary to protect yourself right away. If there is an uneasy feeling that something is not right or a direct assault seems to come out of nowhere, it is necessary to move into a defendable posture. The better you are at 'raising your shields' when necessary, the more at ease you can make people. They will not feel defensiveness or anxiety in the initial contact with you, because your defenses are down. You will simply be comfortable being present with them and that is a great gift to another. Inside a relationship, sometimes it is necessary *not* to raise your shields. Staying in that vulnerable place is what is necessary to create or deepen the trust. Raising the shields will likely stop intimacy from happening. Sometimes it is necessary to risk being hurt in an effort to deepen a relationship. This is not easy, and sometimes it is not rewarded.

Bill had been in a very difficult work situation for some time and was ultimately fired. He had been having casual business consultations with his close friend Edwin about the difficult situation at work. After Bill was fired, he took out his frustrations on Edwin and accused him of not being there for him. None of it was true. But no amount of logic was going to soothe Bill's pain.

Bill and Edwin met in an attempt to talk it out. Bill lobbed one accusation after another at Edwin and was intentionally as mean-spirited as he could possibly be. Edwin never counter-attacked or became defensive, despite the distress Bill was causing him. At the end, Bill said the conversation did not go as he had expected. He had expected a big battle, since both of them had dominant and forceful personalities. Edwin's goal was to hear Bill, understand him and to try to connect with him emotionally. Bill's hurt from losing his job was too great, so he could only express his pain.

They went their separate ways. Edwin processed what happened. Edwin came to realize that, since Bill was unable to punish the people who had fired and humiliated him, Bill had taken all his pent-up rage out on him. Edwin recognized he had been made a scapegoat by Bill.

Bill continued his friendship with Edwin as if nothing had happened, but Edwin could not. Bill's inability and unwillingness to be honest with himself and own his behavior was a deal breaker for Edwin. Edwin told Bill that he really understood how Bill must have been tremendously hurt and in pain to treat him the way that he did, but he could not continue in the relationship and wished him well. As they crossed paths in their mutual social circles, Bill just hung his head and would not look at Edwin. Bill's inability to clean up his part of the disruption to the relationship ended it permanently.

Sometimes, mostly in intimate relationships, we hurt ourselves trying to help the other. David Schnarch, author of *Passionate Marriage,* calls this 'healthy masochism.' Healthy masochism is when you allow yourself to be hurt for the benefit of someone you love. A spouse might let a partner scream at them, because they know it is the partner who is very hurt and trying to find a way to vent. A parent risks helping a sick child, while at the same time understanding that if they get sick as well, it will make life more difficult. But there are limits. Our job in life is to take care of our self. And while there are times we voluntarily suffer pain for another, it has to be limited and reasonable. Being a parent is probably the most masochistic part of being human. Parents sacrifice their needs and wants in order to give their children opportunities for experiences and growth. When a teenager is rebellious, it is important for the parent to not be defensive and to have a firm container of love and caring to hold the pain and confusion of the teenager. Not easy, but needed for the growth and the maturity of the child.

It is necessary to learn this skill if we are going to mature as an adult. In every relationship, there will be an occasional 'empathic failure.' This means that at some point, a spouse, lover, or a friend will feel misunderstood or wounded in some way by what you said or did not say in a moment of vulnerability. It is imperative that if and when this happens, they are able to tell you they feel hurt and that you do not get defensive. If possible, remain open, vulnerable and empathic to both the pain and the content. This will allow them to feel heard and hopefully to get to the source of their pain. If you get defensive, the relationship is at risk. Staying open to what the other has to say is how relationships are repaired and trust is built. However, not all relationships can be saved. Each of us has to decide what our limits are and stand by them for our own mental and emotional health.

We all say things we regret. We may also miss what is going on in front of us. We get distracted or cannot relate to what is being said. Hurts happen. Relationships are damaged. Repairing them through being defendably vulnerable can strengthen and heal relationships.

> *Only to the extent that we expose ourselves over and over to annihilation can that which is indestructible be found in us.*
>
> —Pema Chödrön (b. 1936)
> American Tibetan Buddhist Nun
> from *When Things Fall Apart*

Most of us have experienced both kinds of vulnerability even without realizing it. The defenseless type is much better known and gets far more press. However, if you are aware of your defenseless vulnerabilities, it is a signal that you have some work on shame to do. Any shame inside of you should be worked on because it impairs your self-confidence, well-being and your ability to deepen relationships of all kinds. Clean up the shame, and live a life of defendable vulnerability. You will enjoy life a lot more.

— 16 —

Avoiding Pain
Is The Key To Unhappiness

People are afraid of themselves, of their own reality; their feelings most of all. People talk about how great love is, but that's bullshit. Love hurts. Feelings are disturbing. People are taught that pain is evil and dangerous. How can they deal with love if they're afraid to feel? Pain is meant to wake us up. People try to hide their pain. But they're wrong. Pain is something to carry, like a radio. You feel your strength in the experience of pain. It's all in how you carry it. That's what matters. Pain is a feeling. Your feelings are a part of you. Your own reality. If you feel ashamed of them, and hide them, you're letting society destroy your reality. You should stand up for your right to feel your pain.

—Jim Morrison (b. 1943)
Lead singer and songwriter of The Doors

Bypass: The act of using or doing something in excess to avoid feeling the emotional pain inside you.

Overview

The world is awash in alcohol, drugs and distractions of all types. People are running from themselves in an attempt to avoid emotional pain and discomfort. Most people are taught to control themselves, rather than how to manage their own emotions and responses. It is not real self-control if you have no method of monitoring and processing your inner experiences of sadness, hurt, shame, anger and humiliation. Your emotions need to be processed and regulated from the inside. Using anything, in the long term, to avoid an inner experience is a losing proposition. People are inherently creative. If we encounter emotional pain inside ourselves, we will find something to bypass, drown or distract from the pain. If people would spend as much effort working on creating and cleaning up the relationship with themselves as they do pursuing distractions, life would be a lot easier, more enjoyable and fruitful.

Most actions and feelings have good and bad aspects. Just as there is good guilt and bad guilt, good shame and bad shame, there are good and bad distractions, particularly ones that involve "doing things." It is important to understand when a person has crossed the line and is using a bypass to avoid feeling the pain. Writers often talk about never having such a clean house or a well-tended garden as when they are avoiding a deadline. Exercise is great for you, but if you do it so much that you have no time or the energy to feel and experience yourself, you have crossed the line into using exercise as a deceitfully beneficial distraction.

People who use these methods to excess are doers, rather than people who can just be. "As long as I stay busy and distracted, I do not have to feel anything bad." Words that many people live and die by.

It is possible to use one or more of these methods of bypass, or to use more of one and less of another. The problem with using distractions to excess is that the person hurting will never fully realize they can process and clear the lava-lake of fear, anger or shame causing the pain inside of them. Consequently, their emotional agony will never recede. Usually, layers and layers of bypasses will be built to bury that lava-lake in an attempt to keep pain at bay.

We are curious, intelligent creatures and naturally want to know more about the world around us. Most people have the need to be social. It requires an active, deliberate effort to turn inward. Avoiding the pain inside is natural to some degree, unless we have been trained at an early age to focus inward or are self-disciplined enough to do it as an adult. It is hard to recognize that we easily create distractions in our everyday life to avoid being fully in touch with ourselves.

Getting lost in pleasure or pain is equally bad. The point is not to condemn the bypasses. However, if what is written here triggers you, your unconscious is telling you that you need to pay attention to what you are feeling. What bypass are you using to avoid feeling something inside of yourself?

Jorge is a bright and curious engineer. He has been very successful and was in several long-term relationships. Despite his appearance of success, Jorge realized that he had not yet found whatever he was looking for to define his existence and fill his life. He kept expecting his job, relationship and/or family to make it all okay. Like many young men, he worked long hours, and what little time he had left was home time, where he would focus on his partner. On top of that, he had family commitments. There was not time for him to be truly alone. While he had previously done a lot of work on himself, he still failed to have a relationship with himself. His life was focused on getting other people to like him for his generosity.

Jorge's therapist suggested as an exercise that he imagine himself surrounded by people who did not like him.[21] He did not have to interact; his task was to pay attention to what was happening inside of him. What were his internal voices saying to him? What value did he have to these people? What value did he have to himself? How would he survive this experience?

Jorge courageously did the exercise. He did not like it and it was painful for many minutes. But as he stayed with the feelings and heard the voices inside his head beating him up, he began to quiet and feel himself. Nothing had really changed. If they liked him or not, he was okay. It was all his fantasy that it mattered whether they liked him or not. It reminded him of playing sports in Junior High School and not fitting in. Back then he adapted his behavior to make sure everyone liked him and it became his style of being. Jorge had many more skills now and had no problem fitting in, so this old way of being was now distracting him from feeling himself.

Could you sit in a room only surrounded by people who did not like you? What would come up for you? Do the exercise and see what you discover.

Keep Jorge's experience in mind as some of the more common bypasses are explored in this chapter. These are the ways we distract ourselves. There are too many possible bypasses to list them all. Humans are capable of using anything to avoid being in touch with distressing and undesirable thoughts.

The Bypasses

We use things to make us feel better: Cocktails after work, or a hit of pot to take the edge off and relax. Some people play games, watch movies or just tune out with music or porn to take them away from whatever they are feeling. Most things in small and measured amounts can be helpful for relaxing. But the more you use something to take you away, the more you need it until it becomes the new normal and you are held hostage by that thing that used to take you away from it all. It is just trading one master for another, and there is no happy ending.

Drugs/alcohol

Drugs and alcohol have been used since the beginning of civilization. Today, the abuse of drugs and alcohol seems to be at apocalyptic levels. Odds are you have witnessed first-hand or have been the victim of, a habitual drunk or drug user. When other things do not work at distracting us or require too much effort, we can always have a cocktail, glass of wine, marijuana or any other number of things, legal or not. These will take us out of the moment, take us away from our stressful feelings, take us away from anxiety and chemically force us to relax. It is a mini-vacation from reality and the emotional storms raging within us.

Arturo and Javier, both under twenty-five, busboy and waiter at a popular restaurant, were chatting during a break about the party they had attended the night before. They decided they must have had an incredible time, because they couldn't remember the party. They had blacked out from the alcohol.

From these young men, you could deduce that the path to the successful enjoyment of life is through not remembering you were there. It is sad so many are without any self-awareness about their own avoidance of being in the present and actually experiencing their lives.

Drug and alcohol abuse and addiction are not confined to one class of people. They impact every level of society. Often, having more money or resources simply means being able to consume more and be sheltered a longer time from the consequences. We can be in denial about how much we are using and why. It is a path to temporarily quiet the inner voices or take away the pain. That is the intended use.

Many people use pot or alcohol daily. Some try to stop for a period of time, out of concern of possible abuse. But most return to their daily medication because they have not found an alternative way to deaden their pain. Avoiding pain prevents or delays formation of a solid public self and keeps you from growing up. Many parents and grandparents could not imagine having dinner without wine or beer, ending the day with a cocktail or having a nightcap before bedtime. Having one drink a day does not make you an alcoholic. The issue is, why are you having that drink every day? Do you need it to let go of the day's stress? How would you be without pot or alcohol? What would you do differently if you did not have it?

Food

Food is a tricky distraction. We all need food to survive, but many feed themselves to excess and use it like drugs and alcohol to numb feelings. Food can be wonderful, life sustaining and life enhancing, or it can be an albatross, the negative center of one's life.

When we eat, there is a chemical response in the body and brain. We would normally listen to the signal that we have had enough and ask ourselves if what we are eating is what we really want or even feels good to us. But if the objective is to stop feeling, to ignore the pain or suffocate the undesirable emotions inside, the goal will be to stuff or numb-out the bad feelings and get to feelings of, "I feel loved and cared about" feeling for a few moments, in hopes it will last.

Underneath the stereotypical jolly exterior of many extremely obese people is often a very angry person. By burying feelings, you suffocate your suppressed rage. Overeating and anger control become a game: "If I eat, I do not have to feel my negative feelings." When that angry inner person starts to awaken, there is more incentive than ever to eat more, to keep the feeling cocooned — that if people knew who you truly are, they would not like you.

Eating to excess is a symptom of something. It could be medicating a temporary anxiety or it could be trying to kill a lifetime of emotional pain. The only way out is through the feelings themselves. It is not easy, and it is hard to do alone, but the sooner you start, the closer you will be to reclaiming your body and your life.

Sex

Sex is a "cannot live without" for many people. Life is certainly enhanced when you have a satisfying sexual life. But sex can also be an easy way to focus all of your attention externally searching for that next sexual contact. If you get lost in the search, you will have abandoned yourself.

Sexual compulsives describe the process of their libidinous engines starting up and consequently, the drive to their next sexual contact begins. In most cases when they were asked, what they were really looking for, it wasn't the need for achieving orgasm; they were looking for a sense of being loved and validated. As an exercise, they were asked to stop, if only for moment, once they arranged their next contact and ask themselves, "Am I going to find love here?" Their answers were consistently, "No." The compulsion began as a distraction from the emotional pain of feeling unworthy or incapable of being loved. The drive to go on the hunt for the next sexual contact was simply a way of avoiding their internal pain.

The bypass of chasing sex or having a lot of sex is not about intimacy. The need for compulsive sex comes from the pursuit of the adrenaline rush, the hunt, rather than the intimate physical contact. Hopefully, the more sex a couple has, the deeper the trust, the deeper the connection, and the greater the surrender to the other, allowing for depths of intimacy that can only really be achieved over time. But emotional and sexual intimacy requires going deep into yourself, to expose who you are to the other. It is not about getting lost in the other person, it is about exposing the self and allowing yourself to risk a greater possibility of hurt and rejection, and consequently, love.

Staying on the surface of erotic energy can feel good. It can also be a significant distraction from being in touch with the source of an unsatisfied need. It can reduce sex to, "I am hungry; I need to eat." Quick encounters with anonymous unassociated partners may satisfy for a bit, but like drive-thru-window food, the calories are empty and the need for another fix shows up quickly. There is no satiation and no deepening, so the real payoff of sex can be lost, along with the opportunity to discover your own depths. The 'new' is the distraction. Sustaining a meaningful sex life with one person requires engaging each other's emotional depths and encouraging each other toward deepening vulnerability.

Sports

There are many men and women who eat, sleep and breathe sports. They may be athletes themselves, or take on the identity of a team as an extension of themselves. It is the same as taking on the identity of a religion, school or political party. Any time an external identity becomes too central a part of a personal identity, the person has lost contact with a part of self. Supporting a team is one thing, but to have one's mood be ebullient or bitter because a team won or lost is subjugating one's self to an external entity.

There is nothing wrong with watching or participating in your favorite sports. Participating with the team and its fans is an excellent tool to expand your social world. But like food, drugs, alcohol and sex, becoming obsessive is the avoidance of an ingrained, unprocessed emotion. Perhaps the internal negative messages are:

I have not been successful enough
I am lonely
I feel as if I do not exist.

Some of it might be a cover for a lost dream or fantasy of being a professional athlete. Yet, if being lost in the world of the team seems more real than your real life, then that is a problem.

Religion

Spiritual bypass is the most written about of all of these. First offered by psychologist John Welwood, it is defined as "the use of spiritual practices and beliefs to avoid dealing with our painful feelings, unresolved wounds and developmental needs." Turning every bit of your life over to God, making him/her responsible for everything you do, or do not do, is a cop-out. Finding a connection to a divine entity, whatever that might mean for you, can be a powerful experience. But believing in an all-powerful entity does not eliminate responsibility for your own actions. The more you are in touch with your own being and feel responsible for your life, the easier time you will have finding divinity. People who hide between the pages of the Bible, Koran or any religious work as a substitute for independent thinking, feeling or having true compassion are abdicating their responsibility to the world.

It is common for people who lack a stable internal structure to take on "an external skin" in their chosen religion, which acts as an ego. Much in the same way, insects have exoskeletons to protect their soft, delicate insides. Anything that threatens their external structure threatens their being. Break the lens through which they see the world and they will collapse from the shortsightedness. They invest heavily in not looking, not thinking and not allowing anything into their world that would question or deconstruct their reality. These are the hardest people to deal with if you have a perspective on reality different from theirs. They tend to live in closed worlds in order to protect their structure and to reinforce the strength of their tinted lenses. Such fervor, though appearing as undeniable passion, is still a distraction from the inner emotions.

Meditation

Anything can be used as avoidance of pain. Meditation is a process to make us more aware of ourselves, so that we do not create suffering. Meditation is not meant to avoid suffering. It is about getting clarity about what you are suffering from, so you can change your relationship with the cause, face the pain and work through it. Meditation should also give us more compassion and empathy, not just detachment from pain. Meditation is wonderful, and there are more and more documented claims of benefits, but it is not a 'be-all and end-all.' Just as prayer works for some people as a means of reaching a peaceful place, it cannot be about avoiding the outside world.

Gambling

The world is rife with people who have their heads to the ground sniffing about for their buried pot of gold. Some, in their dreams, have already spent the money in the lottery tickets they just bought. There is the guy betting it all on a sure thing at the craps table. The house wins most of the time, and it is not your house we're talking about. Compulsive gamblers make chance

If pain must come, may it come quickly. Because I have a life to
live, and I need to live it in the best way possible.

— Paulo Coelho (b. 1947) Brazilian Novelist,
By the River Piedra I Sat Down and Wept

and money their God, the giver of good and bad luck. Chance makes good things happen, is outside of their control, and removes responsibility for their actions that create the losses from gambling.

Those with gambling issues choose the riskiest path for their big win, whether that win is money, fame or a relationship, because the pain of the slow or reasonable road feels like death. They cannot stay within themselves and endure the pain of being a normal adult. Their emotional development is that of a child or teenager who has not yet developed a risk-filtering process. At their core, like other bypass types, the gamblers do not like who they are. The big payoff is the validation they never got during childhood or from themselves.

Gambling is a quick fix for achieving the feeling of "I am special." At their core, gamblers do not really believe they are special, but the need to prove they are *not* worthless is overwhelming, so they will risk anything to prove it is not true. Unfortunately, this becomes the central fixation in their life, and can destroy lives and families. The continual need for the excitement from risk-taking grows to be a blanket that covers and hides the lack of developed public self.

Gambling is not restricted to card games, casinos or other obvious games of chance. Starting questionable business ventures, long-shot deals, anything where the adrenaline is in play and there is a potentially big payoff with seemingly little effort, all can be suspect and just another form of gambling.

Electronic Information, Entertainment and Gaming

It is common for many adults and children to be constantly plugged into their music, podcast or audio book sometimes combining with with texting or talking on the phone. They constantly have some external distraction. If you walk the beach almost anywhere, many people are wearing headsets. There is no connection to the sounds of waves crashing on the beach, birds chirping, or dogs and children along the way. These people want to be someplace other than their present moment.

Unadulterated thoughts and feelings drifting through brains get filtered away through an endless barrage of sounds and noise that never subsides, preventing people from tuning into their inner selves.

Some people watch one or two movies every evening after work or binge watch episodes of a series. We all need downtime, *unfocused time*, but people choose not to be alone with themselves. There is so little relationship left with the person inside of them, they go out of their way to avoid the quietness of their own mind and being.

Some people talk about being lost in an online game for hours and sometimes days. They have completely left this world and merged into an alternate universe. There have been cases of young men so lost in the universe of their game, that they literally die because they no longer attend to their most basic needs. They were totally divorced from the here and now of the world we live in. In this alternate reality, gamers feel like they have more control and more power, and they no longer feel like victims. Online, they are more attractive and are able to have relationships. Many gamers know it is only a game and a diversion, or an intellectual challenge (depending on the type of game). Some no longer do.

Another kind of gaming involves creating an avatar that is someone you want to be. Some people end up liking their avatar better than their real life selves. The avatar can be strong, powerful and take revenge on forces that hurt them, often the things the gamer feels they cannot do in reality.

Gaming can be a good outlet for aggression and blowing off steam. It can challenge the intellect to solve puzzles, and improve the ability to think creatively and logically. But there are limits. Learning new skills and working on improving one's real world life is more productive in the long run, and gives the gamer a better chance of healthier outcomes.

It is now possible, and too common, for someone to seldom have a quiet moment of reflection. Perhaps the noise from real feelings will become white noise, but something is lost when there is not just quiet. It is easy to get distracted away from introspection. Not that every moment should be a deep dive into your unconscious, but to truly know who you are requires time, quiet and determination to get past the noise inside your head and find you.

Belinda started each day with music. Her phone was beside her in bed and always a close companion.

With speakers in her bathroom and throughout the apartment, she was never without her constant companion. She never had to feel alone.

Off to work, her headset allowed her to not have to talk or interact with anyone on the subway. In her own universe, she was communing with old friends who filled her with joy and distracted her from any unpleasant thoughts.

Texting with friends, sharing her current song obsession, all allowed her to not be focused on any deep thoughts or concerns of the day.

Belinda's job was computer-based. It gave her minimal contact with other people at work. She used her headset to keep people away and have a constant companion of sound so she would not be distracted from her work by any underlying feelings of insecurity.

On the way home after work, sometimes she would go to a nearby bar to meet other friends who were also decompressing after work. They would talk about their workday and plans for the evening. The alcohol allowed for easier interactions and felt relaxing. At home, a quick hit of pot and the light mood would continue for some time. There was music on while she made a quick, easy dinner, then off to watch her current TV series obsession, until bed and the nightly tuck in with her smartphone before starting the cycle all over again.

Online Profiles

Dating apps and anonymous social media are similar to the online gaming world. People can create online personas who are idealized selves. It is so easy to make yourself taller, a few pounds lighter, five or ten years younger, a different race or gender. You can be polite or rude, outgoing, more handsome or beautiful — you can adjust yourself to suit the people you want to like you. At least they will like your persona. Checking new emails for the attractive persona you've created can be very validating. It can be addicting. It is possible to live in that bubble of being popular and make you feel wanted for a while. But the invented persona is not real. It cannot actually go on a date. It cannot have a happy ending. You would have lied from the beginning, and that destroys any possibility of trust.

Finding an empty e-mail box after putting out a lot of messages on a personals app can be deflating. It is common to tweak a profile that might unconsciously be repelling positive responses, but for some, the need for validation of being wanted or attractive is too strong. They might end up posting pictures of someone else, painting a picture of a person who does not exist. This is called "catfishing."

While there can be great benefit in role playing and trying on different personalities to figure out who you are, getting lost in one that has little or no basis in your real self does not translate to a healthy relationship. It is deceitful and inconsiderate to coerce others into playing with these Frankenstein-like creations. It is using others with no regard to their needs or feelings.

Cora was 38, single and had not dated in years. She was lonely, feeling unattractive, undesired and discarded by men. Cora searched the internet and found a series of pictures of a lovely young woman who looked to be in her mid-20s. She signed onto an online dating site and created an online profile using the unknown younger woman's photos in place of her own. She studied various profiles of women already on the website and noted their most compelling features. Cora completed her online profile with attributes that were an aggregate of the favorable elements of other profiled women.

Soon messages from handsome young men started coming in. She felt great. She chatted with them, focusing on the ones living far away so there was less chance of being pressured into meeting. She established several relationships online and got lost in her fantasies about the men on the other end. One by one the 'relationships' faded, as it became clear to the men that she would never be willing to meet. She now feels worse. Not only is she still alone, but all the fantasies faded as the men drifted away.

While Cora was lost in a whirlwind of chatting and flirting online, she ignored doing anything about all the things that made her believe she was undesirable. She did not improve her self-confidence and, thereby, her sociability. Nor did she make real world attempts to meet people. Instead of using the website as a tool to meet men outside of bars, dance clubs or parties where she felt awkward and objected to the overuse of alcohol, she used the dating site only to find flattery. And even though this was not getting her what she wanted, she kept recreating herself with new fake personas, and going through the process again.

A technique used in group therapy is to have participants put on Halloween masks and encourage them to interact with the other group members. Escaping behind the literal mask, each became a different person. They could expose good parts of themselves they were afraid to let be seen, or unabashedly release the more negative parts of their personality. What they learned was that when they were hidden, they were freer in expressing themselves.

Online profiles allow people to present themselves in ways they might not be in person. They may come to like their online selves better than their real self, or confuse the two and lose track of who they really are.

Relationship

Some people are in constant pursuit of an intimate relationship. They fear being alone. They cannot cope with being unattached, feeling needed or making another feel needed. They move from one relationship to the next when the current one starts to break down. Without a relationship, their lives feel empty, devoid of meaning and not worth living. Sometimes, parents will sacrifice their children to the abuse of the other parent, stepparent or partner, because they cannot imagine living life as a single person.

The need to focus on someone else leads many people to stay in a relationship at any cost. The emptiness inside, the internal critic, becomes deafening when they are left alone. Being with someone else is easier because their focus remains external. No need to deal with those pesky inner voices and discomfort. If you can stay focused on fixing the other or making them happy, there is no need to fix yourself or seek your own happiness.

The popular wedding song, *There is Love*, tells us that "two shall become as one," but that is a fairy tale. While it is necessary to reconfigure yourself to be in a relationship, being in a relationship is not about losing you. It is about enhancing and seeing yourself more clearly through the lens of a relationship. A relationship is not a distraction from our insecurities or our self-perceived shortcomings. It should teach us about ourselves and reveal who we really are.

Victimhood

"The world is against me... God is punishing me... Someone is getting something I am not... They are getting more than I am... Their being alive oppresses me... If they can get married, it invalidates my reality, so they are wrong... I never had a chance... The deck was always stacked against me... No one is ever on my side... I never had a chance."

Being a victim is so easy to succumb to and for many victimhood is synonymous with being alive.

Chapter Nine is devoted to this topic in great depth, but it is important to understand how it can be used as a bypass as well.

There is no limit to the virtuosity that humans are capable of when they perform the mental contortions to portray themselves as being oppressed by others. Reality has no role, and neither does personal responsibility in these creations. In part, these feelings are from a flawed view of how the world works. Most of the time this comes from a childlike, powerless place inside, where they have retreated or have never grown out of. The adult is absent, and the child inside of them wants mommy or daddy to make it better.

Some people are undeniably victims — victims of racism, homophobia, sexism, violence, murder, oppression, and many forms of discrimination where people have been treated as less than human. But to believe "if something bad happens to me, it is always someone else's fault," is a fundamental bypass that keeps people from growing up. To believe everyone and everything is oppressing you prevents you from having the chance to consider your own self or recognize that the pain you feel could be caused by your own actions or inactions.

While there are times we truly are victimized, even those can be healed, but only when we process 'being a victim' and then move on to 'having been victimized.' Perpetually living as a victim is a lose-lose proposition.

Fear

The fear bypass is so common and so detrimental, Chapter Fourteen is devoted to it. Fear of getting in trouble, fear of being wrong, fear of dying, fear of getting hurt, fear of being humiliated or shamed, fear of being found out; the list is endless. We have all felt fear and it can lead us to avoidance or procrastination. Many people work past their fears. Some acknowledge their fears and learn to live with them. Others, like those who play the victim, are consumed by their fears.

Of course, some dangers are real. Soldiers, civilians in war zones, and abused, bullied kids often live in fear every day. Their fear of injury or death is very real, but some people with lives that are 'safe' from sudden gunfire or looming violence still behave as if every decision will have life-or-death consequences. Many people obsess and can only think about bad things that may happen. Being stuck lets you miss the relationship with the person inside you and the opportunity for a sense of self-belief and indomitability in the world.

Worry

Worry is joined at the hip to fear. It is the endless, over-thought, nagging that can fog a person's head. It might not always be that conscious or even verbal. It might just be a pervasive and endless sense of unease — an undertow of anxiety that prevents action without any particular reason. This is a constant distraction that prevents clear thinking and groundedness.

Pop Culture and Celebrity Worship

Living a life vicariously through public figures seems to be an increasing issue. In this society, we believe that when people become famous, they are obliged to have their personal lives exposed to meticulous scrutiny. It is utterly possible to be privy to and feel part of, a media idol's daily life. Waiting breathlessly for the next tweet from a famous person keeps the focus of your energy outside your normal eat-sleep-study-work world. It is no longer enough to live your own good life. You must latch onto the life of the rich and famous.

The idol worship bypass is an obsession of possessiveness with an illusory friend. A fantasized romantic relationship with the hungered-for celebrity is even possible. Because the celebrity is known by the entire world, the illusion of intimate contact via tweet sent directly to a personal phone makes us feel special, part of an elite group. To dwell on the celebrity's emotional highs and lows replaces our own highs and lows, and the dangers of our own emotions. Staying focused on the external is a way to avoid looking at the emptiness of one's own life, from the lack of real relationships and the lack of any real purpose or meaning. People can live vicariously through others. It can be a rock star, a movie star or God. They are all "convenient" and offer more interesting lives than the empty meaningless ones of the masses.

Being Pretty

Children who are continually told they are handsome or pretty, are taught that because people find them attractive, everything about themselves must be desirable and attractive. Any encouragement to pursue inward introspection or strengthen awareness of their abilities and emotions is put on the back burner. Attractive children can grow up to become dependent on other people to notice them and acknowledge their existence.

Physically attractive people get validation more readily than someone less well endowed by genetics. It is easier for them to get jobs and sexual partners, but it is not easier for them to be valued for who they are. Many of the beautiful tend to bypass being themselves in exchange for constantly being undeniably liked, wanted, and sexualized. But this value is based entirely on how their epidermal, muscular and skeletal structures are combined into a pleasant shape.

Why would someone so blessed want to turn their thoughts inside, to figure out who they are? Our society dictates they are to be envied and emulated. It doesn't help that their being attractive also brings an expectation from others that they are also shallow, so there is no great support for them to be introspective as adults, either. To avoid this trap, it is very important for parents not to focus on a child's looks, but to stay focused on reflecting their feelings and validating them as human beings. Such parenting will build an emotionally balanced person, and will hopefully avoid the child becoming lost in the adulation of others.

Being Helpful

If you were asked what makes the most wonderful person in the world wonderful, what would you say? Would you say giving, generous, helpful, humble, and/or sacrificing? Giving people who stay focused on another person's needs, often remaining invisible. These are the selfless who find their validation from your gratitude. They are 'professional helpers.' But all too often they are as empty inside as a narcissist. The generous person's modus operandi is to stay focused outside themself and use the positive reflection to fill the emptiness inside. This also was covered extensively in Chapter Seven, *Selfish/Selfless/Self-Full*.

Excessive generosity can also be a way of hiding. By staying focused on the needs of others, an introverted person can stay safe and hidden. If they are focused on you, they do not have to come out of hiding.

Unceasing giving and selflessness is a very effective and socially encouraged bypass. Despite some of its drawbacks for personal growth, unlike alcohol or drugs, it is unlikely anyone will do an intervention to stop your excessive helpfulness.

Social Media

Social media has redefined how we connect and communicate with people of similar interests. The online social universe continues to expand and evolve exponentially every day. Complusive behavior around social media has emerged insidiously. Distant friends and remotely-related family, people next door and people across the globe are now suddenly part of your circle of 'friends' with the punch of a button — all from the safety of your keyboard. Though there is certainly a positive side to social media, for many people, the internet has replaced in-person communication. Because of the flurry of daily activity on social media, constant vigilance is required to stay on top of what is happening. Sharing our life and observing others' most trivial episodes can easily turn into an obsession that can feed the need for attention and validation, and can divert us from necessary time alone.

Summary of Bypasses

Bypasses are different ways of distracting yourself from your interior existence, drowning the deeper disavowed feelings and supporting the effort to avoid becoming self-aware. The path to self-awareness, like all things, has its ups and downs. Learning to stay present in life, to stay in touch with who you are, how you choose to be in the world, and your real needs instead of just your surface ones, is the task and the goal. With the ability to tap into your depths, you can empower yourself and impact the world around you.

Anything can be used as a bypass, no matter how benign it might seem on the surface. Endless news surfing on the web, or reading one book after another are seemingly good things — and they can be in appropriate amounts, when also allowing time for self-awareness.

However, as we come to terms with how we avoid spending time with ourselves and become conscious about our bypasses, our inherent emotional strengths increase. More self-knowledge will emerge, signaling the process of healing. Some people can awaken in a moment. When the awareness hits, they are ready to face the challenges and to deal with it. Others need to do it in tiny increments, taking years. Still others need the help of a therapist or perhaps a mentor who is farther along on the journey to self-awareness.

Bypasses, by their natures, are satiating, enjoyable, invigorating and even healthy in controlled doses. But anything done to excess opens the door to unforeseen negative aspects. Looking at your bypasses and figuring out if they are useful or not is a big part of being an adult. Some are easier let go than others. Some can be so deeply ingrained that they are almost impossible to be seen on their own.

If you sense your bypass is consuming you, do not be afraid to ask for help, such as friends, a psychotherapist, coach, someone who can see a perspective of your life. Look at what you have been avoiding and ask yourself if you are ready to deal with it. The good news is that as you process the underlying reason for using the bypass, life gets easier and more rewarding. Take a step back and look at what you need to do and then dive in and find you. That is the greatest gift of all.

—— 17 ——

Shame

You can only be shamed about something you already feel shame about

SHAME IS A BIG part of the pain we feel in life. It is hardwired into all of us, and cemented in our childhood experiences. We might talk about shame in whispered tones, but too often shame is the least worked on or acknowledged pain. It is not possible to take a pill and make shame go away. People try, with antidepressants, pot, alcohol and anything else they can find, in a futile attempt to remove themselves from their feelings. How you cope with shame shapes how you behave and how you are perceived.

Shame runs through every chapter of this book. Shame feeds most of the problematic emotions and sensations we have discussed. Shame is something all of us are exposed to, have inside and are capable of carrying around in large amounts.

Families, churches, sexual partners, schools, peers and even strangers we encounter in our daily routine can shame us. Shame is the elephant in the room, the big unspoken emotion that both ties us together as humans and yet prevents us from connecting with love and compassion.

Secrets are shame pockets. If we hold a secret, it is usually something we fear people will judge us about, or not like us, if they knew the truth. In that hidden state, the toxicity of shame increases in strength, packing enough power to destroy relationships and even lives. Pockets of shame can affect your present and future.

There are good reasons to keep secrets. If revealing who you are will possibly get you severely harmed or killed, then holding that secret makes sense. Also, just revealing a secret to make you feel better, may not be reason enough. Sometimes, just holding the secret of a regrettable betrayal is a form of penance and amends; if that secret were revealed, it would only cause the betrayed great pain and there would be nothing gained. Just making yourself feel better in this circumstance is not enough. This chapter is about ending secrets that harm the relationship to our self and usually others. While revealing secrets is usually the best option for staying healthy, it may not always be. It might require some outside perspective to become clear about the best path.

There are gay men who marry women while hiding who they are. There are also many women who were sexually abused, but keep the secret from their partners and are unable to enjoy sex with their partners. Secrets can ambush and derail any chance of intimacy and happiness.

Why would anyone keep such crucial information about themselves from a potential partner? Secretive behavior indicates a person has not come to terms with the truth about themselves. The person is hoping a relationship will magically get rid of shameful feelings and experiences, so the shame will disappear. Hope is good, but the miracle will never come to fruition. In addition to not eradicating pain, the actions will have an irrevocable impact on another person's life.

In many families, not telling the truth is the only way to survive. On the surface, people encourage children to be honest about what they feel and do. But instinctively, children know about surviving. Consequently, they develop a sense of what their parents want from them, and attempt to give it to their parents in an effort to stay in their parents' good graces so the child is not banished or hurt. Children will do or say, or not say, whatever is necessary to stay connected to a parent or family. All too often, children are put into double binds. They harm themselves in an effort not to be discarded or abandoned.

If children are punished for being honest, honesty is not modeled and valued by their parents or family. Where else would children learn that it is okay being who they are and being honest about their feelings and actions? The family is the foundation of learning how to be and what is acceptable and unacceptable. This programming is deeply downloaded into our unconscious. We will replicate the family's behaviors and attitudes until we have mined the deep recesses of our unconscious, and then regurgitate beliefs and ways of being that we swallowed, even if they do not work for us anymore.

Children who are sexually abused realize they are different from their peers. At very early ages, they know to keep this secret to themselves, though they may not understand why. They see and feel themselves as different. Being different is seldom valued or encouraged. Making sense of the world and learning norms is what childhood is about. Being different, overtly or covertly, is painful and brings up the possibility of being rejected or discarded. This is where secrets begin. This is the beginning of shame. I cannot share who I am with you, and it makes me feel bad about myself, which is shame.

It is impossible to grow up as a minority in a majority culture without taking on some shame. Being different is not easy for any child growing up: not conforming, not looking like everyone else, not being as smart as everyone else, the list is endless. Some things we hide. We hide sexual secrets in particular, because sex is still shame-based in most societies and cultures. Some physical attributes we just cannot hide, like race, some disabilities, or deformity.

One should certainly have pride in one's accomplishments and successes, but excessive pride is often a cover for something painful. Too much boasting, or the endless reminder of accomplishments, is a tell-tale sign of the shame inside.

Shame is usually what makes us feel defenseless when we are vulnerable. Shame can make strong men collapse and curl up into balls of despair. Shame, while under-identified and seldom discussed, is a primary emotion and is so debilitating, it can cripple people for life.

There are many books about shame, and a great movie titled *Shame.* The 2012 movie starring Michael Fassbender is about a man with an incestuous childhood who is visited by his sister. All of his methods to avoid the shameful feelings from his childhood start to fail, one by one, until he is trapped in the pain from his past. While shame is a word we are all familiar with, it is not actually well understood. How to deal with shame is even less well known.

Facing shame can bring both emotional and physical discomfort. For many, it might be the most excruciating experience in life. For most, facing and processing their shame is not easy. The more solid a public self we have, the easier it is to face and dive into deep feelings about ourselves. But if we have not formed a solid public self, the dive into those feelings and memories can be overwhelming and feel like drowning in a sea of misery. Too often, people would rather die than face their shame. Shame can be that central to a person's being. Shame at our core is who we think we are.

Shame: "I am bad."
"I am sick."
"I am perverted."
"I am ugly."
"I am stupid."
"I am nothing."

In Alan Downs's profound work *The Velvet Rage,* he details many of the different ways gay men work to compensate for their shame about being gay. They might use sex or drugs to drown out the feelings. Or they might compensate for being gay by having the best car, house, job, income, wardrobe, most friends, best vacations, all to make up for feeling bad about themselves because of their sexual orientation. Until you face the negative self-image at the core of your being, you are doomed to either make it true or to try and find a way to make up for it.

Alcoholics Anonymous, Narcotic Anonymous, Overeaters Anonymous, Marijuana Anonymous, Sex Anonymous and all the other 12-step groups are filled with people who have attempted to use something to avoid the shame they feel about themselves. They have found that drugs, alcohol, eating, whatever done to excess, doesn't work. A great benefit of these groups is the meetings where they get to tell their most shameful stories about themselves and listen to others do the same. The rule against cross-talk, or against having conversations about what has been said, is to prevent shaming each other. The 12-step attendees like everyone else need empathy, compassion and acceptance when they reveal their darkest selves to another. The antidote to shame is light, facing the negative belief about who or what you are, and then bringing it out of hiding and exposing it to others. Owning that thing you believe makes you less than human, and letting others see it, without being humiliated, rejected or invalidated, is the beginning of healing and claiming yourself.

In some churches, when people reveal something that they feel is unacceptable in the theology, they are told they are sick, wrong and will go to Hell. If they continue within the church, they are just downloading more shame and self-loathing. Church members who are judged publicly are convenient distractions for other church members, who judge others to avoid dealing with their own challenges. "My shame is not as bad as your shame," is the real message. "I feel better condemning you, yet I know if I shared my own story, others would think badly of me." Churches are families. People will do whatever is necessary to stay connected to their families, particularly if they think they cannot survive without their family. Many religions and churches tell you that what *they* think about you, is much more important than what *you* think about yourself. This form of mind control is manipulative, pathological and designed to keep the church family together, no matter the cost to the individual or to society.

Sex and Shame

A discussion of sex and shame could easily fill a multi-volume set of books. As we have attempted to civilize humans, it seems that striving to control sexual energy has been a primary focus. Along the way, Western Civilization and many cultures have contorted our sex drive into something dangerous and out of control. As a consequence, we have set-up children to have terrible sex lives as adults. Shaming people about their sexual interest and sexual drives, even inside of a relationship, inhibits a healthy sexual development and has prevented the natural deepening as we dig deeper into finding out who we are and our connection to the world.

Finding a way to reset our perceptions and perspectives on sex is really essential to making better people and relationships. Most religions seem obsessed with sex. Many religious rules are about sex and sexual relationships. It leads to the conclusion that religion is primarily about controlling sex. Erotic energy is one of our most powerful drives. Instead of building adults who have a solid well-developed public self, able to manage their own feelings, drives and responses, we try to control people. It is a misguided attempt to substitute rules and consequences for personal responsibility.

Some religions believe men are incapable of personal responsibility around sex and sexual behavior. They astonishingly assign exclusive responsibility to women. If a woman were not so seductive, men could control themselves. If a woman does not expose herself, then men could control themselves. It is a disservice to both men and women. Such a twisted foundation sets up relationships for failure by creating distrust, imbalance and objectification.

Fertility is a relatively short period of time in a woman's life cycle. Being able to have a healthy pregnancy and child has an even shorter time frame. Instead of focusing on bonding, intimacy, stress reduction and most of all pleasure, why would we reduce sex to being about procreation only? Making sex only about procreation is even more disempowering of women than men. They are reduced to vessels for babies rather than powerful equal co-creators of society.

The shaming of sex is about the shaming of pleasure for both sexes. How sad that one of the primary ways for people to connect and enjoy each other is often taught as something wrong, bad or dirty. As a result, too many people cannot have sex without artificially quieting their minds with a drink or drug to still the voices of shame in their heads.

Children experience pleasure from an early age, at levels of sexual pleasure that are appropriate for their age and development. If this not validated, they conclude they are bad for having this pleasure. When the feelings and acts remain secret, they feel horrible about themselves, because they cannot control their feelings or actions. Children take cues from their parents' behaviors and words. If sex and pleasure is not acknowledged and validated, it is assumed by children that it must be bad. If a child expresses shame about sex, they learned that from their parents.

Masturbation in childhood is the beginning of learning about self-pleasure. Both boys and girls masturbate. Self-pleasure is about building neural pathways in the brain that will allow for building and holding a sexual charge, learning how to experience pleasure and how to create and share that pleasure with others. It is the beginning of a life-long exploration of deepening into the root self and knowing the connection to the spiritual. This is a crucial time in a child's development. Shaming the child, telling it that it is "perverted and twisted" because it is naturally and healthily curious about its body and how it works, creates a negative self-belief that can haunt and emotionally and sexually cripple a child for the rest of its life.

Jesus was born to a large Catholic family in the Midwest United States. His parents struggled to support their large and growing family. At the age of seven, he engaged in some peer-appropriate sex play with a neighborhood girl. "You show me and I will show you," kind of play. Discovered by his father, he was almost beaten to death for this "sick and perverted" behavior. Jesus was forever scarred by the incident and never able to allow himself to be in a relationship because of the negative self-belief downloaded from his father that day. "I am bad," "I am sick," and "I am not lovable" are the messages he swallowed deeply and completely.

Jesus's healing required that he go back to face those experiences and be held by someone who cared. The therapist also reframed the experience and helped him rewrite his internal script about what happened and why. He had to face his fear and anger at his father for hurting him and at his mother for not protecting him. Processing the trauma of the experience was hard but it freed him to begin healing his sexuality. It is almost always necessary to feel the core of the pain for it to be released. That does not mean wallowing in it, but digging in and moving through while someone who understands can hold your hand and lead you through.

Trying to restrict sex to procreation is sexual shaming. While procreation is important, it is not the most common form or purpose of sex. To pretend otherwise diminishes the importance of what sex is to being human and limits the joy of connecting, intimacy, support and pleasure in relationships. It is imperative that we validate sexual expression as a healthy and desirable part of the human experience.

Eroticized shame

Because of our negative programming around sex, most people, carry some eroticized shame. Eroticized shame combines both the feeling of *shame*, "I am bad, sick, perverted," with *sexual arousal*, which are two of the most powerful experiences in our body. It is a potent combination. During therapy sessions, it is common to ask both male and female clients, *what makes you orgasm?* Knowing what pushes them from sexual pleasure to orgasm reveals how they are wired sexually.

Most people are able to enjoy sexual pleasure, but for many to orgasm, something extra is required. It is not just a matter of going over the magical waterfall of pleasure. For many surrendering to orgasm requires a specific thought and/or action. Requiring that extra something is the difference between a purely sensation-based orgasm and a fantasy-based orgasm. Fantasy based orgasms usually have some element of shame in the fantasy.

Akio was a bright and sweet guy. He very much enjoyed sex with his girlfriend. But in order to have an orgasm, he needed to fantasize about being humiliated. His girlfriend had no idea this was going on. Their sex was very ordinary to the outside eye, but when Akio decided it was time to orgasm, he would retreat inside his imagination and think about a woman ridiculing him in some way.

Humiliation was the prompt that triggered his orgasm. He certainly loved his girlfriend and enjoyed sex with her, but he was unable to share his dark secret about his deepest sexual excitement.

In childhood, the way his mother would express her caring was to tell him he was stupid or lazy, so he unconsciously eroticized those words as an expression of love, in order to tolerate them. This interaction with a woman became the center of his sexual fantasy life.

After working on his relationship with his mother and gaining a lot of self-confidence, Akio was able to share his fantasies with his girlfriend. By working through his shame about his fantasies, he could get vulnerable with his girlfriend. The two of them found a conscious way of bringing that into their sex life, which also helped to free him from the shame. He needed to work with a therapist to process his rage at his mother so that it did not show up in his relationship sexually or otherwise. While his core fantasy did not change, it became less the focus of his sexuality, giving him more options to achieve orgasm. It took time, but Akio's courage and efforts to work on himself saved his relationship and gave him the sexual life he deserved.

Often people have so much shame about having sex, they need to fantasize that they are being forced to have sex to enjoy it. While they are voluntarily having sex, somehow, they cannot be personally responsible for having pleasure. In their mind, someone else needs to have coerced, forced or otherwise manipulated them into having sex. This is usually played out in their mind, and is a demonstration of the fantasy-based orgasm.

Sometimes couples use role-play, which allows the shame to be an overt part of sex rather than being covertly fantasized about. In concert with this, alcohol and drug use create common bypass routes for not owning choice and responsibility. The sex drive is so powerful, however, that people need to create a fiction to override massive shame to finally have pleasure and connection with another person.

Erotic programming is set-up early in life. Stanley Siegel, in his book *Your Brain on Sex,* theorizes that at the heart of our erotic life is an attempt to receive love from our families. Based on an individual's interpretation of what is required to get that love, fantasies will configure situations or relationships as a way to get the love you did not get in childhood.

There is no such thing as normal sex. There are societal norms that people compare and often despair about when they look at their desires and actions. Normal sex is whatever two consenting adults or peers choose to do together. The process by which we eroticize anything is very individual. A man who loves women with blue eyes or a woman who likes taller men is well within society norms for being acceptable. However, the way they came to erotize blue eyes or a taller partner is the same process that people might eroticize shoes, feet, hands, hair, etc. The list is endless, as we are capable of eroticizing anything.

Many of the things described in the following paragraphs will sound bizarre and even sick to some, but these are things that can become eroticized for people on their road to establishing themselves as sexual beings. Those moments when you connect that erotic feeling in your body to something outside yourself is how it works. Some men focus on a woman's breasts as the primary erotic object. Perhaps in childhood, while hugging mom, they felt an erotic energy and since then, connect breasts to being turned on.

Erotic connections are not limited to objects, clothing or body parts. Combining shame and erotic energy is, for many a survival strategy. Being humiliated by a parent or authority figure in childhood through physical, emotional or sexual abuse, the child either consciously or unconsciously eroticizes the experience in an effort to tolerate or survive it the best they can. It is neither wrong nor bad, rather a smart thing to do because it helped them survive the experience.

There is a wide range of erotized shame in sex. It can range from the mild, feeling naughty when engaging in sex, to the extreme, where someone needs to be severely beaten, punished or tortured to make sex pleasurable. In the straight world, one of the more common expressions of erotized shame for men is the cuckold fantasy. The husband is not 'man' enough to satisfy his wife. He needs a 'real man' — better endowed, more muscular — just not him, to humiliate him by taking and satisfying his wife. This is how he feels good about her having sex. He is not allowed to have sex with his wife or has some reduced form of sex with her.

Sex is not just about intercourse. It encompasses almost the entire spectrum of human interaction. Someone with a shoe fetish may have no interest in sexual intercourse or even physical contact. It might be just the act of watching a person walk or take off their shoe that brings them to climax. Physical contact might even be repulsive to them. Who are we to say that is wrong, sick, or not acceptable, as long as the person is satisfied and not hurting anyone else?

Some gay, straight and bi men perform sexual servitude or act out emasculation, castration, or feminization fantasies to feel sufficiently humiliated for being less of a man. Their sexual expression comes from acting out these fantasies and/or masturbating while thinking about them.

Men and women of all sexual orientations have rape fantasies. Race play — being dominant or submissive with someone of a different race — is also a common fetish. Humans have done an amazing job of eroticizing just about everything.

When a child watches its parents abusing one another, the child will either identify with the perpetrator or the victim. It is possible to go back and forth, but the primary parent-role the child identifies with will overtly or covertly play a role in future emotional/sexual relationships. In a relationship where there is a dominant and a submissive, each person has taken on a role, acting out what they fantasize a relationship is supposed to be like. Whichever role they are playing, they often feel equally bad. Whether a person is the giver or the receiver of the punishment, they have turned their pain into something erotic in order to tolerate it.

One of the ways a child who is sexually abused can tolerate the abuse is to erotize the shame of the experience. A child absorbs the shame of the abuser, and if there is pleasure involved, will naturally combine the shame and pleasure. Sexual abuse can still involve pleasurable acts. But the power dynamic, the overstimulation of a child's mind and body before a child is ready to handle it, are all abuse. If pleasure is a significant part of the experience, it is a powerful imprinting on a child's sexuality. If the experience is just painful, it is also possible a child will erotize the pain and humiliation of the experience.

A person's first sexual experience is formative, whether the first-time is a sweet experience in the back of a Chevrolet or a brutal rape. It sets up the expectation in the brain of what sex will be. This is why children should be protected from porn, both online or from a parent's collection. Their brains are not yet ready for that intense level of sexual stimulation and it can profoundly impact them. They will absorb whatever they see, and feel its impact, and very likely download shame with those highly erotic images. The shame-based, sexual culture they have downloaded will imprint on their sexual selves. Porn is going to excite children and they may or may not know why, depending on their age and level of sexual education, but in any case, it will usually over-stimulate them and set-up an expectation that sex will always involve that same kind of overwhelming feeling and experience.

There are too many stories of people who, as children, witnessed their parents' sex life. While it is important for children to observe affection and intimacy between their parents, hearing, watching, and witnessing actual sex can overwhelm them with erotic feelings they are not mentally or emotionally prepared to process. To children, it could sound violent, or at best, confusing. They make sense of it any way that they can, not always correctly understanding what it is. Children need to be educated about sex, but not exposed to it before they understand and are emotionally able to handle what it means.

Compulsive sex is a symptom of erotized shame. It is a consequence of the cocktail of sex mixed with shame. Staying immersed in erotic energy attempts to soothe wounds and avoid the pain of shame. Being obsessed with porn, masturbation, hookers or the next hook-up is all part of a quest to not feel shame. Like other easy fixes, compulsive sex has its own downsides. The lack of intimacy, increased risks for STD's and, in extreme cases, job losses and jail for illegal behavior can result from losing perspective about what sex is: intimacy, connection and pleasure. Treating the underlying psychological wound is the cure for compulsive sex. Once the sexual abuse, shame, and original pain are *healed,* the compulsive behavior will go away, replaced by the possibility of deeper sexual connection.

The opposite, sexual anorexia (as in being nonsexual or completely avoiding sex with others), is another path to avoiding eroticized shame. Untreated sexual abuse survivors tend to seesaw between compulsive sex and sexual anorexia. While it is possible to be stuck on one end of the spectrum, it is the dance of striving to feel some pleasure or simply shutting down. Each end of the spectrum is a result of eroticized shame. One extreme is staying externally focused and the other is internally collapsed.

In and of itself, eroticized shame is not always a bad thing. It can add excitement to sex and if shared with a partner, can bring two people closer. Good vulnerability is about being able to expose who we are to our partner and not being rejected or shamed as a result. If there is a shared fantasy, it can be a powerful bond that leads to depths of trust and excitement that enhances all parts of the relationship.

Once shame has been eroticized and has become hardwired into a person's sexuality, it is unlikely to change. The key is to own the sexualized shame in an objective rational way, not as a victim. Then there is the possibility to enjoy it as pleasure, *without* regressing to a child's helpless, submissive perspective. Bringing the fantasy into a relationship is a huge step. For a couple to get to the heart of the intimacy that most people say they want, it is necessary to discuss, understand and accept their own and their partner's sexual fantasies.

What is good eroticized shame in sex? It is whatever works for you. For most people, it is might be as basic as feeling a little dirty, or sluttish. "I am a bad girl." "You are a dirty boy." These terms get used even without understanding their roots or the implications of their meaning. As long as you know it is a fantasy and not who you are, it will not harm you. But if you cannot separate the fantasy from the reality, and are exposed in some way, by a partner or perhaps a sex tape, it will feel like the end of the world. Unprocessed shame feels like death when it is publicly exposed. Bringing light to that core shame in some safe way is necessary to have a healthy and satisfying sex life.

There are many paths to dealing with eroticized shame. The key is to look at the roots of the shame connection and work through any leftover trauma. If the shame is from sexual abuse, it is necessary to work through the trauma of the abuse. Once the erotic connection is made with the shame, it is unlikely, or at least unusual, for the fantasy to simply go away. But it can be experienced from an adult perspective, rather than re-traumatizing the child aspects of a person.

I believe that all BDSM (bondage, discipline, domination, submission, sadism, and masochism) is the acting out of eroticized shame of some kind. As long as a child part of the psyche is not being re-traumatized or brutalized, go ahead and enjoy. I am very supportive of BDSM sex play, and I believe it is healthy only when the adults participating are emotionally developed.

If the sexual shame is religiously based, it is necessary to look at the downloads absorbed from your family and religion and explore how they have impacted your views and actions around sex. Once you own the downloaded belief, you can decide if you want to keep it or discard it. But changing your beliefs may require that you look at your relationship to your religion and possibly your family as well.

Shame and sex are as old as humankind. The more we bring this dynamic into consciousness, the healthier we will be and the healthier our kids will be. Perhaps we can spare the next generation some of this unnecessary shame.

Enrique and Kira had been dating for several months. They were now regularly being sexual after having slowly moved into sex. Kira wanted to go slow. When they did become sexual, Enrique noticed that during intercourse Kira changed. She seemed younger to him, like a little girl. She was passive and compliant, but not as engaged as when they were involved in foreplay, oral or other parts of their pleasure. Enrique tried to talk to her about it, but she did not know what he was talking about. It just seemed normal to her. He felt something was wrong, but did not know how to explain what he was experiencing with her.

Although she had spotty memory of it, Kira had been sexually abused as a child. Her body remembered the sensations clearly. When certain acts occurred during sex with Enrique, her body took her back to those feelings when she was a child. So Enrique was having intercourse with the mind of a little girl, and not the adult Kira whom he loved. This was not good for Kira, or for the relationship. He could feel her disconnect during intercourse and if not addressed, it could sabotage the relationship. This disconnected Enrique from Kira sexually, emotionally, and intellectually. Kira needed treatment for the sexual abuse so she could remain an adult during sex, enjoy her connection with Enrique and give pleasure. The most intimate act of their sex life was re-traumatizing to her.

Biff was 47 and happily married. During his childhood, his father spanked him as punishment. He would pull down Biff's pants while telling Biff what he had done wrong and how he was doing this to help Biff remember what Biff had done wrong. Though he never told him, spanking Biff sexually stimulated Biff's father. The act of dominating his son by spanking his naked butt gave him an erection. Spanking was also a tradition in Biff's family. Biff's grandfather had spanked his father in the same manner and was stimulated as well.

At first, Biff did not like to get spanked. After a while, he came to enjoy it. At times, he found himself looking forward to the spanking. It was the most intimacy he experienced with his father and unconsciously to him, Biff could sense and feel his father's excitement when paddling.

After Biff moved out of his parents' house, he realized that he missed both the intimacy with and the spankings from his father, which had continued until he left. Biff decided to post on an online personals site, looking for an older man that would spank him like his father did. While Biff was straight, he was very turned on by the intimacy with his father and wanted to take the covert sexual aspect of the scene and make it overt. Biff eroticized his submission and wanted to be sexually submissive after the spanking. He needed to symbolically complete the act with his father to complete the unexpressed desire. Once he lived out the experience, either the fantasy would dissipate or it would simply be integrated into his sexual life.

While he loved his wife and had no interest in a relationship with another man, the younger part of him had eroticized a connection to men and he longed for that intimacy.

RELIGIOUS SEXUAL BELIEFS QUESTIONNAIRE

What was your religious training?

Overtly: It was directly part of your upbringing and socialization.

Covertly: While your family did not participate directly, it was part of the culture, such as growing up in Jewish in a Jewish community, or growing up in a Catholic country or community.

What is your religion's perspective on pleasure?

Is some pleasure ok? But not others?

If pleasure is bad, how does that impact sex and pleasure in your life?

How invested in your religion's perspective is your family?

From the religious perspective, what was the purpose of sex?

What was your religion's view of:

Masturbation?

Premarital Sex?

Same sex relationships?

Living together before marriage?

Contraception?

Abortion?

Divorce?

How did all of these messages form your view of sex?

How did these messages and beliefs impact your sex life?

Have your religious beliefs changed over time?

Has this impacted your views of sex?

If you are in a relationship, does your partner share your beliefs?

If not, how has it impacted your relationship and sex life?

If your sexual beliefs or orientation are in conflict with your childhood religious training, how have you reconciled those conflicts?

What have you learned about yourself from answering all of these questions?

Family-based, eroticized shame is handled much the way that religious-based shame is processed. It is necessary to look at what you learned about sex from mom and dad.

This is not an exhaustive questionnaire, but it is a start to look at the bigger picture of your sexuality. Most people have not really done a broad-based look and made the connections from childhood to adulthood. It is a very useful exercise to understand how you got to where you are sexually.

Read the questions and write out the answers. Set the answers aside and come back to them a day or a week later. See if what you wrote surprised you or if you told the truth. Which parts bothered you when you tried to answer them? It is all just information for you to learn about you.

SEX HISTORY QUESTIONNAIRE

Early childhood

What was your first awareness about sex?

Were your parents affectionate in front of you?

Were your parents demonstrative with you and each other?

What were the early messages you got about sex and sexuality?

What messages did you get from religion about sex?

Where your parents comfortable with nudity?

What message did you get from this?

What were the first messages you got about your genitals from your family?

Adolescence

Was your family supportive of your physical and psychological development as a sexual being?

What overt and covert messages did they give you about sex?

Is sex normal?

What is its purpose?

Is sex good or bad?

Do good people have sex?

If they did not discuss sex or acknowledge it, what messages did they impart to you about sex?

Were the messages in your family different for boys and girls?

How did you feel about your changing body?

If you were allowed to date, how did your parents support or not support that?

Did your parents expect you to be sexual?

Did your parents normalize masturbation, shame it or ignore it?

Was one or both of your parents overly concerned or intrusive about your sexual development?

What messages did you get about the purpose of sex?

How did your first sexual experiences inform you about sex?

How did you feel about your early sexual experiences?

Were they good, bad, shameful, fun?

Was one of your parents an erotic obsession for you?

Is there a similarity between the look of your parent and your sexual partners?

Sexual Abuse

If you had sexual contact with someone before the age of 21 with someone of a substantially different age:

What happened?
How did it change you?
    How you interacted in the world?
    How you felt about you?
Did it happen more than once?
    If so, what changed inside of you as it continued?
Did it continue to happen with others, as you got older?
Was the sexual contact with a parent or family member? Who?
    What did that teach you about sex?
How does it show up in your sex life today?
Have you ever fantasized about that, do you find you still fantasize about it or is a re-creation of it a regular part of your sex life?
Are you still in contact with the person this happened with?
How does that make you feel when you see them?
Did you ever tell anyone what happened?
    Were you believed?
    Did you receive help, if so what kind?
    How did that impact you?
Did you become a sex worker as a child or adult?
    What is the connection between sex work and the abuse?
Was the abuser ever held accountable?
    If yes, or no, how did that impact you then? Now?
Do you need help to clear this trauma?
Were you the emotional support for one of your parents?
How did the other parent respond to that?
    Were they glad?
    Were they jealous?

If so, how has it impacted your emotional relationships with your spouse or partners?

Media Influence

What were the early messages about sex you got from seeing images?
What was your first exposure to porn?
Does your current sexuality have any relationship with those first images?

Current Sexuality

Have your sexual activities and perspective of them changed since adolescence?
What would you tell your adolescent self today if you could?
What would you want to be different about your sexuality?
If you have a partner, could you share the answers to this questionnaire with them?
Would your partner be surprised? Be supportive? Still love you?

What have you learned about yourself from answering all of these questions?

Eroticized Anger

Any time a person is deliberately mean to another, that person is using their sexual energy to drive that action, whether overtly sexual or not. It is eroticized anger.

For most people the combination of erotic energy and anger does not seem like a natural pairing. We like to think of sex as fun and safe, while anger is reserved for those moments when it is necessary to protect or defend. However, we are creative beings. Humans are capable of combining many types of emotions and experiences. Eroticized anger is fueled by shame. Instead of taking on the submissive stance of the eroticized shame, it becomes the inflated version of eroticized shame that needs to punish others.

Eroticized anger is using sex or erotic energy as an act of violence with the intention of diminishing, dehumanizing, harming, emasculating, even destroying the other. Anytime people are deliberately mean to another, they are using their sexual energy to drive that action, whether overtly sexual or not. Freud would call this "libidinous energy," which is the life plus sexual energy. Eroticized anger would be the distortion of libidinous energy.

Eroticized anger can be expressed in many forms. The physical abuse of children is often an erotic outlet for adults. They are able to channel their need to be dominant and in control by correcting children with physical punishment. Spanking, slapping, enemas, pinching, hair pulling, twisting of arms, invasive inspections, and humiliating punishments are all eroticized anger.

Emotional violence, particularly in a relationship, has an eroticized edge to it. Both men and women use it in relationships. As a society, we treat physical violence as the most damaging form, but many people never recover from the *emotional* violence in their life. Words can have an even greater impact than a fist. The bruise will heal but the emotional devastation of words may not ever heal. This is in no way meant to diminish the impact of physical violence, but simply to state that words, especially the use of eroticized angry words, can also destroy people.

Bullying has deep roots in eroticized feelings and is, consequently, a form of eroticized anger. Wanting to dominate, control, diminish or abuse someone is equivalent to topping them sexually or being the one in charge in a sexual interaction. For the bully, it is always about their own pleasure.

For many people, whether the giver or receiver, sex is an acceptable way to express anger. From very subtle to overt, there is a wide range of activities that fall into the category of sadomasochistic behaviors. S&M sex-play *that is consensual for both partners* can be great; the only exception is when the one or both parties regress intellectually and emotionally to a child state. When when they are regressed, they are unable to give true consent.

In a consensual relationship, the dominant partner is expressing eroticized anger at the submissive. This can range from some role-play to a full-time lifestyle. Both partners find it sexually and emotionally satisfying. When two or more people choose to play out the eroticized shame and the eroticized anger together, it is an example of a selfish/selfless pairing that is discussed in Chapter Seven *Selfish/Selfless/Self-Full*. In Chapter Two *Defining the Self*, where the graphics show the craters that happen in childhood; this is an example of two different sets of craters that perfectly meet each other's needs.

Sex is complicated, and when we start mixing it with anger, we can lose perspective about what is happening. The underlying motivations matter; being conscious of them will help us make the best choices for our lives.

Relationship and Eroticized Shame

It is very important that there is sexual compatibility in a long-term relationship. While the two people involved might not be a perfect match sexually, there needs to be enough of an overlap, or a willingness on a partner's part to move into the other's realm of eroticism, so that both are satisfied. The lack of any sexual congruence and/or compromise in a couple has doomed many love matches. Love is not enough.

The problem is when the fantasy cripples or prevents intimacy and vulnerability. Just being willing to be beaten does not mean that you are being vulnerable. Vulnerability presents itself when light is shone on the inner-self and any shame inhabiting within. Once the shame is exposed, the fantasy connected to it may be altered or disintegrated. To find out, you must communicate with your partner about desires and expectations. If you cannot trust your partner with your deepest secrets about who you are, then you are in the wrong relationship. At the same time, this kind of vulnerability is not to be pushed. Reveal too much too soon, and you get rejected. Exposing inner secrets should only happen when deep trust has been established. And that requires time. Sometimes a couple of years may pass before the deeply hidden stuff comes out, but that should happen *before* you say 'I do,' and not after.

If we can share our story with someone who responds with empathy and understanding, shame can't survive.

— Brené Brown (b. 1965) *Daring Greatly*

Sexual Transmitted Diseases (STD's)

Because of America's culture of shame regarding sex, getting an STD has a stigma. When a person finds out they have an STD, they are filled with sexual shame. Even though herpes (HSV) and anal warts (HPV) are almost universal, most people do not know they have them, as not all people have breakouts. They simply carry a virus.

When symptoms do arise, it can bring all of the sexual shame to the surface and cause major psychological stress. Panic attacks, depression, and even the extreme of suicidal thoughts are in the possible range of responses. The first common belief is that their sex life is over. There are thoughts of being "damaged goods" and that "No good person would ever have sex with me again." Some people never heal emotionally. To get past it, they would have to process the shame, deal with the downloaded negative beliefs about sex and educate themselves about what STD's are and are not. STD's are viruses, not a physical punishment manifesting a "judgment from God."

An argument made against birth control pills and the HSV vaccine has been that if there were no consequences for having sex, women would sleep with a lot more men. A significant number of people think there should be negative consequences for having sex. This is simply more of the anti-pleasure belief system that has crippled sexual health throughout the world. Punishing people for having pleasure is like being a covert perpetrator. The abuser may not be in the room, but the people who deny others education, vaccinations, and birth control and protection against STD's are perpetrators. Eroticized anger is being acted out on people who dare to experience pleasure.

Economic Shame

As the song says, "Money makes the world go 'round," but combining shame and money takes an already complex relationship with money and can make it much more toxic. There is either too much or there is not enough and either can result in feeling bad about yourself.

Not being able to financially take care of one's self or one's family will invoke shame. Most cultures expect that if a man is an adult, he can provide for himself: food, shelter, clothes, etc. Not to be able says that the man has not only failed to be an adult, but that something is fundamentally wrong with him. To ask for help, to request assistance from family or friends or to apply for welfare is, for most people, hugely humiliating. While women are also humiliated when they ask for help, they are not currently held to the same standard as men. The reason for a man's failure does not matter — being it circumstantial or bad judgment — the need to ask or, as some people judge, 'beg' for help is considered a disgrace.

Josephine had always struggled to make ends meet. She worked hard, got an education and did all the things one is supposed to do to be successful. But somehow, she was never able to get ahead. With a series of layoffs in a bad economy and difficulty in getting a new job, she ran out of options. She was on the verge of being homeless. Her family had never been prosperous and she had a limited number of friends who were in a position to help, even if they could. Asking for help, going to the food bank, applying for government assistance, all felt mortifying. She did dig down into herself, found the courage to ask for help and with assistance, got back on her feet. She was stronger in the end because she found out she could survive anything. But the process of getting there caused her many anxious nights.

In some cultures, people will have the best car or the best clothes and yet live in a shack. It does not matter they have inadequate housing or medical care; it is crucial for everyone to think they are successful. How others might see them is more important than what is actually happening to them. They are ashamed of not being rich or successful enough. But for them, at least on the surface, having other people think they are rich or successful is all that matters.

Aban was a first-generation Lebanese-American. He went to college and graduated with a degree in business. Once he was out of his parents' house for good, he lived with roommates and began a party lifestyle. He spent money like he was rich — buying everyone rounds of drinks, dressing very well, and buying things beyond his means. In a short time, he became more in debt and could not pay his bills. He was deeply ashamed that he could not maintain the lifestyle he was presenting to all of his friends. He was terrified they would see him as a failure, so he hid the extent of his financial problems as long as possible.

In the end, he was forced to declare bankruptcy and sought help to learn about managing his money and to find a way out of debt. Initially, he even ignored the money problems in therapy as he was in so much denial about what was happening. It was more important to him that he appear successful to his friends than to deal with the stress and pain of his situation. It took some work, but he finally faced the pain of the emptiness inside. He had been using his public image to cover to avoid the pain. Aban also realized that this was how his family taught him to be in the world. "What people think of you is much more important than what you feel about yourself." In time, after a lot of hard work, he started to make much better financial choices and turned his financial situation around.

On the other hand having too much money can be problematic for some people. They inherited it, they do not feel worthy of it and they feel like they got lucky. Somehow, they do not deserve it. They can feel guilty that they have more than their peers. These people like having money, but they feel different from their peers. The fear is people will only like them for their money or in some way it makes them different, and they are uncomfortable dealing with that. They need to be liked and having money can move other people one more step away and can make for awkward relationships.

Coming into money means changing one's identity. You are not going to be like everyone else anymore. You have options other people do not have.

There will be envy and jealousy, and not being able to deal with that will bring to the surface some shame that there is something wrong with you.

Money is the currency of love in many families. If there is not enough money, there is not enough love. Not having enough makes you bad and unlovable. This happens in families at all economic levels, where parents use money to reward or control. This is a set-up for a lifetime of "money equals self-worth" and thus a core of shame.

If the measure of your being loved is how much money you have, how much money you are paid, or how much money you are given, then your value is tied to money. When money is tight, or you are going through a tough period, this complicates your ability to tolerate and work through a hard time. It will make it much harder (if at all possible), to make good decisions about a situation because it is not just a financial decision. It is a decision about who you are and whether you are going to be loved.

Some adult children stay connected to abusive parents in order to get an inheritance. This is how people can be controlled by inheritances. They believe if they do not get the money then they are not loved. The way parents choose to leave money to children can be the final assault and a demonstration of who was truly loved and who was not. Kids can spend a lifetime trying to keep their parents' approval in order to get the final payout. As long as they are tied to the money and it is controlling them, they cannot grow up and they cannot truly value themselves as individuals or adults. Since love was conditional and demonstrated through money, rather than by caring and acceptance, the children never learn how to be loved or give love. It is a set-up for a lifetime of pain with the shame of not really being loved.

Some people suffer guilt from having money; they feel fortunate and are acutely aware that others are not as fortunate. The shame comes from having what others lack. Like it or not, we live in a world with social classes. There are the haves, the have-nots and the in-betweens. Each level will have people who feel bad about being a part of their class. It makes no sense to the poor person that someone with money should feel bad about it. A middle-class person can feel just as bad about having more money than a poor person, just as a rich person might feel about the middle class. It is relative. It does not have to make sense to anyone outside. It comes down to how you think others see you. If they see you as more fortunate, they may not like you. Apologizing for having assets seems the only way to stay in others' good graces. It is a twisted braid of shame, but it still comes back to being ruled by how you think others see you.

Having money or not makes no difference. It is about how having or not having makes you feel about yourself. There is no question that having more money gives you more options, but when the amount of money you have is the measure of your value and worth, you are surrendering who you are to something outside of yourself.

Body Shame

Above all else, kids want to fit in. Anything that makes them different is a problem for them. As they are still in the process of developing a solid sense of self, peer and family responses are really important to how they see themselves. What is really happening is that on the inside, they feel bad about themselves. When something about their body gets pointed out or they fear they are obviously different in some way, whether others see it or not, they externalize that bad feeling onto their physical characteristic. It might be having red hair, or too much hair or not enough hair. Their nose is too big, too small, too flat, not Caucasian enough, or not European enough. It might be they feel they are too tall or too short. It might be having breasts too large or too small, or having a penis that is not big enough. They are too heavy or too skinny. The list of possible *perceived* imperfections and flaws is endless, even while the perception might be wrong. Yet the need to make sense out of this bad feeling inside is what drives the desire to change or hide this physical issue so that they can feel better about themselves. Said more accurately, they would feel less judged by others because they have changed or hidden their real or imagined flaw.

People sometimes try to make sense of the shame they feel inside by focusing on something on the outside. We can concretize our internal feelings by identifying them as an external characteristic. Our bodies are convenient scapegoats. We see our bodies every day, and tend to have little perspective as to how our bodies appear to others. To obsess about some real or imagined flaw becomes an easy outlet to prevent us from dealing with the real pain inside of ourselves.

There are probably equal numbers of people that inflate their sense of beauty versus people who denigrate themselves for how they look. Both the inflation and the deflation of the exterior looks are masks for shame. An obsession with external parts of ourselves is missing the point of who we are on the inside. If who we think we are is bad, there is substantial incentive to look externally in order to distract from the pain and deflect from the source of it.

Kids who are sexually abused are much more likely to have physical shame. They are brought into a premature hyper-awareness of their bodies and sexual feelings long before they are able to process or handle the information. Since kids usually blame themselves for being abused, they often decide it has something to do with how they look or how they act, resulting in shame about their bodies. Disgusting or evil are just a couple of the various ways they can sense their bodies. It can be a long road to healing and owning their bodies in a healthy way.

Unresolved issues, particularly around physical and sexual abuse, can be the basis of body issues in adulthood. It is common for abuse victims to armor themselves through extreme weight gain or extreme body building in an effort to protect themselves. Conversely, self-starvation to disappear or to be unattractive can be another attempt to stop or prevent future abuse.

When someone comes to a therapist with a physical complaint about something they'd like to change, the first step should be to send them to a physician if they have not been to one already. Most therapists are not physicians, and anything that is physical should be cleared or at least examined. If the potential client considers their nose to be an issue, then they should see a plastic surgeon. A good doctor will tell them if their issue can be changed or corrected, and what the likely outcome would be.

After the medical screening, it is possible for the therapist to assess for an emotional or psychological issue. Well-trained doctors and plastic surgeons, in particular, are aware of the psychological condition, Body Dysmorphic Disorder, commonly known as BDD. It is a disorder which people do not see themselves accurately in the mirror. They see imperfections, flaws and skin disorders that are not really there. BDD is very difficult to treat, and usually requires high doses of SSRI's (such as Prozac, Paxil, Zoloft, etc.) to reduce the discomfort of the client.

Somatization is when people are unable or unwilling to express emotions which instead turn into physical symptoms. While it is normal and healthy to feel emotions in the body, if there is a split between the mind and body and the emotions are not processed directly, the repressed emotions can become physical disorders. Somatization can range from an upset stomach to illnesses that require treatment. Once people begin to make the connection between their physical and emotional states, the work of resolving the pain can happen. Feelings will end up being expressed in some form. Shame can both show up on the outside and inside of the body. It is better to deal with the underlying pain so that most of the somatic complaints will dissipate.

Race Shame

I believe it is impossible to grow up as a minority in any culture without taking on some level of shame. When you are young, you want to belong, and if tangible qualities prevent you from appearing like the majority, you feel self-conscious. If the images a child sees of the socially powerful in the community are consistently different from their race, a child will come to its own conclusions as to why that might be so. Children blame themselves for most things going on around them. This is particularly true if it involves their security or self-identity. If they feel out of place or invisible, they will blame themselves.

The majority because they are in the majority often can't see that being different from the majority can create a different perspective on the world. They don't see the compromises to opportunity and the struggle to be accepted that people of different races experience. The obliviousness or lack of empathy on the majority's part increases the difficulty in changing attitudes and behaviors. If you can't see it, there is nothing to correct.

Race shame looks a lot like sexual orientation shame, except the person of a minority race doesn't generally have the option to hide who they are. Because they are visibly different they have the feeling, real or not, that they have to be many times better than the majority race to succeed in the face of direct hostility and constant micro-aggressions, which reinforce the feeling of not being good enough.

Compensatory behaviors are some of the major unconscious ways of dealing with racial shame — having the most money, the best car, the most or best jewelry, whatever makes people feel better. But underneath those behaviors is the 'I am not good enough' shame. It can show up in being the kindest, most generous person, or attempting to save the world in some form. Many of the compensatory behaviors can be very useful in pushing people to be the best they can be and to help others. But the underlying feelings must be addressed, so that there is more freedom to be in the world. No one should have to compensate for being their race.

The downside of racial shame is giving up or collapsing: *The system is stacked against me. I am never going to make it so I am not going to try.* The physical defeat validates the internal feeling of not being good enough. Giving up can lead to the formation of collectives of gangs or groups of frustrated individuals who feel the same, are angry and act out in violent, anti-establishment forms. For the solitary type, shame can result in chronic drug abuse, alcoholism or other forms of medicating and checking out. Until the shame is addressed, it is very hard to change how it is being expressed.

There are different degrees of shame that people download. How their families deal with being a minority will directly affect how their children feel about themselves. Some parents do better jobs of addressing it than others. Most people do not talk about shame, as it is not at the forefront of our consciousness and thus not a part of our conversation. This is a particularly sensitive and difficult issue to address.

The following is a contribution from a colleague, after reading a rough draft of section on race shame:

"As a light-skinned black man, I see that the racism between light/dark-skinned people also works to divide and conquer within communities of color. I got more shit from darker-skinned black folks than I ever did from white folks. One dark-skinned bully used to shield his eyes when he saw me, saying, "God, you're so bright I'm going to go blind." Other kids would of course laugh.

In communities where people are of different shades (blacks, East Indians, Hispanics, on and on) there is often hatred from the darker people toward the lighter people. Of course, there is also elitism from the lighter people, looking down at the darker people.

The elite black social clubs in Chicago where I grew up, might have well have said.... "No dark blacks allowed." I recently came across a picture of a social club my mom belonged to — the wives of black doctors, lawyers etc. Out of maybe 40 women, at least 35 were "high yellow." A few darker ladies were allowed in, perhaps because their husbands were SUPER exceptional. It is kind of sick.

Here is another crazy story. When I had hair, it was more obvious that I was black. I would get pulled over, and twice was given roadside sobriety tests when I literally had nothing at all to drink. I was NEVER given a break on a ticket.

After I shaved my head, the first time I was pulled over, I was going 75 in a 55. The cop reduced my ticket to "6 mph over speed limit." Saved me several hundred dollars. On the ticket he wrote, "white male." The next time I was pulled over for an illegal lane change, the cop gave me a warning ticket. No fine. On the ticket it said, "white male."

I cannot make this up. I am one of the few people in this country who can actually report the difference in treatment from being seen as a "black male" to being seen as a "white male." Pretty crazy, eh?[22]

Shame as the sense of self

Childhood, for many, is one long shaming experience. Children are told they are bad, stupid, ugly, perverted and any derogatory expression that can be used to assault the growing self-awareness of children. The continuous assault takes a huge toll on them, on their mental health and can destroy any positive sense of self or self-esteem.

Shaming children is a way to control them. It makes them more submissive and subservient. The problem is that those downloaded beliefs can last a lifetime, and the damage will likely go unrepaired. Too many parents disable their kids from the beginning and then wonder why their grown children are never able to be self-sufficient or succeed.

Criticism that is not about a specific act or action, which is instead directed at who the child is, is damaging. Once a child has received enough of these messages, they will develop a negative sense of self. When the child then thinks of themself, they will see someone unworthy, stupid, incapable, weak or any number of a long list of negative self-statements. These can be carried into adult life. The adult can then develop compensating behaviors like having the best car, making the most money, having the best job, or owning the biggest home entertainment system, in order to distract themself from how they feel inside. Anything that threatens those compensatory outward expressions is intolerable. They will attempt to go to great extremes to avoid that loss of face and risk having their shame exposed to everyone.

For children to develop a healthy public self, they require years of being reflected by their parents and teachers. Having their experience reflected back to them is how they begin to make the connections inside and start to pull together the pieces of who they are inside. Children who do not get enough reflection of themselves grow up without an internal sense of self. When they go inside, there is nothing there. They feel empty. It is only when they are reflected back by others that they see themselves. The emptiness is experienced as shame, the sense that they are intrinsically bad. If the reflection received from external reinforcement is not positive, it pushes them into a deep, shameful internal experience. People who are easily wounded are examples of this. The kid on the street who is always picking fights because they feel disrespected is telling you they feel bad about themself. Anything that does not validate them as good is pushing them into that shame-filled interior, which creates anger and overwhelming pain.

Developing a healthy sense of self is not easy, and navigating the treacherous waters of childhood is difficult for most people. Without healthy parents there to help chart a course and make course corrections, it is almost impossible to emerge into adulthood fully intact.

Facing the Truth of Your Life

PART FOUR

CHILDHOOD RE-IMAGINED

—— 18 ——

Making Sense
of Childhood

CHILDREN HAVE TWO PRIMARY psychological jobs to accomplish when they come into the world.[23] From the first moments of birth, babies start trying to make sense out of all that is happening. We know that a child is not a completely blank slate. Genetics play a key role, but the brain is not ready at birth to organize all the data that starts to pour in. Babies are naturally undifferentiated. They have not had the chance to form a sense of self. They exist in the reflection they get back in the smiles and giggles from their caregivers. Babies operate on the most basic of survival functions, but they are still actively observing. They are taking in information that they will organize and reorganize, and immediately start reaching conclusions about how the world works and who they are.

Job 1

Conclusions formulated while you are a baby or a child, theorizing how the world works, are based on incomplete information. A central part of psychotherapy is the process of going back and rediscovering those very early conclusions that were reached much too early in life, with too little information and no bigger perspective.

If you carry your childhood with you,
you never become older.

— Tom Stoppard (b. 1937)
Playwright and Screenwriter

A baby cries itself to sleep and concludes that it is not lovable.
A child accidentally abandoned at the sports field concludes it is not important.
A child shamed for breaking a toy concludes it is bad.

The first task is discovering and then own the conclusion reached such as: *I am not lovable. I am not important. I am bad.*

Next, the task is to chew it up and discard whatever doesn't work, and keep those parts of the belief that make sense from an adult perspective.

For a long time, the professional advice to parents on getting babies to sleep alone was to "let them cry it out." Parents and babies were tortured by letting the baby wail for hours at times, with the baby feeling abandoned by the parent while frightened and overwhelmed with emptiness. Some babies and young children reach the conclusion that their needs do not matter, and they never will. So what appears to be a selfless child might be one that just gave up trying to get its needs met. This happens at such an early age, the adult doesn't remember it happening, but the wiring and view of the world is in place, and will be until that painful experience is unearthed and healed.

EXERCISE: EXPLORING CONCLUSIONS FROM EARLY CHILDHOOD

This exercise needs to be done with another person. Hopefully, they are someone who has done some therapy and has insight into their own early life process. Pair up and one at a time, go back as far in childhood as each is comfortable and tell a story about an early painful experience. It might seem minor to someone else, though it might actually be a major trauma. You get to decide. But the memory should have at least a fair amount of emotional charge.

With the other person's help, the two of you figure out what conclusion(s) were reached by the child in that story — about who the child is and how the world works.

The conclusion you came to might be a surprise and it might not, but understand it is a substantial piece of how you still see yourself and how you think the world is organized.

Once you have this realization, and you get that this is your truth, you have the opportunity to decide if it is still true for you, or if you need to reorganize your belief system based on your adult perspective, rather than a child's.

Before the belief can be changed, it has to be acknowledged and owned. Only then is there the possibility of change.

Jim adored his father. When he was just six, he was left at the library to play and his father was supposed to pick him up later. At the appointed time, Dad never showed. This experience had a lasting impact on Jim and his ability to trust anyone, particularly men. It was not until he could get in touch with the abandoned six-year-old inside of himself that he began to understand where his belief that he was not lovable came from. Only by rescuing that child and helping him understand that it was not his fault, could Jim begin the process of healing and interacting with men as an adult, instead of as that six-year-old.

Juan Carlos was 10 years old. He played left field for a Little League team. He was neither the best nor the worst player on the team. His team was in the championship game and down to the last out. The batter slammed a ball to left field. Juan Carlos dropped the ball and the boy on third base scored. The game was over. Juan Carlos was devastated. He felt totally responsible for the team's loss. This became the foundation of his belief about himself that he was a loser and would never succeed.

For many people, these early core beliefs, born out of seemingly minor incidents, become self-fulfilling prophecies that color their worldview for the rest of their lives. It is the job of the parent to help children make sense out of these potentially traumatizing and life-changing experiences, so they see the bigger picture and reach reasonable conclusions. It is crucial that children also know they are loved, even when bad things happen.

When a child's parents fight or even divorce, the child usually believes it is somehow at fault. Children are healthily narcissistic and to them, everything that goes on around them is consequently about them. They have yet to form an internal sense of self that allows them to separate the inside from the outside. Inside and outside is all the same thing.

The first two years should center on intuitively meeting the needs of the child. Babies do not really have the ability to make sense of most of their parents' words. That starts between two and three years of age. The parent's primary job those first few years is to make the child feel safe, secure and loved.

It is crucial that a parent spend the early years of a child's life reflecting back the child's external experience to the child, helping make sense of it. That is how a child develops a healthy sense of self and separate what is internal from the external world. For example, when a child is sad, the parent reflects back what they see so the child can connect internally what the experience is. Without that, a child thinks everyone feels the way it does. Reflecting a child's experiences back to it is required to form a solid sense of self and grow into a healthy adult.

Examples of reflective statements and questions:

Billy, you look sad.
Sara, how excited you must feel.
George, you feel really frustrated and angry to me.

The point is not to create those feelings in the child, but to accurately reflect back the feelings the child is having at that moment.

Job 2

The second job of a child is to download the love of a parent. This will determine the child's attachment style. The attachment style is how a person receives and gives love. The relationship of the child to each parent will have a huge influence on the child's relationship to people of that parent's gender. It will also determine if a child is able to feel loved by someone. If a child never felt loved by a parent, and is not secure in the belief that they are lovable, the child will have a difficult time being in a healthy relationship.

Bill and Joe's parents divorced early. They lived with their mother while their dad got visitation rights. Mom used the boys to feel

What attachment theory essentially says is that being loved matters—and, more than that, it matters who loves us and whom we love in return. It's not just a matter of the warm body holding the bottle; it's not object love at all; we love specific people and we need them to love us back. And in the case of the child's tie to the mother, it matters that the mother loves that baby and that the baby knows it. When you are a very small child, love needs to be as tangible as warm arms around you and as audible as the lull of a gentle voice at night.

—Deborah Blum (b.1954) Pulitzer Prize-winning American Journalist

loved. All of the attention they got from her was conditional, requiring them to make her feel loved. So the way they got their needs met was to meet Mom's needs. She would force them to attend to her needs, like brushing her hair, listening to her talk for hours and doing other things for her to prove they loved her. Anytime the boys showed interest in a girl, she would disapprove. The girls were "trash" or "not good enough for her boys."

The boys were an extension of their mother and her needs, rather than separate individuals with their own wants and needs. Bill and Joe did not have a true childhood. They learned that to survive, they had to keep Mom happy. It was never about them. This would have a huge impact on being in relationship with women later in life.

Dad did the best he could, but could not protect his sons from their mother, because he was not there all the time. When the time was right, their father assumed custody, but the damage had already been done.

When it came time to date, Bill was very attracted to women, but he had a strong ambivalence about being in a relationship. The childhood experience with his mother taught him the message that being in a relationship meant giving up all of his needs and meeting the needs of his partner. Understandably, this felt out of balance to the adult Bill, but deep inside, no matter how attracted he was, the closer he got, the more ambivalent he felt about being with her.

Joe, on the other hand, took on his mother's style and constantly needed his partner's reassurance that he was loved and wanted. He also found it difficult to be in a relationship because his needs drove partners away.

Conversely, both boys had really good relationships with men. They were able to download their father's love and thus felt secure in their relationships with men. Dad made the relationship about his sons and not himself. Being a parent means meeting the child's needs.

After a lot of psychotherapy on their childhood and the relationship with their mother, both sons were both able to have sustained satisfying relationships. Each of them was committed to healing, so that they could be in a relationship, and their determination and dedication paid off.

If a child is able to take in and hold the love of a parent or an adult, it can sustain them for the rest of their lives. They know they are loved. How well a child is able to download their parent's love is one of the best predictors of having a successful, healthy adult relationship and of being successful in the world. Too many parents have kids so they, the *parents,* can feel loved. That is child abuse. And it will impact the child for the rest of their lives.

No one escapes from childhood unscathed; however, it is not intended to be pain-free or, all that easy. Childhood is about creating a person. It is about making mistakes and figuring out the world. When clients come into therapy and report they had an idyllic childhood, it generally means long-term therapy ahead. *Romanticized childhoods suggest the need to bury any pain underneath the story.* It is necessary to break through the denial of the fantasy before being able to address the pain. Generally speaking, the greater the denial, the greater the buried pain in a person.

Not all childhoods are created equal. Many are better or worse than the average. Parents are supposed to be there to help guide their children through the pain, give them a means to deal with it and understand it, so that the children eventually have the tools to be an adult. Of course, the problem is most parents have not figured that out for themselves. All too often, people had children when they were merely children themselves.

Most non-chemically-based mental illness develops when parents are the source of a child's pain or fail to help the child navigate the pain of growing up. The children are trapped and have no avenue for support or education. They survive the best they can, trying to make sense of the situation they are in and then extrapolating it to the rest of the world.

Parents who attempt to give their kids pain-free childhoods are creating adults who may never grow up. The adult children will have no tools to deal with the disappointments of the real world and can end up being hypersensitive to everything. It is a setup for a painful adult life. These children's parents have no understanding about raising a child to adulthood. It is probable that the parents had never dealt with the pain of their own childhood and may be trying to save their children from the kind of pain they experienced. Instead, they are condemning their children to another kind of hell.

Childhood is a long, painful, and confusing training school. There should be lots of wonderful moments and deep bonding along the way as well. The more good moments, the better. Pain needs a balance. Parents are the primary teachers. The parents' responsibility is to protect, and make their children feel safe, loved and secure enough so the children can come to the parents for help. This is a core part of the parenting job, so that when kids grow up, they end up with a secure sense of self they can pass on to the next generation.

—— 19 ——

Giving Me Up,
To Be Loved By You

The capacity for friendship is God's way
of apologizing for our families.

—Jay McInerney (b. 1955)
The Last of the Savages

THE HOLIDAYS BRING UP fantasies of hearth and home, a family gathering to reconnect and reaffirm love and commitment to each other. When it works and goes well, it can be a powerful antidote to the stress and isolation of modern life. Families can be exotic collections of personalities, each with their own realities. Unique childhood experience defines them. So many expectations, so many movie clichés of the way it is supposed to be, or should have been. Sadly, despite propaganda to the contrary, the problem-free family is the exception rather than the rule. Disappointments, hurts and reverting to survival mode are all too often the elements of a holiday gathering.

Family

So what is a family? What should a family be? What if it were based on love rather than bloodline? Many cultures teach their children it is the children's job to take care of their parents and siblings. Parents gave life, so it is the children's alleged duty to fulfill the contract by staying connected, no matter what negative history they may have had together. Frequently, the more abusive the childhood is, the greater the download of guilt and obligation to repay their parents for the parents' sacrifices.

Mic Hunter, author of several books about boys who were sexually abused as children, defines child abuse as, "*anytime* a child is used to meet the needs of the adult." Having a child in order to have someone love you, or take care of you, both fall within Hunter's definition of abuse. All too often, mothers who raised children can suddenly become helpless when their children become adults, making the adult child their caretaker. This is not about caring for a seriously ill or elderly parent, but rather an adult who is otherwise able to function independently. A parent who regresses to a helpless, child-like place is putting responsibility for the parent's happiness onto the adult child, depriving the adult child of their own life.

Jamie was the middle child of three children. He had an older brother and a younger sister. While his childhood was not perfect, he was able to launch himself into the world. His sister Sara, on the other hand, took up the mantle of caring for their mother. She never left home emotionally. She sacrificed everything for her parents, never married and even lived next door. Even though both parents worked, Sara was there to give them whatever help they might need. This was long before dementia and health issues overtook them in old age. So instead of being a separate individual person, she became an extension of them.

When people are considering marriage, one of the most important consid-
erations is this: Are you ready and able to put your partner first? Before your
parents, your siblings and your friends? Are you willing to make this person
the most important person in your life?

For some, this seems a shocking consideration. Cutting the apron ties and
creating your own family is your first priority. Separating from your family
of origin and setting them free to their own choices is hard to imagine, let
alone the thought of *not* sacrificing yourself to save family and friends from
themselves.

Gab and Amelia had been married for 30 years. By all accounts,
they had a happy marriage. Their three sons launched into the
world successfully. But after the boys left home and two of the
three married, they were upset they did not visit often enough.
They no longer came home for all the holidays. The oldest, Mat-
thew, spent almost all of his holidays with his wife's family. The
middle son, Ethan, simply chose to travel or be with his friends. The
boys stayed in contact, but did not focus their social life on their
parents and did not feel compelled to reassure their parents they
were loved.

Gab was very upset and tried to set his boys straight about his
expectations as a parent. Amelia was upset that her oldest was
choosing his wife's family over her. She felt rejected. They needed
the boys' attention, especially as a distraction from each other. As
the nest emptied, they really needed to reacquaint themselves with
each other and find out how life had changed. It was less threatening for their relationship to blame their unhappiness on the boy's
inattention.

An easy definition of codependency[24] is: Giving *me* up, to be loved by *you*. "I will sacrifice myself and put aside my needs and wants to make you happy in hopes that so you will like and love me." Many family scripts teach kids they have to sacrifice themselves for their parents in order to be loved. If love is conditional in childhood, it builds codependency into the family dynamics and relationships.

Jenna grew up in an abusive home. She was sexually abused as a child and also raped several times as an adult. She was fearful of life in general, and the somatization of her fears had turned into many physical issues. She had never been able to process the trauma and PTSD of childhood, let alone the adult trauma. She was a giver. She was constantly trying to give food, or literally the clothes on her back, to make people like her. She just saw it as caring about people. It was painful to watch, as she did not understand how her constant giving was actually pushing people away. People genuinely liked her and wanted the best for her. But her underlying neediness made most people keep a certain distance, which, in turn caused her to try harder to get them to like her. There was a disconnect inside Jenna that made it impossible for her to understand what was actually being offered. She had no emotional frame for unconditional love, so she could not really accept someone caring for her in return.

So what should a family be?

A nuclear family (in whatever formulation) is necessary for the raising of children. Children need to be held in a safe and nurturing container so they can grow and develop into healthy adults, and importantly, leave the nest.

The point of family is to launch the kids and teach them not to need their parents. That does not mean they are never in touch again, or not there in some form to care for elderly parents. But that kind of love and caring should come naturally from the relationship, not driven by guilt, shame or obligation.

A broader, more realistic definition of family should be the people who love you for who you are. As mentioned before, one of the gifts of being different is that you get to find out if your family really loves you unconditionally. Becoming an adult is about living your own life. Robert Bly's book, *Iron John*,[25] talks about the need of the son to steal the key to his power from underneath his mother's pillow. We all need to take back our power from our parents and live our own life.

If members of your biological family are loving and supportive, they can and should be part of one's 'family of choice.' If they are not, they really are no different from strangers or acquaintances. To call someone "family" is to know they love you and they are there for you.

Years ago, a man tried to sell Jerome a franchise business. One of the things the salesman asked Jerome was how many people he could call at 3 AM that would be there for him without question. The salesman's purpose was to find out if Jerome could relate to people and if he could form deep connections, because it is an important personal quality in sales.

It is a profound question — to really know who your friends are, people who you can call at any time. It is also an excellent measure of who you can call 'family.' Members of a family of choice do not always approve of what you do (and they should let you know), but they love you and wish the best for you. Those people really do make a family, and yet blood is not a required part of the definition. Take a look at your family and your friends. Who are the real members of your family of choice? Part of being an adult is knowing and choosing who belongs in your life and who doesn't.

FAMILY OF CHOICE EXERCISE

While there is a graphic, you are welcome to make a list on a piece of paper or draw the circles so you can write the names under each heading. Your family of origin members can fall into any of the five circles.

Who is member of your **Family of Choice**? These are the people that are there for you no matter what, like those people that you can call at 3 AM.

Who are your **Friends**? They are people who care about you and may know you reasonably well, but do not really know your deepest thoughts. You share much with them, but not everything. There are limits to the intimacy and trust.

Who are the **People You Know**? These are the people you might see in a shop or cafe each day, or the neighbor next door you say hello to and might chat with, but you do not really get into deep things or share too much. Family members often fall into this category.

Who are the members of your **Community**? These are the people you pass by on your way to work in your car or on transit — the nameless faces that may or may not come into focus now and then, but you do not really know each other.

Your biological family can be in any or all of the circles. It would be a fantasy to think they are all in the inner circle. Just knowing you a long time or having given birth to you is not enough. It is about knowing you, who you are and what you stand for that invites people into your inner circles.

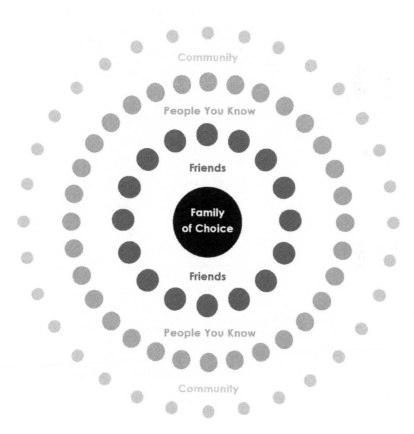

—— 20 ——

Keys to Raising Healthy Kids

The most important thing that parents can teach their children is how to get along without them.

—Frank A. Clark (b. 1860) Politician

OVER THE PAST 34 years in therapeutic settings, I have learned a lot about what works and doesn't work when it comes to parenting. There are some universal truths about successfully navigating the landmines and potholes of childhood so a child can grow into adulthood successfully. What follows are tips from the men and women who have trusted me with both their pain and their joy.

Key 1
Make Your Love Obvious

As mentioned before, it is one of the primary tasks of childhood to download the love of a parent. Most parents really love their children. However, many children do not understand it fully, or feel that the love is so conditional that they do not trust the love from their parent. And as a consequence, they may not trust love from anyone else later in life.

Parents need to tell their children they love them, often and in many ways. Gary Chapman in *The 5 Love Languages*[26] suggests there are five primary ways that people express and feel love: Words of Affirmation, Acts of Service, Receiving Gifts, Quality Time and Physical Touch. This book has been an invaluable resource for countless numbers of people.

Everyone has a unique style of giving and receiving love. Children learn how to give and receive from their parents. We generally download their style. It is not something we generally think about; it is usually automatic. Often the style of love people want most as an adult is one they did not get as a child. A child who is not touched longs for touch and that becomes a primary love language. A child who is not told they are loved may long for the words they rarely or never heard as a child. If the style of love expressed in their family was conditional or incomplete, wanting an untainted expression of love makes sense.

Parents have a different perspective. Most parents love their children. They feed them, comfort them, clothe them, and send them to school. The many things parents do for their children are all acts of love. But a child largely takes these acts for granted, as they should. As children age and gain a greater perspective of life and hopefully they acquire the awareness that not all families are the same. By gaining consciousness of what it takes to make all of the magic of a family and home happen, they will likely be grateful as well. But a parent can educate a child about expressing love in all the different forms, especially until the parent understand how the child takes in love. To a child, no amount of money or physical comforts can be substituted for feeling truly loved.

There are too many tragic tales of adults never having been touched by their parents or never told they were loved. Money is often substituted as the currency of love, but it does not heal or sustain the heart.

It is especially important for a child to know that when a parent is angry or disappointed with them, they are still loved. Correcting a child is an important requirement of being a parent, but if a child fears being abandoned or harmed in some way, the lesson ceases to be about what was done wrong and becomes about survival.

It is also crucial that parents keep boundaries between them and the child. Too many parents try to be their child's best friend. Or they use the child as a support or confidant. That is not the role of a child. That is not love. It is the parent using the child to meet the needs of the parent.

Love your children. Love them in many different ways and educate them about the ways love can be expressed. Do not confuse a child's love for you as that of an equal or make them someone you lean on. A parent certainly wants to be loved by their child. It does not always happen, and it may not show up in a form that makes the parent happy, but it is the job of the parent to make the child feel loved. Most kids love their parents, but it is not the job of the child to make the parent feel loved.

Key 2
Keep shame to the minimum.

What a child *did* was bad; who they *are* is not bad.

Let's differentiate between guilt and shame. Guilt is feeling bad about what you did, what you did not do, or what you thought about doing. Shame is feeling bad about who you are, carrying around beliefs about yourself, such as: "I am bad," "I am awful," "I am sick," or "I am perverted."

One of the most common experiences we all have as human beings is being shamed. Parents unintentionally shame children all the time. Instead of a parent saying, "Billy, that was a bad thing to do," they say, "Billy, you are a bad boy." Children swallow that. They tend to believe parents literally and these beliefs can become foundational in how children see themselves. Children experience themselves in the reflections that their parents and caregivers give them. All of us have shame, but the question is, how much shame did we retain? It really depends on how we are raised and our experiences as a child.

In daily interactions, a stressed, frustrated and critical parent can easily make children feel bad about themselves, especially when it is a common style of interaction. In the short run, it may get the parent what they want — a contrite, quiet, punished child. But in the long run, it can have serious consequences to a child's sense of self, self-esteem, and ability to function later on in the world as a healthy adult.

A better approach to parenting emphasizes empathy and teaching. It is really important for a parent to be as conscious as possible when punishing a child. Parents can get angry and short-tempered. But it is still a child they are dealing with, not some demon from hell sent to annoy them. The task is to understand what is happening, helping children understand what has happened, checking in with them to see what they were thinking or how they got to the conclusion they did, then teaching them a better path. That is parenting.

Chloe was 9 years old. She went to school and had friends. One day she saw a classmate with a shaved head. She made fun of the girl, accusing her of being weird and ugly. This got her into a lot of trouble at school and later at home. Chloe's mom, Scarlett was horrified and enraged at her daughter. She felt shamed by Chloe's behavior and was sure that the school thought she was a bad parent. So she decided to teach Chloe an unforgettable lesson by shaving Chloe's head and forcing her to feel the same humiliation and taunts.

Scarlett managed to make the situation worse. She proved to the school she was a bad abusive parent and they better understood Chloe's behavior. The girl obviously learned that you shame and humiliate people, so that is what she did. Chloe's mother simply reinforced that behavior and no good lesson was learned from this experience by anyone.

A better outcome would have been achieved by asking Chloe what made her humiliate the little girl? What feeling did Chloe have when saw the girl with the bald head? How did she feel after she did it? Chloe said when she saw the girl, she did not know what to think about it. She felt bad inside and just started to make fun of her. Chloe did not understand that she was trying to dispel her own anxiety about seeing something very strange in another girl her age.

The next step would have been to ask her, "What would you have felt if someone did something like that to you?" Chloe said it would make her feel bad. At this point, it is time for education. It was time to explain that the little girl was sick and getting help in order to recover. Perhaps Chloe would benefit from a trip to a children's hospital ward to actually interact with others who are sick. She would learn that some people, even kids, get sick, and we need to be kind to them because they need all the energy they can muster to get well. Bringing about this kind of understanding is parenting. This is how to help a child grow instead of making a bad situation worse.

Key 3
Avoiding Emotional Incest

Easily the most overlooked and under-treated issue in psychotherapy is emotional incest. Psychotherapy is often very critical of parents' relationship with their children, but emotional incest seems to be too uncomfortable or too close to home for most therapists to address. There are many books about momma's boys and why you shouldn't marry them, but we do not hear nearly as much about daddy's girls or about mother and daughter merging.

Emotional incest is when a parent uses a child to meet their psychosexual needs. A parent who relies on their child for emotional support, companionship, touch, or emotional intimacy rather than getting these from another adult or spouse is abusing the child and crossing a boundary. This can be overt or covert behavior on the adult's part.

It is hard for some parents to maintain a healthy boundary with their kids. Parents have a greater degree of power, and kids are going to do whatever it takes to get and keep their parents' love. If the parent has boundary issues, and if their own needs are not getting met elsewhere, it is very easy for them to use the child to get their psychosexual needs met. With healthy boundaries, an adult would understand the different stages of development and the child's needs and truly understand that a child has no real power over an adult. If that boundary is not held, a child is not able to do anything about it, because they have limited power in such situations. The child's survival is dependent on the adult liking and taking care of their child.

A child is not there to meet the parents' emotional or sexual needs. While we are expected to be appalled when parents cross the line sexually with children, that collective judgment does not exist when it comes to crossing those boundaries emotionally.

Hudson and Ruby got married after a short courtship and lots of intense sex. Both of them expected that heat to continue forever. It did not, however. Hudson had been the only child of a single parent. His mother loved him a great deal. He was her best friend, confidant and the rock she leaned on. Hudson learned that to be loved was to be consumed by the other. His mother was not thrilled when he got married, as she had never felt any woman was good enough for him. He even dated Ruby while making sure his mother did not know.

After the heat of the initial attraction waned, the couple settled into a typical routine. Then Ruby got pregnant. Soon she had this amazing baby boy who loved her and whom she loved completely.

Hudson and Ruby had sex less often, even though sex was still their primary connection. He was not comfortable with the emotional intimacy and so, while he was willing to be sexual, he was not really meeting Ruby's psycho-sexual needs or emotional ones either. She increasingly turned to her adorable little boy to fill that empty space inside.

Ruby unconsciously stopped trying to get her needs met with Hudson. She increasingly turned her attention to her little boy. She often had him sleep in her bed, pushing Hudson out. As the little boy grew up, she was there to meet his every need before the needs of her husband or the relationship.

Ruby's baby boy grew up to be a handsome and seductive young man. He had no problem attracting women, as he was intuitively able to read a woman's needs. His goal was sexual conquest and he was well prepared for that. Sex was fun and easy, but the emotional part of relationship felt suffocating to him. Emotional intimacy was scary and confusing and he simply tried to ignore those parts of a relationship with any woman. He retreated into work and had affairs in order to keep that sexual juice alive while keeping the intimacy of emotions at a distance so he did not feel like he was drowning. The son becomes the father, and marries his mother; the cycle continues.

Ruby and Hudson's story is not unusual. In sexual abuse terminology, both the father and son experienced what can be called covert sexual abuse. There was no physical line crossed. Neither mother fondled her son or had any kind of overt sex, but the emotional intrusion is as bad, if not worse, because the source of the problem is not as obvious.

Men more easily can acknowledge being hurt when they see a physical wound, but emotional wounds are often harder for them to recognize and to own. Since they are often not trained to deal with their emotions, they ignore the ones that do not fit into a box or are confusing. It is difficult to make the connection between their avoidance of emotional intimacy and what happened to them emotionally in childhood. This is why it is as bad, if not worse in some cases, than incest. It is *not* possible to heal if you cannot see something as a wound.

So let children be children. Do not treat them as little adults, especially when it comes to family relationships. Kids need to be told about problems in the family when they notice something happening and/or it will affect them overtly. They need to have appropriate levels of information and to know it is not their responsibility to solve the problem. It is the parents' job to manage and take care of the family. Children are not confidants. They are not the go-betweens for adults, and they are not there to meet either parent's needs. In a single parent household, the parent needs to find another adult, even a friend, to help with their own emotional needs. Burdening the child will make the adult child's future relationships much more difficult, if not impossible. Being out of balance means the child will easily repeat the same pattern and pick partners that replicate the family's own dynamics.

Key 4
Teach children to problem-solve.

Part A: *Skill building is part of parenting children*

A big reason many people come to therapy is a lack of problem-solving skills. Parents do not always teach them such skills. A parent might have rushed in and done the homework for the child, or solved the problem, rather than helping the child think and feel through the process. Learning to problem-solve is probably one of the most valuable skills that a parent can teach a child. If people can solve problems and be confident in that skill, they are able to go out into the world and feel as if they can handle whatever happens. If they do not know how, and they do not have the skills to figure out how to figure it out, they will not succeed and will be dependent upon other people.

Parents should start small giving increasingly difficult tasks to children as they grow physically and developmentally. When children fail, it is crucial to go back and help them understand what they did wrong. In my first book, *Reflections for Managers*, we talked about the importance of a manager understanding the thought process of an employee who made a wrong decision. A manager can tell an employee what to do, but instead by understanding the process of that decision and helping the employee understand where they took a wrong turn, they might solve the problem better next time. This lesson applies to parents and children as well. Being a parent is a lot like being a manager and being a manager is a lot like being a parent. Ask any manager.

Learning to solve problems also means letting the child experience a failure. Trying and then not succeeding is crucial to growth. We learn from our mistakes. Getting a failing grade on something is a learning about life. If kids cannot fail, then they are not taking enough risks. Childhood is about trying to figure out what works and what does not. Failure and missed goals are good and important in the process of growing up and learning about how the world works.

Parents should help children learn to problem-solve. Teach them the steps they must follow to work through problems. This is fundamental to their learning to survive and thrive in the world.

Teaching problem-solving is as much about understanding one's feelings as it is about figuring out the steps to solve a problem.

Part B: *When children are stuck, do not ask 'why,' ask 'what' they are feeling.* When children are solving problems in both school and life, a parent or teacher should help them sort out their feelings first, instead of asking why they cannot do something.

Regina had been assigned a project for her fifth-grade class some weeks ago. Her mother, Wanda, had not been able to persuade her daughter to even start the project, let alone finish it. Wanda kept asking Regina, "Why aren't you doing the project?" but never got an answer. Regina would just shut down and withdraw.

Wanda consulted Rex, the school guidance counselor, and asked what she needed to do to get Regina to complete her projects. After listening to Wanda's description of her interaction with her daughter, he advised her to change her questions from why to what.

Rex suggested Wanda ask Regina what feelings happen inside her when she thinks about working on the project. He also suggested she ask Regina what she thought was the first step she should take to work on the project. Both of these questions would allow Regina to show what was happening in her head and help her sort out and create a process for problem-solving. Children, like adults, cannot know what they do not know. Asking questions and understanding their feelings and thought processes will allow for understanding and create pathways to success.

Children are probably not conscious as to why they cannot get started or why they are stuck. If they are aware, it saves time. But kids are trying to make sense of their feelings and actions, and if they do not know what the block is to moving forward, it is the job of the adult to help by asking:

What are you feeling?
What happens inside when you try to do that?
How does it make you feel?
How do you feel when you are at school? At church? With that person?
When you start to work on your math homework, what happens inside of you?

It is understandably easy to get frustrated with children who cannot seem to accomplish what seems to be a normal task, like a homework problem or cleaning their room. Instead of asking why they cannot do it, ask them what they are feeling. If you can get to the feeling, such as "I am overwhelmed," "I feel stupid," you have a real chance of getting into the problem-solving phase. Kids are often overwhelmed with feelings and they may have no idea of what they mean or how to process them. This is part of helping them "making sense out of the world." Helping them identify their feelings and make sense out of them, will serve them the rest of their lives. Just asking 'why' they cannot do it when it is clear they are stuck, is a form of shaming.

This is so important, it is worth repeating. When working with children, there is a temptation to ask the child 'why' they cannot solve this problem or 'why' they cannot do a required task. For most kids, that is simply the wrong question. The real question is "What are you feeling?" The way to build a sense of self and self-esteem is by constantly reflecting back the external experience of children to their internal experience. By asking children 'what' they are feeling, rather than 'why,' you are really not asking them what is going on in their head. It is more useful to ask what is going on in their *body*, and with their *emotions*. They may not be thinking, because they are stuck. Most of life's problems are really feeling problems, rather than thinking problems. If you can sort out the feelings, the thinking often becomes clarified and then they can move forward. If you do not have a vocabulary and awareness or understanding of one's own feelings, then it is impossible to sort out what you are thinking. Helping children to understand their feelings, and how those get in the way of moving forward, is a gift that will never stop paying dividends.

Key 5
Kids and Sex Education

Children are truth detectors. They often know when a parent is lying, and they certainly know when a parent is embarrassed or ashamed. Whenever possible, it is best to tell the child as much of the truth as possible. This also means educating children about important things like sex.

The sex education that most children get, if any, is severely lacking. It is important to separate religious education from pure factual information about sex, sexuality and relationships. It is important to teach them basic biology, contraception, the developmental process of relationships, and most of all, the difference between sex and love. Without that information in a non-judgmental way and in an age-appropriate way, children are led to believe that their sexual feelings are bad or wrong. This is the root of sexual shame. If we cannot talk about it, if we whisper about it, kids come to believe it is something bad. When kids are educated to know that their sexual feelings are normal and they are educated about sex, they have a good chance of feeling good about their sexuality. They will also have useful benchmarks for observing their own sexual development.

It is a parent's responsibility to either teach their children directly about sex or see that they get the information. Many parents are understandably uncomfortable having some of these conversations with their children and are not sure which information is age-appropriate. Sadly, many parents have had minimal sex education themselves. When parents communicate their discomfort, it transmits another layer of shame and embarrassment to children about what the children's relationship to sex and sexuality should be.

It is very helpful if parents understand this information for themselves and work through any sexual shame first. Then they can best prepare their children for the world.

Normalizing masturbation is key to validating and empowering sexual feelings. It is the foundation of a person's sexuality. The ability to self-pleasure and release sexual tension without a partner is essential. Because of religious and cultural programming, even this simple act of self-pleasure can be made into a landmine of guilt and conflict. Some people feel their partners are cheating on them when the other masturbates alone. Or there can be shame from the programming about being selfish or wicked and giving into one's own needs and desires. It can leave people deeply conflicted about the purpose of sex and pleasure. When we can talk with friends about sex and be honest and vulnerable, it breaks the isolation of believing it is "just me who feels this way." Talking openly also promotes sex as a normal experience and is an important part of a happy life.

It is also very important that children are not overexposed to overt sexual imagery or sexual situations before they are psychologically able to process it.

This is a psychological perspective fully apart from any moral posture on the subject. Too early an exposure will lead to overstimulation and potentially set-up a lifetime of sexual dysfunction. There is a world of difference between casual nudity and children hearing or watching their parents or anyone else being sexual. Consciously or not, a child can feel and absorb other people's emotions. If being naked sexually arouses an adult, on some level, children will feel that too and they will absorb that as the way to interpret that experience. It is also critical that kids learn that being nude does not just mean "sex." Being comfortable with the naked body without shame is very helpful in adulthood.

Far from "scoring," young boys or men have their first sexual experiences with much older girls or women can be severely traumatized. The same can be said for young girls with older males, yet we seem to have a double-standard in our culture — we are less outraged by an older female with a younger male.

When it comes to consent and healthy behavior, laws should be based on biology rather than morality. The brain is mostly developed around the age of 25. Overloading a younger brain with more stimulation than it is prepared to handle will damage it. A sexual partner much closer in age should produce roughly the same amount of excitement, so that neither is overwhelmed by the experience. As we grow physically, the brain is growing and developing and part of that development is the ability to experience pleasure. Part of the adolescent growth process involves learning how to hold a sexual charge and experience pleasure in the body. If a child or teen has sex with someone older, that process can be disrupted.

Exposure to pornography or extreme erotic material can have a damaging impact on children. Many men report that their mothers openly bought them subscriptions to Playboy, or they spent a lot of time secretly looking at a parent's porn. Adults viewing erotic material is fine in moderation, but it is too stimulating for a child to see and experience. It can have similar effects as when a child is sexually abused or is exposed to people having sex around them. It is like plugging a 110-volt appliance into a 220-volt outlet. It will blow the circuit. When that happens, children get stuck in a loop, whether pleasurable or not, until it is healed. What happens is that they will try to recreate the overwhelming experience of erotic energy over and over. It is called a repetition compulsion. They are erotically traumatized and until that is resolved they are stuck doing it repeatedly to get sexual satisfaction.

By the time boys and girls start to date and approach tentative sexual exploration with others, not just themselves, some exposure to pornography is almost impossible to avoid. It is important to educate kids about sex, even the parts that make adults uncomfortable. Non-sensationalized information about the range of sexual possibilities is crucial.

By age 7 or 8, kids also need to know how to protect themselves from people who want to entice them with the exciting unknown. Just make sure that as a parent, you have ready answers to their questions or that you can refer them to a credible source. It is probably not the family physician. A sex educator or a psychotherapist who specializes in sex is a better choice for straightforward information.

Protect them, normalize their feelings, and do not shame or punish peer experiences. Kids playing doctor or "show me yours and I'll show you mine" are normal. They should not be shamed. This behavior should be used as an opportunity to talk about the physical differences between boys and girls. Allow them to have their innocence, but at the same time, educate them so they are not naive. Keeping them completely in the dark about sex sets them up to be victimized. Information does not destroy innocence, but actually protects it for a much longer period. One unfortunate proof of this is seen in the fact that the more restrictive a community is about providing sex education to children, the higher the rate of teen pregnancy.

Real sex education without moralizing or shaming is the key to creating a sexually healthy adult. Information is protection. Kids going through puberty have a new toy, but their sexuality can now also be explored online. Of course, they want to play with it and see how it works. This is normal and healthy. But without education about sex, intimacy, STD's, relationship dynamics, sexual orientation, gender orientation, and the process of physical and emotional development, we are setting them up to have endless shame about their sexual feelings at the very least, or at worst, to be victims. If there is a desire for religious education, that should be done separately. If the religious education is designed to make people feel shame about sex, please consider how that will impact your child. Taking the shame out of sex and our bodies will empower people to be responsible for their actions and feelings.

Key 6
Do not overemphasize looks or constantly tell children they are special.

It is important to validate that children are attractive, but do not tell them repeatedly how beautiful they are. Validate their self-worth, their accomplishments, their efforts and being a good person.

It is striking how often we hear parents tell children how beautiful they are, or that they are "lookers" or that people are going to adore you because they are pretty. While it might be true that the child is attractive, and most parents believe their child is attractive, it is not helpful for a child to learn to value their worth based upon their looks. Because looks change and fade with time, what may be a very attractive child could still turn into a very unattractive adult. If self-esteem is based on how other people respond to looks, then adult children will be dependent upon others to make them feel better about themselves.

As children grow, they will get plenty of messages from the world about how attractive they are. Or are not. Being considered attractive by conventional standards certainly has its value, but it is not enough to build a self or the internal fortitude to survive bad times in one's life. Knowing one's worth and value transcends looks and can sustain a person for a lifetime.

For a healthy sense of self and self-esteem, it is essential that people have a strong internal core as a foundation for being in the world. They will trust and value their skills, have empathy and compassion for others, and will be emotionally self-reliant. This is how you build a strong adult, capable of succeeding in the world.

Telling children they are "special" and "better than everyone else" is damaging. To accomplish extraordinary things and be able to really own that accomplishment, it is important they own their ordinariness first. Otherwise, it is a set-up to fail. Life will tell them whether they are special or not, soon enough. What children need to be accomplished and succeed in the world is a belief they are truly loved. That is the greatest gift a parent can give. From there, children will find out if they are attractive or special in some way.

If children are overweight, the key is to find out why. Is it the family genetics? If so, how does the family deal with that in a healthy way? Does it? Does the family need another approach or perspective? If a child was sexually abused or is being abused and is using food as self-comfort or protection, then that needs to be discovered and treated as soon as possible. Being overweight is usually a symptom of something else. Find out the cause and deal with that, and the weight should become a non-issue.

If there is some kind of physical problem, like breast growth (gynecomastia) on a boy, a cleft palate or severe birthmarks, it is the job of the parent to find a way to have that addressed, if possible. But a nose job or some other plastic surgery should only be pursued after issues of self-worth are addressed. Rushing to have plastic surgery too soon can tell children that all solutions to make them feel better come from the outside. Growing up is stressful enough, and looking different, while having some of the advantages of being different as discussed in prior chapters, should not be framed as "bad." If it is within the realm of possibility, unfortunate birthmarks, deformities and similar issues should indeed be addressed with the option of surgery, to give children the best chance to succeed in life. Never forget that who they are on the inside is far more important than whatever their external appearance might be.

Focusing on the external as the source of the primary value of a child is damaging, and will create an underdeveloped adult.

Recap

First – Make your love for the child obvious and use all of the love languages to express it.

Second – Do not shame a child intentionally. Too much shame can set a child up for a lifetime of self-hatred.

Third – Do not use your children to meet your own needs. Keep good boundaries with them so they can have good boundaries with others, especially when they become adults.

Fourth – Teach them to problem-solve. Teach both how to understand and process their feelings as well as what steps are necessary to solve a problem. Problem-solving is also about clarifying feelings that can obscure or block the problem-solving.

Fifth – Teach kids the facts about sex, biology and relationship. It will free them to feel good about their sexual feelings and experiences.

Sixth – Do not over-emphasize looks or continually tell children they are special or better looking than everyone else. They are beautiful and special to you. That is what they need to know and believe.

PART FIVE

CONCLUSION

—— 21 ——

Bringing It All Together

A true teacher doesn't teach you to think like him,
but to think without him.

—Tariq Ramadan (b.1962) Professor

We are All Family

In early times and a less developed world, the family and extended family was indeed the protection and centerpiece of life. But we now live in a much more crowded world, one that requires ever more cooperation for us to survive. We need a new paradigm that expands our caring and expands our seeing everyone as family, not just the blood relations or people who raised us. We need to expand our view to being the family of the human race. Until we love everyone as our self, we are not going to be able to make this world work. It will always be your family against mine, unless we replace the old family paradigm that keeps everyone separate and in conflict.

The core of spiritually is that we are all the same and we are all connected. The artificial differences we dwell on are just a part of our construct of the world. Once we reach a certain level of development, we begin to under-

The bond that links your true family is not one of blood,
but of respect and joy in each other's life.

— Richard Bach (b. 1936) American Writer

stand there are no differences. As long as we are divided by race, religion, country, gender, sexual orientation, gender orientation and all the other ways we see differences, we will not be able to come together and raise us all up, to save us all.

This book has been about the ways we distract ourselves from recognizing that we are all the same. But it also acknowledges the difficulty of facing who we are. It requires that we love our neighbor as our self and that we let go of the biological family as the centerpiece, finding the community of humanity to be our family.

We have to face our pain in order to find genuine compassion for others. We have to go inside to find our connection to others. We have to quiet our minds and really get in touch with our feelings to have empathy and love. Too much of modern life is about using others as distractions or objects of pleasure. It is time to find our humanity, our connection and most of all, to find ourselves.

Goals to Live By

Do No Harm
Leave the World a Better Place than We Found

These are very simple rules that relate to the core of how you choose to be in the world. They inform your every interaction. The world is constantly in

We do not have to accept the world as we find it. And we have a responsibility to leave our world a better place and never walk by on the other side of injustice.

—Ed Miliband (b. 1969) British Politician

need of improvement, just as are we as individuals. The person we were at age 20 and who we are at 60 are very different. We are constantly changing and so is the world around us. To stop trying means you are just waiting to die.

There are two different types of retirees: those who are counting days until they check out, and the ones that continue to make themselves and the world better.

In our daily lives, we usually encounter a lot of different people. Each interaction can be a potentially life-changing moment for each person. The universal laws of cause and effect and action/reaction tell us that there is nothing benign in the world. It is all energy, both positive and negative. Each action brings another action in response.

Do No Harm

What does this mean? Every word we speak to someone has an impact. Customer service representatives are often convenient targets of people's frustration and anger even though the situation was probably not the representative's fault. While there might be a short-term satisfaction in venting, are you really proud of making them feel bad as the recipient of your rage? Did that make you a better person? Will their thoughts about you be good? If you put that out into the world, what do you expect to get back in return?

We often make unkind remarks and observations that belittle people. It diminishes them and reduces us to being less than we could or should be. Throwing a bottle or trash out of your car's window might reduce the clutter in your immediate world, but it is increasing the clutter and litter in the rest of the world, of which you are still a part.

You can hold people accountable for their words and actions in constructive ways rather than reducing yourself to someone who abuses, no matter how justified it might seem.

There is a difference between the ferocity of a parent protecting a child and merely expressing rage. There are times we all need to own and express our ferocity. This is part of being alive and taking care of ourselves. It is not easy in painful situations to keep the bigger picture in mind. Reactions are automatic. The task is to develop sufficient consciousness to be aware of and a witness to our own feelings, thoughts and actions so that we can respond, rather than react. Only then can we actively improve ourselves and do much less harm in the world.

For some people, doing no harm might include being a vegan from an enhanced sensitivity to our animal companions on this planet. For others, it might mean not being critical of something — choosing to spare a person's feelings when there is nothing to be gained by either party in sharing an opinion. Feeling empathy and compassion before speaking is a proven method of doing no or at least less harm. You may choose not to harm the planet through recycling or some other means. There are many paths traveled each day. How we decide to journey them speaks both a lot about who we are as well as what kind of energy we choose to put into the world.

Leave the World a Better Place than We Found It

Making the world better can be as simple as a gracious conversation explaining something that someone else is perplexed about. It could also just be picking up a piece of trash and disposing of it. Perhaps it is starting an organization to address a community need or giving a homeless person money, food or shelter. Giving directions to a stranger may be another way, or passing on a few dollars so that the person in front of you in line can pick up a prescription or buy something to eat.

Making the world a better place happens through big and small actions. It is about energy. We collectively create the energy to make this a better world for everyone, not just ourselves or 'our family.'

Going From Here

Thank you for having read this book and I congratulate you for courageously making it this far. I understand for many this book may have been difficult to take in, and I hope the journey was worth it. Whatever you are feeling now, I hope that you are able to do something with what you have learned about yourself and take it to the next step.

The next step might mean talking to a therapist, talking to friends, writing a journal, learning to meditate, taking a class, breaking some dishes, whatever you feel the next step is for you. Trust your intuition, and do the work that is necessary to put your pain in the past.

I am sure that there are concepts and ideas encountered here that you have never heard of before. There are probably a few things that you did not agree with, and likely a couple of things that really upset you. Take your time to

Real change happens when the pain of staying the same is greater than the pain of changing.

—Sheldon Kopp (b. 1929) Psychologist,
from *If You Meet the Buddha on the Road, Kill Him*

process what came up, but if at all possible, do not sweep those feelings and memories under the rug. They are your best chance to change your life for the better. The good news about what you read that upset you personally, is that it is *accessible* to you. With access it is possible to do something about it.

The goal of this book is not only to help you face your truth but to allow the 'original you' to shine and be present in the world. While we do not always intend to be like someone else, our programming turns us into copies. Make sure the original you shines.

If You Need a Psychotherapist

While this book is not a light and easy read, there may have been one or two things that brought up memories, gave insights or just pushed some buttons that you did or did not know you had.

Perhaps it is time to get some assistance in looking at whatever came up for you.

While some ministers are taught to do counseling, most have little to no special training and certainly no substantial training in deep personality change. Most coaches are also not really trained in working with trauma and family-of-origin issues. For many issues brought up in *Facing the Truth of Your Life*, psychotherapy will probably be required.

Never, never, never wish to be like anyone in the world
unless you want to be a copy. Copies only produce mediocrity.
If you are not an original, you are nothing. The world, you see,
worships the original.

—Spoken by Ingrid Bergman in the movie *A Matter of Time*[27]

My belief and experience is that if you want to really heal the past, a body-oriented, or somatic psychotherapist is required. In layman's terms, that means a therapist who is aware of how trauma and emotions are stored and experienced in the body and even more importantly, how to clear them out of the mind and body. If it is not cleared out of the mind and body, whatever the issue, it is not fully healed.

Easily the fastest and most effective treatment for the remnants of past trauma is EMDR Therapy. EMDR means eye movement desensitization reprocessing. EMDRIA.org has a referral directory for EMDR therapists in the United States. Canada, Australia, and Europe all have their own National EMDR associations. All are available online.

Most states in the United States have psychotherapist organizations, usually on a state level that have free referral services.

A licensed therapist is always a good start. While it does not guarantee a really good therapist, any more than any lawyer who has passed the bar is competent, it is a baseline to start with.

If people in your life are in therapy and you can see it has made a difference, ask them about their experience. If the friend is too close, meaning you would likely be talking to the same therapist about each other, you could obtain a referral from their therapist, rather than seeing the same one. Good therapists usually refer to other good therapists.

If you have little to no resources, there are usually free to low-fee community counseling centers in most medium to large cities. In California, they are either specific issue-oriented centers, for spousal abuse, child abuse, addiction, and/or they are training centers for postgraduate students gaining experience to become licensed in their state.

Most centers and psychotherapists now have websites. This is a great way to get some idea of who they are and how they do therapy.

Once you have a short list, first talk to each therapist on the phone. A 15-minute conversation will give you a sense of them, their intuitiveness, and their ability to ask good insightful questions.

If the phone conversation goes well, make an appointment to meet the therapist in person. The two most important things to ask yourself are: "Can I relate to them? and "On a deep intuitive level, do I feel like I can trust them?" Trust is a key ingredient in working with any psychotherapist. If you do not trust them on some level, they are not right for you. Move on to another therapist.

Never see a psychotherapist who has not done personal work on themselves for many years. If they have never been in therapy then they have no idea what it is like to be on the other side of the couch. Be sure to ask them about their own healing process. They are not going to give much specific information, but they should give enough information for you to know if they understand what it takes to heal. If they are unwilling to say anything then *move on* and find another therapist.

Try one to three sessions and see how you feel. You will not magically be cured right away. Psychotherapy does not work that way, but you should begin to feel your comfort level increasing and you should have increasing interest in telling your story. The therapist's first job is to get your story and get a deep sense of how you are wired inside. Soon, the therapist should move into action to assist both your insight and in making your life easier.

Psychotherapy is an art, much more than a science. Studies show that the relationship between therapist and client is the most important part of a successful outcome. Having a tool like EMDR in the therapist's toolbox is essential to impact trauma quickly and relieve suffering.

It is your healing and your life. Find the right therapist match, and it will save you time, money and suffering.

In Closing

Pain, confrontation, discomfort, sadness and hurt are all unpleasant parts of life. Sometimes, helping someone get through something they do not like will make them and the world a better place. But there might be consequences. Experiencing joy, ecstasy, pleasure and happiness can be great as well, but they are not the goal. They are some of the benefits of being in our human body. Life is to be experienced. With more consciousness of who we are and how we fit into the bigger picture of existence, the more likely we can make good choices both for ourselves as well as our human family.

So many people are angry because the world does not work the way they think it should. People fail, people cheat and people disappoint. Who is to blame and who is going to fix it? Holding onto perfection or the perfect answer is committing to a life of suffering. What is perfect to one is not to another. Different perspectives on the same problem have different answers. If you are climbing to the top of a hill, you might have the best view from there, but maybe not. From the top, there might be a lower peak that obscures part of that view, where the perspective from the lower peak might not be blocked. The higher up you move in the management of a business, the less simple the solutions are because you have to take into account more parts of the business. What seems perfectly simple to a person working on the front lines of production may be quite complex for someone responsible for more parts of the business.

This is an imperfect world of imperfect people who create imperfect organizations that produce imperfect results. All we can do is set our intention each day to do the best we can, not to harm anyone and leave the world a better place.

We are all a work in progress. Compassion and understanding for each of us being in our own process makes this a much easier world in which to navigate and thrive.

Afterword

Dear Readers,

Thank you for buying and reading this book. It has been a labor of love and I hope you found much that inspired, challenged and changed you.

Please join the conversation on Facebook. We have started a closed group for people who have read the book and want to discuss it with others and get some direct feedback from me as well. Facebook: *FTT Community*

Please consider starting a group in your area or online to go through the book together to do the exercises and to process your thoughts and emotions that are triggered from the material. Having that support can change your life.

You are welcome to contact me directly for consultations or to set-up live events, in person or online. I am also willing to answer questions, as much as I can.

My email address for questions and comments about the book is: FTT@merleyost.com

In addition, I need your help to get the word out to others about *Facing the Truth of Your Life.*

First, if you liked the book, please review it on Amazon, Good Reads, B&N, and any other book review sites you might know of. Local and professional newsletters and newspapers are also good possibilities; it can be your chance to get published as well.

Second, tell your friends. Buy copies of the book for people in your family, friends and enemies, anyone that you think would benefit from it and grow as a person. Encourage book clubs to read and discuss the book.

Third, put together a group of people and have your own FTT reading/ discussion group. The experience could be invaluable in understanding the book and how it relates to you and your life.

Facing the Truth of Your Life is about starting a conversation with yourself and others. The more that people are talking about it, the more conversation will become possible. You do not have to agree with everything in the book, but it should spark conversation and thought. That is what I intended.

Be well and thank you once again for taking this journey with me.

Merle Yost

Appendix

Differential Diagnosis for Victim Identity Disorder (VID)

This is a clinical description of VID and the related psychological disorders primarily written for psychotherapists to assist them in getting a deeper understanding of the VID.

This disorder can look like a Narcissistic Personality Disorder[28] (NPD). The deflated and the inflated versions of NPD can look like VID. The VID type that is loud about their victimization and the type that is quiet and collapses into the self are parallel to the inflated and deflated versions of the NPD. Some people will have aspects of both. The difference is that the VID person has some sense of self or ego. Though their view of themself is negative, they are aware of an internal self — "I am bad." They therefore feel they deserve punishment even as they protest against it. The NPD has no sense of self or ego. The other key difference between VID and NPD is that the VID can have empathy for other victims, where the NPD will not. The VID is developmentally older than the NPD. It is possible to be a victim while not being a narcissist. It is not possible to be a narcissist and not be a victim.

The VID has similar traits to the Borderline Personality Disorder[29] (BPD). The major difference is the central reason for the pain. While the VID person is focused on his victimization and not being victimized again, the BPD person's main concern revolves around a fear of abandonment. Abandonment can be one piece of the victimization reality for the VID, but it is not seed of the VID's fear or lens of perception.

The Masochistic Character Structure (MasCS) is the third closely related pathology and the closest and most difficult to differentiate from VID. The MasCS is sometimes called The Endurer in contemporary Bioenergetics,[30] which is a type of body-oriented psychotherapy created by Alexander Lowen, MD, based on the work of Wilhelm Reich, MD. In the MasCS external type, there is usually an eroticized component to the victimization. They feel deserving of punishment and with the pleasure they move toward the pain or discomfort. This is most closely associated with VID Type Four. As stated before, the Type Four is more about being erased and/or objectified but certainly regressed to a child-like level of responsibility.

Types one through three of the VID do not really receive pleasure from being victimized; they do feel validation in some way, but not pleasure. In the internal version of the MasCS, the sufferers are pleasure-phobic and avoid the feeling of pleasure. They endure the pain because it is safer than risking experiencing hope or pleasure. If they allow themselves to welcome pleasure, they are aware it can also be taken away. Pleasure makes them feel vulnerable and exposed. The VID often searches for pleasure and can welcome, absorb it, enjoy it, and strive for more but will never find enough to overcome the feeling of being victimized.

Someone with a Paranoid Personality Disorder (PPD) has a constant hypervigilance, looking out for potential attacks. At their core, they do not trust themselves. Consequently, they feel they are unable to protect themselves and are constantly on the alert for potential dangers. They will find order in chaos in an effort to make sense of it and to construct a worldview that attempts to help them to be prepared for the oncoming attack. Making connections where none exist and finding validation for their perspective, they can never stop trying to protect themselves.

VID sufferers certainly have medium to strong PPD traits but are not as hypervigilant. While they make connections, it is less total fantasy as to the existence of the connection or threat.

And it is possible to have both VID and a PPD.

About the Author

Merle Yost, LMFT
Author, Consultant, Speaker and Psychotherapist
Licensed Marriage & Family Therapist,
California License # MFT32346

M.A., Counseling Psychology, Transpersonal Specialization, *John F. Kennedy University*, Pleasant Hill, CA
B.A., Management, *University of Phoenix*, Tucson, AZ

Merle is a full time writer, speaker and consultant. Retired from private practice in psychotherapy after 25 years, he now lectures and consults to help people make sense out of their lives and often the pain they are in, so they can move forward. With over 35 years of personal and professional work, Merle has taken the summary of his experience and training and uses it to help others.

All of his books are about helping people live better lives. Merle is committed to continuing his teaching and efforts to educate people about themselves.

Merle's own healing journey informs deep compassion for the emotional pain people experience, as well as his profound belief in the possibility of healing and claiming one's life.

End Notes

1. Jim Jones, American cult leader of the Peoples Temple, ending in mass murder-suicide in November 1978.

2. Sigmund Freud, *The Pleasure Principle*, 1922, International Psycho-Analytical,

3. Viktor E. Frankl, *Man's Search for Meaning*, 2006, Beacon Press

4. Abraham Maslow, *Motivation and Personality*, 1954, Harper & Brothers, hierarchy of needs

5. Frances Vaughan, *The Inward Arc*, 1986, The Transpersonal Self, page 39, Shambhala

6. Gary Yontef, Ph.D., *Awareness, Dialogue, and Process*, 1993, The Gestalt Journal Press, "Through introjection, foreign material is absorbed without discriminating or assimilating. Swallowing whole creates an "as if" personality and rigid character. Introjected values and behavior are imposed on self. As in all contact boundary disturbances, swallowing whole can be healthy or pathological, depending on the circumstances and degree of awareness. For example, students taking a lecture course may, with full awareness that they are doing so, copy, memorize and regurgitate material without full 'digestion.'"

7. Richard Niolon, Ph.D., *The Therapeutic Relationship* - Part I, 12/99: "The 'observing ego,' or the part of us that watches what we do and say in some objective manner, watches all this and tolerates the anxiety that is produced."

8. The first time I heard a version of this exercise was in a training for Enneagram with Helen Palmer, 1989

9. John Naisbitt, *Megatrends: Ten New Directions Transforming Our Lives*, 1984, Warner Books

10. From http://juliacolwell.com/archives/110 "This word was coined by Mary Tebbs, in a Life Alignment Program call where we were talking about this." She described this as the necessary and healthy middle ground.

11. Observing Ego – the term originates in psychoanalytic psychotherapy and is commonly used in most psychotherapies. It is the ability to step back and see our own behavior. I have heard it referred to as the part of us sitting on our shoulder and just watching. It is our own witness, hopefully, without judgment.

12. The Jar in the Heart Exercise: I first heard this from Anna Gomez during a psychotherapy training with her on using EMDR with kids with EMDR. https://anagomez.org

13. This is a version of an exercise I learned in an EMDR training from Landry Wildwood.

14. Somaticize: converting negative emotions into major and minor physical disorders.

15. https://www.enneagramworldwide.com

16. Helen Palmer: *The Enneagram*, Harper Collins, 2001 and *The Enneagram in Love and Work*, 2010, Harper Collins

17. Don Riso: *Personality Types*, 2011, Mariner Books and *The Wisdom of the Enneagram*, 1999, Bantam

18. Klinefelter syndrome is a genetic condition that results when a boy is born with an extra copy of the X chromosome. Klinefelter syndrome is a common genetic condition affecting males. (From the Mayo Clinic Website http://www.mayoclinic.org/diseases-conditions/klinefelter-syndrome/basics/definition/CON-20033637)

19. Laozi, *Tao Te Ching*, Chapter 1, Verse 1

20. EMDR, www.emdria.org

21. This is an exercise from Cai Bristol, Hypnotherapist www.caibristol.com

22. This is a personal anecdote from an African-American colleague whom I consulted with about the Race Shame section.

23. Two Tasks of Childhood – I originally heard this story and concept from Suzanne Slyman, LMFT in supervision/consultation a very long time ago.

24. Codependency: "A psychological condition or a relationship in which a person is controlled or manipulated by another who is affected with a pathological condition (as an addiction to alcohol or heroin); broadly: dependence on the needs of or control by another." Merriam-Webster Online Dictionary http://www.merriam-webster.com/dictionary/codependency

25. Robert Bly, *Iron John*, 2015, Da Capo Press

26. Gary Chapman, *The 5 Love Languages*, 2014, Northfield Publishing

27. *A Matter of Time*, 1967, Staring Liza Minnelli, Ingrid Bergman, Charles Boyer, directed by Vincente Minnelli

28. The Narcissistic Personality Disorder was described earlier in the book. There are many ways the disorder is displayed. Two common versions are the inflated and deflated types. The inflated version is the person that is constantly and overtly drawing attention to themselves. They need the constant reflection of themselves to exist. The deflated version is generally considered the nicest person in the room, the sweet, grandmotherly type that is always attending to others needs and being of service. She is still using the positive attention and being seen as a saint to validate her existence. And internally, it is still all about her, just as it is for the inflated type. When around each of these types, it will feel like all of the energy in the room is being sucked out. They are taking everything they can get.

29. Borderline Personality Disorder: While this is a complex disorder, a simple explanation is that this personality disorder is characterized by a pathological fear of abandonment. This type of person can be very seductive and charming. If they feel the potential for abandonment, they will either run away, or get confrontational and possibly violent. The Glenn Close character in Fatal Attraction is an excellent depiction of a BPD,

30. Bioenergetics is a therapy created by Alexander Lowen, MD. A body-oriented psychotherapy, it continues to evolve. While the Masochistic Personality Disorder is no longer part of the DSM, the disorder still exists. This personally structure is sometimes referred to as The Endurer in Bioenergetics. http://energeticsinstitute.com. au/psychotherapy-counselling/characterology/endurer-masochist/

Made in the USA
San Bernardino, CA
20 February 2018